"Steven and Jodie's intuitive yet scientific approach makes this a wonderful guide to interpersonal relationships. Their sound astrological principles are undeniably helpful, informative and make good practical sense."

—Danny Kee, Director of A&R, Warner Brothers Records.

"Steven and Jodie Forrest are two of the most genuinely wise people I have ever known, and the miracle is how fluidly that knowledge flows through their writings and teachings. Their work has given guidance, insight and a profound understanding to my life and that of countless others."

—Rob Lehmann, author of *Cooking for Life*; professor, Philadelphia University; Philadelphia Humanitarian of the Year, 1992.

"En la literatura astrológica son raros y preciosos los matrimonios perfectos: Buen inglés y magnífica astrología, sentido común y profunda espiritualidad, objetividad y optimismo, precisión técnica e imágenes conmovedoras. Definitivamente *Skymates*." (Translation: Perfect marriages are rare and precious in astrological literature. Good English and magnificent astrology, common sense and deep spirituality, objectivity and optimism, technical precision and moving images. These are *Skymates'* achievements.)

—Luis Lesur, author of *Astrologia Cotidiana*.

"I have been receiving readings from Steven Forrest for ten years now. What he`s done for me is not to predict my future but to help me meditate on some of the warnings I might look out for, based on a scientific but more importantly a compassionate approach. These readings have improved the quality of my life."

—Dominic Miller, guitarist for Sting, The Pretenders; composer, solo CDs *First Touch* and *Second Nature*.

"*Skymates* is an unforgettable literary journey that will enrich your personal consciousness while ultimately leading to more fulfilling relationships."

—Laure Redmond, author of *Feel Good Naked*.

"One of the first appointments I made after the birth of my daughter was for an astrology reading with Steven and Jodie Forrest. Now, fifteen years later, I still refer to its contents and am grateful for their insight in helping me honor her uniqueness and support her strengths and weaknesses. I can't imagine a more valuable gift that parents could give to their child."

honor her uniqueness and support her strengths and weaknesses. I can't imagine a more valuable gift that parents could give to their child."

—Susan B. Reintjes, psychic, author of *Third Eye Open: Unmasking Your True Awareness.*

"To write a powerful book on the astrology of relationships takes two things: a vast knowledge of astrology and a fantastical, loving relationship in life. When these two things merge, well, the results are nothing short of miraculous. The Forrests have both. Caution: insight and miraculous relationship knowledge inside."

—Philip Sedgwick, author of *Astrology of Deep Space,* and *The Sun at the Center.*

"From their insight and understanding, you'd think Jodie and Steven were your closest childhood friends. They have an uncanny ability to gently unravel the tightest knots of your inner self."

—Eric Silver, award-winning songwriter: Dixie Chicks, Donna Summer, Diamond Rio. Record producer: Michelle Wright, Neal McCoy, Reba McEntire.

SKYMATES:

Love, Sex and

Evolutionary Astrology

Volume One

by

Jodie Forrest

and

Steven Forrest

Copyright © 2002
by Jodie Forrest and Steven Forrest

Published by
Seven Paws Press, POB 2345, Chapel Hill NC 27515
tel. 919.929.4287; fax 919.929.7092
www.sevenpawspress.com
info@sevenpawspress.com

We gratefully acknowledge the following quotes from the original edition:

From *Some Sort of Epic Grandeur: The Life of F. Scott Fitzgerald*, © 1981 by Matthew J. Bruccoli, used by permission of Harcourt Brace Jovanovich Inc.

From *The Theory of Celestial Influence* by Rodney Collin, used by permission of Robinson Books Ltd. 1954/Shambala 1986.

Cover designed by Steven Forrest.

ISBN 0-9649-113-5-3
Library of Congress CIP Number: 01-26666

First edition of this revised and expanded volume.
First printing, February 2002.

Some portions of the text were previously published in the original edition from ACS Publications (1992) and Bantam Books (1989).

Open eyes, open heart:
this book is dedicated to you.

The key to the understanding of sex is the knowledge that sexual energy is the finest and subtlest naturally produced by the human organism. This sexual energy can be turned to any purpose, can express itself on any level. It contains the potentiality of the highest forms of creation, and it also contains the possibility of destroying a man, and wrecking him, physically, morally, and emotionally. It can combine with his most bestial side, with criminal impulses of cruelty, hatred, and fear; or it can combine with his most refined aspirations and keenest sensibilities. And in either case it will immensely heighten the tendency to which it becomes attached . . .

By pure sex, the ordinary man may gain in a moment what the ascetic denies himself for years to achieve, what the saint prays a lifetime to feel. But this is only on the condition that he approaches it already free from fear, from violence, and from greed. And on condition also that he does not afterwards deny what he learns in sex, but on the contrary allows the understanding attained in sex to pass into all other sides of his life, mellowing, harmonizing, and enriching them also.

-RODNEY COLLIN,
The Theory of Celestial Influence

ACKNOWLEDGMENTS

We would like to thank the following people for their friendship, support, insights, patience, practical assistance, or opening their lives and homes to us:

The Forrest astrological apprenticeship program members one and all; the Blue Sky Ranch community; Judy C. Bemis, Walt Crockett, Hadley Fitzgerald, Richard Fuller, Nan Geary, Tom Goyett, Mary Kay Hocking, Bill Janis, Barbara Jensen, Rob Lehmann, Mark McDonough, the Nalbandian family, Vinessa Nevala, Pyanfar the Cat (four of the Seven Paws), Lois Rodden, Sonja Runar, Savannah Scarborough, Cristina Smith, Lauryl Stone, Mark Urban-Lurain, the late Vincent the Cat (three of the Seven Paws), and Roger Windsor.

We would like to thank the following couples, "skymates" all, for opening their hearts to us: Willard and Bobbie Aldrich, Scott Ainslie and Barb Ackemann, Cyril Beveridge and Sinikka Laine, Maryska Bigos and Jeff Hamilton, Nick and Karen Callen, Keith Cleversley and Lia Roldan, Mike and Carol Czeczot, Mitch Easter and Shalini Chatterjee, Sue and Tommy Field, Dick and Bunny Forrest, Kelli and David Fox, Karen Galey and Steve Briggs, Ginger Gaffney and Glenda Fletcher, Tracy Gaudet and Rich Leibowitz, Wolf and Martina Green, Robert and Diana Griffin, Dave and Donna Gulick, Dan and Teri Kee, Alphee and Carol Lavoie, Luis Lesur and Barbara Kastelein, Jim and Sharon Mullaney, Michael Rank and Kate Tolley, Dag and Sharon Rossman, Phil Sedgwick and Eileen Lehn, Eric Silver and Adela Rios, Paul and Lauryl Stone, Trudie Styler and Sting, Tem Tarriktar and Kate Sholly, Jeff and Jan Ward, James Weinberg and Mary Beth Cysewski, Charles and Cindy Wyatt, Scotty Young and Lina Pratt.

We would like to thank Ingrid Coffin for the loan of her house where we wrote this new edition, for her generosity, and most of all for her friendship.

TABLE OF CONTENTS

SKYMATES:
Love, Sex, and Evolutionary Astrology,
Volume One

Preface to the New Edition

This new edition of *Skymates* is based on the previous edition in about the same way a Boeing 777 is based on the contraption the Wright brothers flew. Even if you have a dog-eared copy of the older book, we encourage you to open this one at random and take a look. You'll see the differences right away.

Our previous *Skymates* came out toward the end of the last century, in 1989, as a Bantam Books original, and the identical text was reprinted in 1992 under a new cover by ACS Publications.

Saying "toward the end of the last century" may seem precious here in the summer of 2001, but it feels right. When we wrote that book, we had been married only four or five years—whistling past the graveyard, we joked a lot about tempting the Fates by writing a book about marriage so early in our own journey together. Now we're twenty years down the road, still loving each other one day at a time. We've learned a thing or two, and we've incorporated all of that into these pages. That's one big difference.

Another difference is that we're both in bed with our publishers nowadays. Seven Paws Press is our own business. That gives us a lot of freedom to write in our own voices, independent of the pervasive pressure on astrological writers to dumb everything down. We're still stinging from a conversation with an editor who insisted that "enhanced" was too hard a word for the astrological audience. We *know* that you, our readers, are smarter than that. On the other hand, perhaps we should be thankful to that editor—Seven Paws Press owes a lot of its direction and intent to that exchange.

There are also many concrete differences between this new book and the previous one. The most obvious distinction is that we've added extensive "cookbook" sections. Learning *to think astrologically* is really the higher ground, but many readers have expressed appreciation for simply being able to look things up. If your natal Sun squares your partner's Venus, turn to Chapter Thirteen. If you are wondering about the sexual significance of Saturn being in your eighth house, try Chapter Eleven.

We've come to particularly "enhanced" understandings of the intimate meanings of two of astrology's core symbols: the fourth and sixth houses. We've added those perspectives to our previous "arc of intimacy" material—and supplemented that entire section of the book with detailed analyses of what it means to have each particular planet in houses four, five, six, seven or eight. Name the configuration: it's there.

Back in our Bantam Books days, we were discouraged from making our writing "too spiritual." That led to a diminished focus on the evolution of consciousness, and specifically on the psychological dynamics of reincarnation. We've filled that vacuum here—although if you are uncomfortable with the idea of reincarnation, we think you will still find the book mostly accessible. Some of our assumptions are unabashedly metaphysical, but we try to speak the verifiable language of experience, and also of psychology. You can, in all cases, try on what we say and see if it works for you.

Finally, to make room for the extra content, something had to go. We decided to excise all the material about the composite chart which made up Part Four, "The Eternal Triangle," of the original *Skymates*. That was a hard choice, but it was made even more pressing by the fact that we have learned enough about the composite chart over the last fourteen years to fill another book.

Writing that one is our next project. We hope to have *Skymates, Volume Two: The Composite Chart,* available sometime in 2003.

Jodie and Steven Forrest
Borrego Springs, California
July 21, 2001

CHAPTER ONE: MAGIC OR MURDEROUS MYTHOLOGY?

Nothing strips us so naked. Nothing is quicker to reveal the angel we hide behind our eyes, and nothing is so quick to unmask our private madnesses. Who has not been lifted high by love? Who has not felt the world change in a moment of secret tenderness? And who has not been ripped open by love and left bleeding and alone, wide-eyed at four in the morning?

People speak of "fear of intimacy" as if it were some kind of modern disease. That's lunacy. We've never met anyone with enough brains to fill a teaspoon who didn't fear intimacy. It's dangerous. It's an awesome force. Once we've been around love's mulberry bush a few times, we learn that—and usually have some scars to prove it. Kids from happy, stable families generally don't know it, and maybe they serve to remind us of some innocent state of grace. But for most of us, in matters of love, it's "once burned, twice smart," and maybe that's not so bad. Maybe that hesitation to trust another person has something to do with wisdom. Certainly it has to do with experience.

Yet most of us come back. Heterosexual people, gay people, cultural conservatives and people experimenting on the wild and woolly edges of human possibility—love draws us all like a magnet. And only those whom love has truly battered into hopelessness see that return as madness. We return to love for the same reasons we hesitate: wisdom and experience. Once we've allowed ourselves to love, whatever the outcome, we're hooked. We have realized that little else can give us even half that much joy. And perhaps if we're reflective, we've also learned that no force can so radically accelerate our long evolutionary march toward sanity and inner peace.

On rare occasions, when love goes bad, the fault lies squarely on the shoulders of one person. One lover might simply be too irresponsible, too selfish, too damaged, or too confused about sex to make that kind of leap right then, and the other lover is left hanging. But that's rare. Most of the time, when love goes bad, we find two sets of fingerprints on the murder weapon.

Why? Part of the answer comes when we take a minute to contemplate a simple fact: most of us date a lot more people than we marry—and we're using the word "marry" here in the organic sense, not the legal one. Chew on that fact, and it's not long before we realize that the vast majority of our relationships are "doomed to fail," although "doomed to fail" is perhaps an overly grim prognosis. Certainly we *learn* from most of our courtship experiences. The critical idea is that not every man or woman is right for us.

We may learn to turn away from the ones with "poison" written in neon letters across their foreheads. But that still leaves a lot of good people in the world, and sometimes we're halfway to deep commitment before we realize that the magic is falling victim to the craziness. Sometimes we're a few years beyond the commitment.

Another part of the answer, and the part that forms the soul of this book, is that no matter how good our intentions and no matter how inspired our choice of partners, relationships are still perhaps the greatest challenge life will ever offer us. Nothing so stretches the soul. They even make nuclear physics seem simple by comparison, as I suspect many a loving nuclear physicist will attest.

In *Skymates* we're writing about the Holy Grail of loving: a sexual, existential partnership aimed at lasting for the long haul. To make that kind of love work in our lives, we need help. In fact, we need all the help we can get. Astrology cannot create love. What astrology can do is serve as an ally in the process of loving.

The gift astrology offers is simply one of clear seeing. It serves as a wise third party, mirroring each lover's viewpoint, needs, and nature with neutrality and evolutionary insight. Used sensitively, it does not pontificate and judge. That's not how conscious, evolutionary astrology operates. Instead, it seeks only to promote mutual understanding. (For the principles of evolutionary astrology, please see Appendix Two.)

Where there are irresolvable dilemmas, astrology can often suggest adult compromises. Where there are basic harmonies, astrology can help you fan those delightful flames with concrete strategies for joy and play. Where your dictionaries contain the same words, but with different definitions, astrology can often help straighten out the tangled lines of communication.

If you are single, astrology can assist you in understanding what kinds of people best suit your needs in the long haul—and it can warn you about illusions that leave you with nothing but empty hurt. If you are currently in love, astrology can help you nurture the relationship, counseling gentleness here, force there, self-scrutiny in this area, hard questions for your partner in that one, slowly guiding you as you mold that love into a treasure.

All that, astrology can do well. Loving, you must do for yourself.

Half the Truth

Romance is dangerous. Most of us can affirm that fact from our own experience. But there are those who take an even darker view. Some people think romantic feelings are a kind of mental disorder. They point out that kind of love often takes an otherwise sane individual and turns him or her into a babbling psychopath: jealous, insecure, possessive, and monomaniacally consumed with one other person, as if that single individual held the key to all the happiness and meaning in the universe.

That's perhaps an overly cynical view, but we've all certainly seen it in our partners—and, if we're brave, in the mirror too. What makes us act that way?

The Jungian analyst Robert Johnson, in his book, *We: Understanding the Psychology of Romantic Love* (Harper and Row, NY, 1984), offers some convincing arguments on the subject. His thesis, which he develops through insightful analysis of a twelfth century chivalric myth, is that romantic love is a relatively new invention, unique to Western civilization, and that, so far as healthiness goes, it's generally up there with HIV and spent nuclear fuel rods. His notion, in a nutshell, is that with the collapse of the absolute authority of the church, our ancestors took a lot of emotional needs that had always been satisfied through religion and attempted to satisfy them through "courtly love"—the endless pining of a knight for an unattainable lady, usually married to someone else. Johnson implies that the unattainable lady was a pretty fair psychological substitute for God. At least it worked until the knight got sick of pining for her and managed to get himself invited into her bed. Then the trouble began. The perfect woman soon proved to be a monkey like the rest of us.

Think about it: when you imagine the ideal sexual relationship for yourself, don't you think of ecstasy, mystical communion, psychic or extrasensory understandings, a sense of ultimate meaning? Spiritual experiences, in other words. The stuff we used to expect from God, not from a man or woman. And that's a lot to ask of a monkey.

Johnson suggests that these unrealistic expectations, fueled by the Hollywood myth-machines, have led inevitably to pain and disillusionment for everyone. He also says that these expectations have become so much a part of our world view that they persist and continue to damage people. He compares our Western notions of marriage unfavorably with those current in India and Japan. He describes marriages in those cultures as often more loving and caring than what we see here, but without the inflated mythology.

3

He then points out how we, with our spiraling divorce rate and our soap operatic lives, arrogantly dismiss those kinds of marriages as "unromantic."

We is a powerful book, and to us, at least, its key insights have the ring of truth. We all expect love to work healing wonders in our lives, and by the time we reach our thirtieth birthdays, most of us have been disastrously disappointed more than once.

How does all this relate to astrology? Very directly. Through the birthchart, you can often glimpse the silhouette of your *soulmate* in clear and explicit terms. Getting that message is easy. What's hard, as we'll be exploring in the chapters that follow, is knowing what to do with your soulmate once you've found each other.

Soulmate! That concept lies at the core of all the romantic mythology that has ever existed. The one true love with whom you are destined to be united! The one who fits you like a key fits a lock! Robert Johnson, and anyone who understands his work, must cringe when they hear the word.

Let them cringe. The word "soulmate" is too beautiful and too elemental a part of our sanity to dismiss. Without it, one more psychologically essential piece of magic goes down the drain. The problem with the word is that for far too long we've let teenagers and romance novelists define it.

The Other Half of the Truth

There's a wise woman from northern Idaho who was kind enough to befriend us some years ago. Once I heard a tape of a psychic reading she had done for a couple we know. In it she said, "You two are soulmates." After a dramatic pause she continued, "And soulmates often kill each other."

Just what does it mean to keep company with a soulmate? The first step is to forget the idea that the seconds, months, and decades you spend with such a person are some kind of blissful, orgasmic dream. That may be part of it sometimes, but the core of the idea is that in a soulmate we meet someone who is capable of helping us alter our fundamental natures, helping us alter our *souls*, in other words. And that process can make a ride on a roller coaster look like teatime with your maiden aunt.

Johnny plays guitar in a rock band. He's a natural musician but has never really pushed himself to explore the limits of his talent. He's been on the road for ten years and is increasingly reliant on alcohol, drugs, and cynicism to get him through the day.

Into Johnny's life comes Terry, his soulmate. As is often the case with such meetings, they react to each other quickly, moving into a sexual relationship. The honeymoon is short-lived. Terry sees clearly what Johnny is doing to himself. As his soulmate, she also *sees what he could be*. She keys into his nature in such a way that his "decadent rock star" pose suddenly seems awkward and transparent to both of them, little more than a thin defensive posture. Terry's very being seems to confront Johnny, challenging him. Is this the best of what you are? Is this the highest truth you know?

In the Hollywood version of the story, Johnny obediently cleans up his act, marries Terry, hailing her as his savior, and they blissfully drive off to fame, fortune, and the eternal suburbs.

In real life, they have one hell of a fight.

In real life, that fight brings up such defensiveness in both of them that Johnny and Terry very likely break up, at least for a while. Something deep inside Johnny senses that if he stays with Terry, the life he knows will be irremediably changed. Profound fears, locked behind elaborate defense mechanisms, loom large and demand battle. Brittle, comforting lies come crashing down. Psychological "devil's bargains" he made back in childhood suddenly come up for review.

Why should Johnny vex himself with all this trauma? Is this woman really worth the trouble she's causing? There are plenty of other women. Those are good questions, and ones he no doubt asks himself. Conveniently, Sexy Sadie appears on the scene, and Johnny finds her overwhelmingly attractive. He has a cup of coffee with Terry and solemnly tells her that her nature is just too intense for him, and besides, Sadie accepts him as he is. They both agree that their affair was a "learning experience," but that it's finished.

Why is Terry so quick to agree with Johnny's bogus analysis? For the same reason he was so quick to produce it—she's terrified too! Just as with him, half of what she potentially is has never been revealed. *A soulmate relationship is never a one-way street.* In this kind of human love, saviors always come in matching pairs.

Terry is a poet, and a fine one. She writes grown-up love poetry, verses full of love and hate, passion and fear. But no one knows that about her. Her poetry is a deep secret. The few poems she's published appeared under a pseudonym. Long ago Terry learned to keep her feelings hidden. She has always been the one who takes care of other people. That pattern goes right back to her childhood, where circumstances forced her to play the role of parent to her younger siblings. Being the rescuer is comfortable for her. Equality and emotional nakedness are experiences she's never known. They frighten her.

Johnny, despite all his own issues, sees through Terry's mask as if it were a windowpane. When his eyes lock on to hers, something deep inside her feels profoundly uncomfortable. "Here's a man who could flush me out of hiding. Here's one who already seems to know about my secrets—not only my poetry, but also my hunger, my possessiveness, my need to remain in control. *I'm getting out of here!*"

What happens? There's no way to know, not even with astrology. People write their own scripts. Maybe Johnny and Terry part, the potential of their soul-bond left untapped. Maybe they stay together, and still leave the potential of their soul-bond untapped. How? Perhaps Johnny remains the perennial child, playing the eternal "bad boy" to Terry's "martyred mommy." Together they could methodically build a marriage in which eyes never meet, sex occurs only in the dark, and a private joke is made out of what they mockingly describe as other couples' "growth experiences."

Those are sad choices, but they are available. How often have you seen love blow up in an explosion that was more smoke than fire? How many zombie marriages have you seen?

The alternative, for Terry and Johnny—and the rest of us—is to recognize that if love is going to heal us, it must sometimes take us to the limits of our endurance first. Honesty, courage, humility, trust, forgiveness—adult love's ancient allies—must hurl explosions of light into the darkest, most painful, most embarrassing corners of our psyches.

There's joy too, of course. This is not a pessimistic book you're holding in your hands! Quite the opposite. But couples often part nowadays, and it's rarely because of excessive joy. When soul touches soul, we experience perhaps the deepest happiness we'll ever know. We also experience evolutionary growth, and it's there that we encounter those far limits of our potential as men and women.

Johnny and Terry, you and me, we're all free to do as we please. Astrology is no panacea for the hurt that love sometimes gives us. The panacea, if there is one, lies in the radical development of those virtues—honesty, courage, forgiveness, patience—that make ongoing, grown-up love a possibility for us.

What if Johnny and Terry, after their breakup, find themselves drifting back together again? What if they realize that some invisible cord links their spirits, but that their fearful games are gnawing at it like a hungry coyote?

Perhaps in their confusion, and with their hearts and minds open, they approach a modern evolutionary astrologer. What happens? Johnny might learn that he is a fourth house Pisces with Sagittarius rising. Translated, he

6

would learn that his entire identity is locked into a magical, mystical realm of imagination and creativity, but that as a result, his ego never quite crystallized. He would learn that people such as himself can serve as precious oracles for the rest of us, if they don't ruin that potential with dissipation, vain posturing, and escapism. He would learn that his Sagittarian Ascendant gives him a breezy, colorful "gypsy mask" to hide behind—which is just fine, as long as he doesn't start believing his own press releases.

Terry would hear that she's a Cancer with Capricorn on the Ascendant and the Moon in Virgo. To use a formula we'll introduce in the next chapter, she is the *Healer* (Cancer Sun) with the *Soul of the Servant* (Virgo Moon) wearing the *Mask of the Elder* (Capricorn Ascendant). Beautiful energy at times—but it also accounts for her urge to protect herself from true intimacy with Johnny by hiding behind the role of his guru, mother, and psychotherapist.

With Johnny and Terry sitting there looking into each other's eyes, that astrologer would lay the cards on the table. They could read their scripts like automatons in an ancient melodrama, with Johnny playing the tragic rogue and Terry playing the doomed angel who loves him come what may. Or they could drop those deadening, soulless games, face each other like three-dimensional adults, and help each other grow.

That astrologer could go a lot further. Wisdom and sensitivity artificially boosted by the two birthcharts, he or she could X-ray the bond that joins Terry and Johnny, checking it for any kind of interactive weakness, and in many cases offering practical solutions and supportive, positive interpretations of their dilemmas. Johnny, for example, has a fourth house Piscean need for occasional periods of absolute, uncontested privacy in order to cultivate his creativity and spiritual life. If he doesn't get those periods alone, then he's likely to become withdrawn and moody, inclined toward staring at the television. Terry needs to learn that when Johnny asks for some space, it has nothing to do with her character or with their relationship, and she doesn't need to feel threatened.

Terry, on the other hand, needs a bit more orderliness, predictability, and emotional support in her life than Johnny might instinctively provide. That goes with the territory of Cancer, Virgo, and Capricorn, the signs that figure so prominently in her psychological makeup. Situations that would seem merely adventuresome and interesting to Johnny can feel dangerously out of control to Terry. One taste, and she clams up, hiding her fear behind one of her controlling masks. If she is going to feel safe enough to reveal the poet inside her, she's going to need a lot of reassurance first.

7

Johnny is Johnny, and it would be wrong to ask him to mold his life around Terry's insecurities. But with the astrologer's assistance, he could perhaps recognize the true nature of those insecurities for the first time and treat his soulmate with more sensitivity. For her sake? Yes, of course; that generosity is in the nature of love. But also for his own sake: life is simply more pleasant with a sane woman than with a mad one.

Going further into each of their charts, taking in planets, houses, and other technical details that we'll explore in chapters to come, the astrologer might strike a vein of gold: Terry and Johnny, for example, might love to garden together, or travel, or learn a foreign language. Those shared experiences might help forge a powerful link in the chain of pleasures that binds them together—and without a full measure of those pleasures, nobody but a masochist is going to last long in a relationship with a soulmate! Figuring out ways to emphasize and support the natural joys of the partnership is just as essential as negotiating solutions to the inevitable conflicts. In some ways, it might even be more important. For most of us, it's joy that keeps us working on a relationship, not the abstract promise of spiritual growth.

This, then, is the territory of *synastry*, the astrology of partnership. As you can see from what we've written so far, our aim is an active, dynamic one. We are not fortune-tellers. In this book, you will learn more than how to issue postmortems on failed relationships, or to come up with astrological reasons for why a particular bond is working. Far more excitingly, you will learn how to use astrology actively to intervene in the process of loving, helping yourself and your loved ones experience improved communication, deeper happiness, personal growth, better sex—and clean, fair fights that tear walls down rather than build them up.

If you know some astrology already, you will probably not find this book terribly demanding at a technical level. Even if you are a complete beginner, we'll get you up to speed as quickly as we can in the following chapter. But the personal questions this book raises will very likely push you into emotionally explosive territory.

Fortunately astrology can also help guide you through those explosive places. It can calm you, counsel you, lift you above the hormonal fog. If you're just starting with astrology and the symbolism seems a bit technical or abstract at first, stick with it. There is nothing mysterious about it. Astrology is just life, translated into a kind of symbolic shorthand. It's only a craft, with clear-cut procedures and techniques. To use it, you don't need anything that you don't already have between your ears. In a few hours, you'll learn enough to help yourself. With a few weeks of effort, you'll acquire enough skill to begin helping others.

If you've read *The Inner Sky*, you've already learned half the language. In that case you might want to skip the next chapter entirely, which is a crash course for beginners. If you've never learned about astrology before, please pay close attention to the next few pages. You'll need that knowledge to make sense of the material that follows.

CHAPTER TWO: INSTANT ASTROLOGY

Never explored astrology before? Then this chapter is for you. A grand tour of all the basic symbolism, squeezed into a few pages, is enough to get you started. That simplicity is one of the beauties of astrology—but don't let it fool you. Even though all the essentials can be expressed in a handful of elementary ideas, a lifetime of endless fascination can pass as you discover all their nuances and subtleties. Johannes Kepler never got to the bottom of the astrological well. Neither did Pythagoras or Plato or Galileo or Carl Jung, nor did any of the similarly gifted women whose names seem to have slipped our minds. Yet all of them started with the same raw material: thirty-four basic astrological symbols and some connective tissue. Here we briefly survey that territory. If you'd like a deeper understanding of these ideas, try reading Steven's book, *The Inner Sky*.

Signs, Planets, and Houses

Astrology is not one single system of symbols. It is three: signs, planets, and houses. Each set of symbols is separate and distinct. Each serves a unique purpose. Learning to keep them untangled is the first step in any orderly, effective approach to astrological interpretation.

Briefly, signs represent a set of twelve psychological processes, each with a clear evolutionary goal, appropriate resources, and a few classic pitfalls. Aries, for example, represents the process of *seeking courage*. Its central resources are enthusiasm and love of adventure. But if the process goes sour, then instead of courage, we see nothing but pointless explosiveness, bluster and temper—Arian energy run amuck.

Planets, quite distinct from signs, represent a *map of the mind*. Every one of us, for example, has some capacity for reason. Everyone has some capacity to feel. Many times we find it useful to divide those two categories of experience. "My heads says I should do this, but my heart says I should do that." Planets work exactly the same way—except that they divide the mind into ten pieces of mental circuitry, not two. There's a planet for reason (Mercury) and one for feeling (the Moon), but there are also planets for many other functions, such as self-discipline (Saturn), assertiveness (Mars), even our ability to resist the herd instinct (Uranus). Everybody's got all ten planets; they just work differently in each of us.

Houses represent life's basic existential arenas. There are twelve of them, and each symbolizes a territory we can enter and explore. There's a "house of learning," for example. There's also a "house of career." Some of the houses represent internal rather than external territories—there's a "house of the unconscious mind." The key with houses is to know that they are concrete areas of life where we can make choices.

Put signs, planets, and houses together, and they give us humanity's oldest and most evocative map of the mind. Here's a very simple way of keeping them straight:

Planets answer the question *"What?"* What part of the mind are we talking about? Ego development? Rational thought? Mate selection?

Signs take us a step farther by answering the questions *"Why?"* and *"How?"* What is that planet's goal? What is it chasing after? What is its hidden agenda? How can that goal be realized?

Houses complete the picture by answering the final question, *"Where?"* In what part of life will we observe the most characteristic behavioral expression of that planet-sign dynamic? Will it be in creativity, in love affairs, in the professional life?

Put the three symbols together and you have a description of a rather precise and unique human situation. Understanding it will give you real insight into certain dimensions of the person's nature, and a spectrum of possible behaviors available to him or to her. Some of those behaviors will be self-evidently positive—they'll involve a more creative, interesting, loving engagement with life's possibilities. Others, equally consistent with the message of the symbols, will be darker. They'll reflect letting fear or self-importance or even simple denial make too many decisions.

It is profoundly important to remember that every configuration is like that: there really are no good or bad configurations—*all of them are potentially both good and bad.* What happens in our lives depends on the choices we make within the framework of the astrological questions.

Underlying all these ideas is one basic philosophical premise: life is purposeful, and its purpose centers on the evolution of consciousness. What we see in these planet-sign-house combinations is nothing less than the *evolutionary intentions* of a soul in this lifetime.

Here's an example of how all this works in practice. Dustin Hoffman was born in Los Angeles on August 8, 1937, at 5:07 PM PST. That gives him the planet Mars in the sign Sagittarius late in his tenth house. What can that mean? Think like this: Mars is the *what.* In this case, we are talking about assertiveness. Everyone has assertiveness issues in his or her birthchart, what makes Dustin Hoffman unique? His assertiveness is motivated by the logic of the sign Sagittarius, so that sign supplies the *why* and the *how*. In this case we see that his Mars is developmentally motivated by an urge to seek new horizons or to break up familiar routines (Sagittarian goals). Where will we see the most characteristic expression of this desire? In his tenth house—the house of career.

Dustin Hoffman has apparently made a strong, self-aware response to his Mars configuration. He has shown eagerness to explore new, controversial, unfamiliar territories in his career. As an actor he has resisted Hollywood's tendency to typecast its stars, as anyone who has seen his hilarious portrayal of a woman in *Tootsie* will affirm.

Did Dustin Hoffman have any choice in the matter, or was he simply "programmed" by astrological forces? That is perhaps the single most important question any student of astrology could ask. Astrologers are divided: traditionally, one's "fate" could be read in the stars. Many astrologers still think that way. We disagree. To us, an individual's willpower and imagination play a huge role in determining how the astrological forces actually manifest. A truly modern astrologer rarely speaks of "fate" in rigid, inescapable terms. Dustin Hoffman, and everybody else, makes choices. He's apparently risen to the evolutionary challenge and done well with his tenth-house Sagittarian Mars. He could have done otherwise. His freedom includes the right to "chicken out" (Mars failure), abandon his expansive principles (Sagittarian failure), and wind up in some kind of boring, irritating work that has nothing to do with him (tenth-house failure), probably with a petty tyrant for a boss. We should credit Dustin Hoffman's courage, not his birthchart, that he has accomplished so much.

For easy reference as you progress through this book, we are including an overview of the signs, planets, and houses in Tables One, Two and Three, on pages 14, 15 and 16. This is shorthand, to put it mildly. People have literally written books about each one of these symbols. Ultimately they are all sufficiently multidimensional to deserve that kind of in-depth treatment. But if you're a beginner, this overview will get you started. As you read on and watch the symbols put to practical use, you'll quickly learn much more. There's a good reason for that—you already know all this material! It's just life, translated into a kind of supercondensed code. You don't have to learn the ideas; those you know right now. All you need to learn is the code itself, and that's not so hard once you practice for a little while.

TABLE ONE: THE PLANETS

Planet	Glyph	Function	Dysfunction
Sun	☉	Identity Formation Vitality	Selfishness Laziness
Moon	☽	Subjectivity Emotion	Moodiness Self-indulgence
Mercury	☿	Intelligence, Curiosity, Communication	Nervousness Worry
Venus	♀	Empathy, Love, Connection	Vanity, Dissipation, Manipulation
Mars	♂	Assertiveness, Territoriality	Rage (Self) Destruction
Jupiter	♃	Faith Enthusiasm	Overextension Pompousness
Saturn	♄	Self-discipline Reality-testing	Depression Unresponsiveness
Uranus	♅	Individuation Autonomy	Eccentricity Rebelliousness
Neptune	♆	Mysticism Imagination	Confusion Escapism
Pluto	♇	Truthfulness Penetration	Cynicism Meaninglessness
South Node	☋	Consciousness of Old Patterns	Repetition of Old Patterns
North Node	☊	Definition of Soul-Intentions	Ignorance

TABLE TWO: THE SIGNS

Sign	Glyph	Aim	Strategy	Shadow
Aries	♈	Courage	Adventure	Rage
Taurus	♉	Serenity Naturalness	Silence Simplicity	Laziness Materialism
Gemini	♊	Openness Curiosity	Experience Learning	Chaos
Cancer	♋	Caring Healing	Nurturing of Self & Other	Invisibility "Mothering"
Leo	♌	Joy; Self-expression	Creativity Play	Melodrama False Pride
Virgo	♍	Perfection	Analysis Precision	Self-doubt Fussiness
Libra	♎	Balance Peace	Aesthetics Grace	Indecision Inauthenticity
Scorpio	♏	Depth Soul-retrieval	Introspection Honesty	Moodiness Heaviness
Sagittarius	♐	Understanding Expansion	Immersion in Experience	Foolishness Fanaticism
Capricorn	♑	Great Works Integrity	Self-discipline	Coldness Repression
Aquarius	♒	Individuality	Questioning Authority	Alienation Dissociation
Pisces	♓	Mystical Oneness	Compassion Meditation	Confusion Escapism

TABLE THREE: THE HOUSES

House	Traditional Name	Territory
1	House of Personality	Personal style; social "mask"
2	House of Money	Resources; self-confidence
3	House of Communication	Information exchange
4	House of Home	Personal roots; the deep Self
5	House of Children	Self-expression; play; pleasure
6	House of Servants	Duties; mentoring; skill
7	House of Marriage	Intimacy; commitment
8	House of Death	Instincts; sexual bonding; wounds
9	House of Journeys	Education; travel; beliefs
10	House of Career	Profession; reputation
11	House of Friends	Goals; allies; strategies
12	House of Troubles	Release; spirituality

Aspects

There's another link in the astrological chain: *aspects*. These are simply *geometric angles* formed between planets. Long ago, astrologers realized that certain angles had specific personalities. Planets separated by those angles interacted powerfully, with each planet flavoring the meaning of the other. These interactions can take many forms. Sometimes two planets appear to be best friends, helping each other and sharing common goals. Other times, the relationship between two planets can be more problematic. They seem to be natural enemies. These angles, by the way, are pretty intuitive—triangles and squares and six-pointed stars.

We still read about "good" aspects and "bad" aspects, but those ideas are misleading ones and are gradually fading from the astrologer's vocabulary. The so-called good aspects are better described as harmonious—and that doesn't always mean good. Two wild teenagers can be in perfect harmony with each other about "borrowing" that shiny red Lexus for an hour or two. Their singleminded accord still doesn't make stealing that car a good idea. Maybe a third friend introduces a "bad aspect," pointing out to them that another term for their proposed joyride is "Grand Theft Auto," and mentioning that he saw the Chief of Police climb out of that very Lexus just an hour ago. So-called bad aspects may be disharmonious, but they often breed caution and sound judgment.

One more idea: although aspects are technically very precise angles, they tolerate a certain amount of slushiness. We call that slushiness the "orb" of the aspect. For example, a square is technically an angle of ninety degrees. In practice, a pair of planets separated by ninety-five degrees still interacts he same way. In Table Four on page 18, we give our suggestions for these orbs, but please don't take them rigidly. Aspects never simply "turn on" or "turn off." They build gradually in intensity, then slowly fade out. The orbs we suggest are no more than rules of thumb to help get you off to a sound start.

Table Four summarizes the action of the major aspects. If you'd like deeper understanding, you might want to read Chapter Nine of *The Inner Sky*.

Here's an example of how aspects work in practice. We've already looked at Dustin Hoffman's tenth-house Sagittarian Mars. He also has Saturn in early Aries in his second house. It makes a trine aspect to his Mars. How do we analyze this interaction?

TABLE FOUR: ASPECTS

Aspect	Glyph	Separation	Orb	Interactive Process
Conjunction	☌	0°	7°	Fusion; synthesis
Sextile	⚹	60°	5°	Stimulation; excitation
Square	□	90°	7°	Friction; clashing
Trine	△	120°	7°	Enhancement; support
Opposition	☍	180°	7°	Tension; polarization

Start by grasping the significance of each planet. We got a handle on Mars a few paragraphs back, so that leaves Saturn. What part of Dustin Hoffman's mental circuitry are we discussing? Saturn, his capacity for self-discipline and for adjustment to living in the real world. What *motivates* his Saturn? What is Saturn's *hidden agenda,* and what are its *resources?* The sign, Aries, provides our answer. At the highest level, his evolutionary intention is to use self-discipline (Saturn) to learn courage (Aries's aim). His resources in that process are a sense of adventure and a taste for risk (Aries material). Now add the final ingredient: houses. Where will we see the most characteristic behavioral expression of his Saturn in Aries? In the second house: that is, in Hoffman's efforts to gain self-confidence, to prove himself to himself (second house terrain).

In plain English, if Dustin Hoffman is to *feel good about himself* (second house), he must work in a self-disciplined, perfectionistic way (Saturn) and be willing to take risks there (Aries).

This Saturn function is in a supportive, harmonious *trine* aspect with his exploratory Mars in the house of career. The two planets clearly share common ground and common goals. As one prospers, so does the other. But since each is inclined to mammoth outlays of energy, this mutually supportive harmony also threatens the potential danger of emotional or physical burnout. He might, for example, be working near his limits, determined to take a much-needed break as soon as possible. On the eve of that vacation he's offered an exciting, challenging acting opportunity, starting tomorrow. His tenth house Sagittarian Mars might find that offer irresistible, and his second house Arian Saturn might give him the discipline and drive he needs to complete the project. But what happened to that vacation? And how long can his mind and body endure that kind of stress? Always remember those two rambunctious kids agreeing to take the Lexus for a spin!

The Birthchart

Figure One on page 20 shows Dustin Hoffman's complete birthchart. While a detailed analysis of the chart would carry us too far afield, a guided tour of its layout will help you relate the ideas we've covered in this chapter to all those seemingly incomprehensible squiggles.

The first point to grasp is that a birthchart is simply a stylized map of the sky as it looked on the date of a person's birth, at the instant of his or her first breath, from the point of view of the birthplace.

19

FIGURE ONE

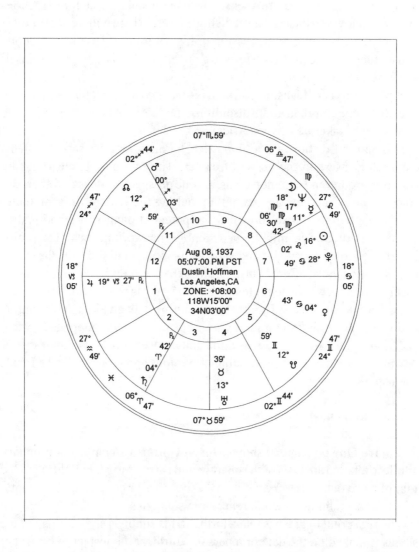

The horizontal axis of the birthchart represents the horizon. Everything above that line was in the visible half of the sky at the instant Dustin Hoffman was born. Everything beneath the line was invisible, beneath the earth. The prominent "pie-slices" are the twelve houses. Here's the tricky part: east is on the *left,* not on the right where we customarily find it. This break with convention has more behind it than simple perversity, but since we're trying to cover a lot of ground quickly here, we won't waste time with explanations. If you're curious, look at Chapter Three of *The Inner Sky.*

Planets are scattered in what appears to be a random way through the houses. The Sun {☉} is in Hoffman's seventh house; find it on the right side of the chart above Pluto {♇}, which lies above the horizon line. (Remember, west is on the right!) What you are looking at is a setting Sun, low in the western sky, and that makes sense for a birth that occurred at 5:07 PM. If we found the Sun anywhere else, we'd know immediately that a mathematical error had been made. The birthchart, in other words, is a kind of clock. Learn how to read it, and you can do a rough check on the accuracy of the astrologer's computations. How? Simply by remembering that the Sun sets in the west in the afternoon, rises in the east at dawn, and so on.

Next to the glyph for Dustin Hoffman's Sun you see the notation 16°02'. This tells us where his Sun is in terms of the twelve signs. It lies in sixteen degrees and two minutes of Leo. (A minute is one-sixtieth of a degree.) Each sign is thirty degrees wide, and a planet can be anywhere in the sign. Its meaning is not affected directly by the degree it occupies; just knowing the sign is enough for that. Why do we bother with degrees then? They become important when we start thinking about aspects, and they are also necessary to help us see exactly which house a planet occupies.

What about all those numbers around the outer rim of the wheel? Those notations show us where the wheel of signs has "stopped" in relation to Dustin Hoffman's houses; they establish the all-important relationship between the two wheels—houses and signs.

Think about it like this: earlier on the day of his birth the Sun was still in Leo—it spends a month there each year—but of course it was higher in the sky. If Hoffman had been born just before noon, for example, that Leo Sun would have been in the tenth house, not the seventh. You see the apparent motion of the Sun around the Earth every day: it rises, passes overhead and sets. Just take that observation a step further and recognize that the signs do exactly the same thing. Like the Sun, they rise, pass overhead, and set.

Look toward the eastern horizon of the birthchart. There, on the left, you see the notation 18° ♑ 05'. This tells us that eighteen degrees, five minutes, of the sign Capricorn was rising at the instant Dustin Hoffman took his first breath. If he had waited an hour or so before being born, then the next sign, Aquarius, would have been rising. Even though we can't readily see it, the wheel of signs is spinning around the wheel of houses. In twenty-four hours each sign will rise once.

The rising sign, along with the Sun and the Moon, is one of the three most significant factors in astrology. Together, they form the *primal triad.* Symbolically, the rising sign (or Ascendant, to use the more formal term) represents the *social personality.* It is the mask the psyche must adopt if it is to relate to the superficial realities of most human interaction. Insincerity is not the point. You don't, for example, necessarily tell the traffic cop how you feel about his giving you a speeding ticket! That's a superficial relationship, and it's best to keep it that way. Think of the Ascendant as the stained glass through which the light of your spirit is shining into the world; as it makes the translation from inner experience to outer expression, it's given a certain tint or hue.

With Capricorn rising, Dustin Hoffman wears the mask of the hermit. He would be hard to read at first, but he would radiate the Capricorn qualities of competence and responsibility, and probably a hint of mischievous humor. Jupiter was almost exactly on the eastern horizon when he was born, so his Ascendant is more complex than most. The clownish expansiveness of Jupiter mitigates some of Capricorn's typical reserve. Hoffman's mask would include some good-humored playfulness, but behind that surface we would sense qualities of solitude and caution.

Numbers appear around the entire rim of the birthchart. They all work pretty much like the Ascendant. Each one shows where the **cusp** (that is, the beginning) of a house intersects the wheel of signs. Look, for example, at the cusp of his second house. There you will see the notation 27°♒ 49', telling us that twenty-seven degrees, forty-nine minutes of the sign Aquarius lie at the beginning of that house. The top of Hoffman's birthchart shows 07°♏59'; he has seven degrees, fifty-nine minutes of Scorpio on his *Midheaven,* or tenth house cusp. That's the part of the birthchart that refers to his relationship to the community: his "job" in the largest sense.

Aspects are shown in the triangular grid in Figure Two on page 23. We've discussed the trine formed between Mars and Saturn. Where do we see it? Find the glyphs for Mars and Saturn in the aspect grid. Look down the Saturn column until it intersects the Mars row. In that box you see a little triangle, the glyph for the trine. Similarly, there's a sextile between

FIGURE TWO

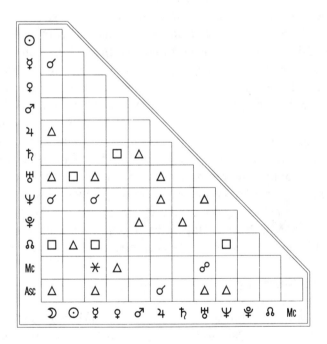

Hoffman's Mercury and his Midheaven, a conjunction of the Moon and Neptune, and so on.

The Nodes of the Moon

Two more symbols appear on the birthchart: the north (☊) and south (☋) *Nodes of the Moon*. These are some of the deepest and most slippery symbols in astrology. Here's the best way we know to think about them: a baby is born. He or she is only thirty seconds old. Look into that baby's eyes. *There's already someone in there!* One infant looks wise, another jolly; a third one seems kind of vacant. How did a personality get in there so quickly? The Hindu or the old Druid would speak of previous lifetimes. The scientist would tell us of heredity. The Pope might speak of some disembodied prebirth state in the mind of God.

Pick the model that works best for you personally. Anyone with the right attitude for astrological practice understands that the core message of the symbolism lies in having respect for human differences. Throughout this book, we will mostly use the language of reincarnation. That's our belief, but if it's not your belief too, you can think of the South Node as representing the reality of what you can see in the eyes of that newborn infant. Whether it's reincarnation, DNA, psychological family history or how God made the baby, all these perspectives refer to "past lives" in some sense of the word.

The north node, always opposite the south node, refers to the individual's evolutionary future. It represents the most challenging, the most unfamiliar and therefore the most awkward, *and* the most spiritually rewarding activity available to the person.

And that's the birthchart. Hopefully, if you're a beginner, this ancient wheel of hieroglyphics is not quite as cryptic as it was a little while ago.

A Helpful Shortcut

A birthchart can be almost as complex as a human being, and figuring one out completely is one of those endless, impossible tasks that can fascinate us for a lifetime. What's often less obvious is that a birthchart can also be extremely simple.

There's a trick, first introduced in *The Inner Sky*, that allows us to convert the essential message of any given birthchart into a single sentence. Naturally, in employing this shortcut, we lose sight of a lot of juicy details. But we gain that most precious of interpretive qualities: perspective. In all astrological work, and most especially in synastry, our great bugaboo is the threat of losing track of the big picture. The following technique, while utterly simple, is more than a free ticket down the path of least resistance. It's a strategy that supplies a framework to help you keep your balance as you move into more subtle levels of analysis.

The shortcut is based upon the three most critical factors in any birthchart: the Sun, the Moon, and the Ascendant. The Sun is taken to represent *who the person is*, his or her identity. The Moon, with its emotional, magical dimensions, represents the individual's *soul*. Finally, the Ascendant, our social personality, plays the role of our *mask*.

These three factors, Sun, Moon, and Ascendant, are then expressed as *archetypes*, according to the sign that's flavoring them. Archetypes are simple mythic images, like "the wise old man" or "the impetuous youth." A less charitable word for archetype is "cliché." That translation is accurate enough, but to call an archetype a cliché is to risk missing its real power, which is the capacity to convey a lot of information in a single image.

On pages 26 and 27 is a *Table of Archetypes*. In this table, the spirit of all twelve signs, in both their higher and less than healthy manifestations, is expressed in simple human images. Some of them are more cultural icons than archetypes in the strict sense of that word, but in those cases we thought they worked so well that we included them anyway. There is nothing rigid about this Table; they are merely suggestions. As your own experience with the sign deepens, we encourage you to add to the lists. Also, bookmark these pages, because you'll want to refer to this table in Chapter Eight on interaspects.

Dustin Hoffman is a Sun sign Leo, with the Moon in Virgo and Capricorn rising. Unless you've been studying astrology for a while, that sentence might not mean a great deal to you. But now let's apply our formula. We might say that he is the Performer (Leo Sun) with the soul of the Perfectionist (Virgo Moon) wearing the mask of the Hermit (Capricorn Ascendant). Or that he is the Clown with the soul of the Martyr wearing the mask of the Prime Minister. We can mix the archetypal images in any way we please. However they are assembled, they reveal a lot about an individual's character in a few words.

Try the technique yourself. It's powerful. You've heard of number-crunchers. This is a symbol-cruncher. Within its limitations, the Table of Archetypes works wonders. Practice a few minutes, and you'll be able to glance at any birthchart and almost instantly say something intelligent about it.

TABLE OF ARCHETYPES

Sign	High Archetypes	Low Archetypes
Aries	The Warrior; The Survivor; the Daredevil; The Pioneer	The Bully; The Reckless Fool; The Warmonger
Taurus	The Silent One; the Elf; The Totem Animal (pick your favorite creature!)	The Stubborn Mule; The Reactionary; the Materialist
Gemini	The Witness; the Storyteller; The Communicator	The Chatterbox; The Eternal Adolescent; the Trickster
Cancer	The Sensitive; The Healer; The Parent; The Psychotherapist	The Smothering Mother; the Crybaby; Invisible Man/Woman
Leo	The King/Queen; The Performer; Clown; The Child; The Aristocrat	The Autocrat; The Megalomaniac; The Spoiled Brat; the Prima Donna
Virgo	The Analyst; The Servant; The Critic; The Perfectionist; The Craftsperson	The Martyr; The Drudge; The Whiner; The Fault-finder

TABLE OF ARCHETYPES

Sign	High Archetypes	Low Archetypes
Libra	The Lover; The Artist; The Diplomat; The Peacemaker; the Counselor	The Flirt; The Fence-sitter; The Snob; The Clinging Vine
Scorpio	The Shaman; The Psychologist; The Detective; The Hypnotist	The Seducer; The Spy; The Intruder; The Wicked Witch/Evil Sorcerer
Sagittarius	The Gypsy; The Scholar; The Philosopher; The Pilgrim	The Guileless Fool; The Overbearing Jerk; The Fanatic
Capricorn	The Father; The Prime Minister; The Hermit; The Elder; The Strategist	The Tyrant; The Curmudgeon; The Schemer; the Power-Tripper
Aquarius	The Exile; the Genius; The Scientist; The Truthsayer; The Revolutionary	The Misfit; The Flake; The Sociopath; The Criminal; The Iceberg
Pisces	The Mystic; The Dreamer; The Poet; The Seer; The Visionary	The Addict; The Lost Soul; The Helpless One; The Space Cadet

If you don't feel that you remember everything you've just read in this chapter, don't worry. For a quick fix, the archetypes won't let you down, and for more detailed information you can always refer to the other tables.

The main point to recall is that astrology is composed of three symbol systems: the *planets,* which describe the structure of the mind; the *signs,* which describe its motivations and needs; and the *houses,* which describe the arenas within which that mind explores and makes decisions. If you can remember that much, you are doing fine. The details will become clearer in the following pages as you watch the astrological drama of love and intimacy unfold. As you'll discover, nothing reveals the inner logic (and illogic!) of a birthchart faster than putting it in the pressure cooker with another birthchart.

CHAPTER THREE: INSTANT SYNASTRY

You've seen how signs, planets, and houses work in an individual birthchart. Now we'll examine what happens when two charts interact.

Two of your faithful friends have eagerly offered to let you practice your astrological skills with them. Twenty minutes ago they showed up at your door. The nervous giggles have died away, and now you're facing two pairs of expectant eyes—and two sets of planets that suddenly make as much sense as an ancient Chinese crossword puzzle.

What you need is a systematic approach. In this brief chapter, we want to give you an overview of the basic procedures we'll be explaining throughout the rest of the book. That way, we hope you'll have a kind of skeleton on which you can hang the many details we're about to explore. Essentially, synastry boils down to two steps: first, you try to understand the individuals as separate, independent entities. Then you try to understand their interactions.

Understanding the Individual

Woody Allen's classic romantic comedy, *Annie Hall*, contains a scene where the couple's therapists ask each of them, in separate sessions, how often they have sex. Diane Keaton's character grimaces and says, "All the time! Three times a week." Woody Allen's character looks injured and says, "Practically never! Three times a week."

Relationships mean different things to different people, and individual needs and expectations vary widely. Look at each chart and ask yourself: Who is this person? What does she want? What does he need? What attracts her? What does he fear? How much privacy does she want? How passionate is he? Try to understand this individual as if he or she were operating in an emotional vacuum, with no reference to anyone else.

In the previous chapter, we made a solid start. Throughout the rest of the book, you'll learn a lot more. At first we'll be considering various astrological configurations in a piecemeal way—the meaning of Mars, for example, in each of the signs or in the houses that are important to relationships. Towards the end of the book, we'll be concentrating on how to put it all together. In fact, there's a chapter by that name, followed by a demonstration of the analysis of two separate birthcharts, those of Zelda and F. Scott Fitzgerald.

Understanding How the Birthcharts Interact

Once you've absorbed each chart's individual message, it's time to compare them. This step really consists of three "giant steps," whose technical procedures form a large part of what you are about to read. Right now, we're only surveying the territory. Later we'll analyze each step in detail.

Here they are:

* *Analyze the aspects the planets in one chart make to the planets in the other chart.* Aries and Libra are opposite signs. If my Moon is in the early part of Aries and your Sun is in the early part of Libra, then we have a Sun-Moon opposition between our charts. That's called an *interaspect*, and it reveals a lot about how we would get along. We'll analyze this technique in detail in Chapters Seven and Eight.

* *Note where the planets in one chart would fall if you placed them in the houses of the other person's chart.* If your Libran Sun were in the first house of your chart, then my Aries Moon (which is opposite your Sun, as we saw) would also have to fall in the opposite house—your seventh. In this technique, it doesn't matter where the Moon is in my *own* chart. Here we're only concerned with where my Moon would be if we put it in *your* chart. This technique is called *House Transpositions*. We'll learn how to work with it in Chapter Nine.

* *Compare the overall feeling of the two charts.* This is the most important step because it's where your intuitive strengths come into play. How do the two people complement each other? Where do they clash? What we're looking for now is the big picture. Search for basic strengths and harmonies between the two charts. How do you think the couple can emphasize them? Where can they maximize what they have in common? What are their blindspots? There are many specific techniques for answering these questions; mostly, however, it's a matter of using imagination and common sense. We think that by the time you come to the end of the book, if you've applied some of what you've learned to the charts of people important to you, this part will be a lot clearer. It's really the soul of synastry. In the final chapters of the book, we'll explain it as best we can. Then we'll demonstrate it when we look at the interactions between Zelda and F. Scott Fitzgerald.

So there are the two steps in synastry: start by honoring the individuality of the two people, then understand their connection and how best to support it. Master them, and you are well on your way to the rewarding experience of performing an effective synastry interpretation.

Let's move on to a close examination of the individual birthchart from a relationship perspective, in Chapters Four, Five and Six. Next we'll focus on interaspects and house transpositions, in Chapters Eight through Fourteen. Then we'll put it all together in Chapter Fifteen, and analyze the Fitzgeralds' synastry in Chapter Sixteen.

CHAPTER FOUR: LOVE AND INDIVIDUALITY
Sun, Moon, Ascendant and the Twelve Signs

A man and a woman sit together in silence, each engrossed in reading. An evening passes. Not a word is spoken. At eleven o'clock the man gets up and walks across the room. He bends over, plants a kiss on the woman's forehead. She looks up warmly and whispers, "I love you." He smiles and his eyes linger on hers for a moment. Then he walks off to brush his teeth, grateful that she's part of his life.

Down the block, another couple sits in silence. He's reading. She's playing solitaire. An hour passes. Suddenly the woman explodes, "If you don't start talking to me, we'll both go crazy! I feel like I'm living with a stranger!" She storms out of the room, slamming the door. He mutters "bitch" behind her back and goes back to his book.

Every partnership needs communication. Every partnership needs some silence too. That much is universal and can safely be applied to everybody. Beyond that, we enter the gray zones. For the first couple, long periods of shared silence are a source of renewed closeness and connectedness. For the second couple, at least for the woman, that same silence is a painful problem. What nourishes the first marriage poisons the second one; what might seem like pointless, annoying chatter in the happier relationship could be a source of joy and healing for the strained one.

Two marriages. That means four people. Four unique human beings, each with his or her own separate hungers, tolerances, and prickly places.

The woman in the traumatized marriage charges out of the house angry and drops in on a friend. She complains that her husband's obsession with reading is his way of avoiding meaningful contact with her. She expresses the opinion that he is an emotional basket case, and that if he had any sensitivity, he'd recognize his problem and make an appointment with a psychotherapist, as she has pressed him to do on countless occasions.

Her husband, meanwhile, finds himself unable to concentrate on his book after the tiff with his wife. He strolls down to the corner bar and meets a buddy. They settle down to talk. Now we hear the husband's side of the argument. Unsurprisingly, the situation has a different complexion to him than it does to his wife. "What can I do? Everything seems fine. She's playing cards. I sit down for an hour to read and she goes off like Mount Vesuvius." Like his wife, he then goes on to offer psychiatric perspectives. "She's like a spoiled kid. She needs constant attention. To hear her talk, the minute I stop gazing into her eyes, I'm a psychopath! The instant I get interested in anything, I'm avoiding her. I can't win."

Who's right? That, of course, is a silly question. They are both right. That is, both people are expressing perfectly legitimate, if differing, human needs. The problem is that the woman needs more active, intensive interaction than her husband does. He, on the other hand, is not quite so psychological as she is. For him, feelings of personal fulfillment arise more from an exploration of ideas than from an exploration of feelings. Perhaps he has been longing for the day when she would read a book herself and share an intelligent discussion with him.

Should they be married? That's a legitimate question. One might read a few too many self-help books and get the notion that any two people chosen at random will spontaneously experience marital bliss, if only they learn to paint by the right numbers. Who knows? Perhaps there is a grain of truth in that assertion, but for practical purposes, half the battle in creating a satisfying bond with another person lies in choosing the right partner. Maybe the man and the woman in this story are ill-suited to each other. Maybe meeting each other's needs would involve such a fundamental betrayal of each one's own nature that they would be better off apart.

These questions are not for an astrologer to answer. They belong strictly to the two individuals. An astrologer's task is to help the man and the woman understand each other and to provide them with practical support and suggestions. Beyond that, it's up to the couple to decide. No matter how impossible a relationship might appear astrologically, the astrologer's central responsibility is to describe ways in which the bond *could* be made to work. This is especially true when, as in our example, the couple has already made a commitment.

Just about everyone wants love. That is one of the few unqualified statements we can make on the subject of intimacy. Beyond that, we enter the infinitely complex world of human differences. One person thrives on silence; another needs talk. One needs adventure and stimulation; the other craves security. Placid harmony versus growth and challenge. Total sharing versus radical individuality. A love of family versus an appreciation of childlessness. How much intellectual input do you need from your partner? How much playfulness? How much seriousness? How much sexual contact? What kinds? The list of variables goes on and on. There is no "generic" experience of human love. For each of us the experience of loving is unique, utterly special, and totally unprecedented.

Our first step as astrologers is to come to grips with that uniqueness. Before we consider any kind of astrological interaction between people, our first requirement is to acquire a thorough understanding of the people *as individuals.* And that process starts with a long, hard look at the two birthcharts—separately.

Sun Signs: Blessing or Curse?

Most people know their Sun signs. Even people who laugh at astrology usually know enough to say "I'm a Taurus" or "I'm a Virgo." Astrology, at least at that level, is woven into the fabric of our culture as tightly as the tales of Mickey Mouse or Batman.

The parallels between that kind of astrology and Mickey Mouse or Batman run deep. Sun signs and comic book characters both serve essentially the same purpose: they provide evocative, mythic images of fundamental human principles. Batman represents the Triumph of Justice. Mickey Mouse represents Irrepressible Pluck. In much the same way, Aries represents Courage while Pisces represents Sensitivity.

And just as it might shock the pants off you to find Batman standing in line behind you in the grocery store, you'd be quite surprised if you ever met the pure unadulterated principles astrologers call Aries or Pisces. They're comic book material too.

Unlike a Sun sign, a birthchart is no two-dimensional cartoon. It is a multidimensional entity, full of ambiguities and shadowy corners. Comparing the insights we get from Sun sign astrology with those available from an accurate birthchart is like comparing *Lara Croft: Tomb Raider* with the works of Ernest Hemingway or Hermann Hesse.

Still, Sun signs survive. There are two reasons for that. First, they are simple and accessible. "What's your birthday? Oh, you're a Gemini." It's that easy. No calculations. No daunting columns of figures. No gap between question and answer.

The second reason why Sun signs survive is a better one: they actually work. Despite their limitations, they serve a practical purpose. Astrology's critics often object to the way it "puts people into twelve neat little boxes." Sun sign astrology is certainly guilty of that, but those same critics often categorize people with even simpler typologies. "She's such an introvert!" Well, there are only two categories there: introversion and extroversion. And yet we find that language useful.

35

As typologies go, Sun signs are reasonably sophisticated, despite the protests of astrology's detractors. There are twelve sign categories, enough to allow for some subtlety. But it is essential to remember that no human being actually is a category. We're all vastly more complex than that. It is also essential to remember that the twelve signs of the Zodiac are not strictly *Sun* signs—the Moon, the Ascendant, and all the planets pass through the same twelve signs too.

Are Sun signs a blessing or a curse? That's a very difficult question. Many professional astrologers develop a knee-jerk reaction against them. We feel like poets who are writing for an audience that recognizes only twelve words. That's the dark side of the coin: Sun signs, with their easy temptations, have trivialized astrology, converting it from the repository of ancient humanity's psychological wisdom, as Carl Jung put it, into a commodity that can be sold in the grocery store alongside pulp newspapers and glamour magazines.

The blessing? Because of the effortlessness of Sun signs, almost everyone in this society has some exposure to astrology, and that has undoubtedly helped to keep the system alive. Without Sun signs, astrology might have faded from the popular imagination along with alchemy, cloud-reading, and divination by animal entrails.

Perhaps the wisest course is not to condemn Sun signs, but rather to make an effort to resurrect them from triviality and understand them in the context of the larger astrological framework.

Sun and Moon

Everyone knows his or her Sun sign, but how many people are aware of their Moon signs? One in a hundred? A pop-astrologer might defend that lapse by claiming that the Sun is more important than the Moon. Don't be deceived! To imply that the Sun is more important than the Moon is to imply that ego is more important than imagination or that logic is more important than emotion. It's not a question of which one lifts the most weight. They're different energies, and they're both essential to our sanity.

Both the Sun and the Moon, and every other planet for that matter, operate as distinct functions in the psyche. One of the most critical skills in astrology is learning to keep straight in our own minds which of these functions we are discussing. An Aries with a Pisces Moon is not the same as a Pisces with an Aries Moon, even basically.

Traditionally the Sun has been associated with so-called "masculine" qualities such as reason, leadership, and individuality, while the Moon has been viewed as "feminine"—nurturing, emotional, and moody. But every birthchart contains both! Any human being who lacks a fully developed solar function and a fully developed lunar function is at best half-mad. And the idea that "the Sun is more important than the Moon" flows from the same spring of "wisdom" that once convinced us it was better to have a son than a daughter.

The Sun helps us build an identity and to support that identity with concrete accomplishments. The Moon helps us feel pleasure and pain, joy and sorrow, and to nurture and restore ourselves. As we learned in Chapter Two, the Sun tells us who we are, while the Moon describes the "soulful" side of life. Each function is further shaped by a sign, and that sign serves to describe a specific evolutionary goal toward which our solar ego or our lunar soul is journeying. The sign also offers a road map to that goal. It describes a set of experiences we can gather and digest that move us rapidly toward that goal. Finally, all that material can be fouled up by laziness or fear, and can turn into an unpleasant syndrome of attitudes and behaviors we dub the sign's "shadow."

Toward the end of this chapter, we'll go over each one of the twelve signs in detail—and remember that while you can indeed think of what you'll read there in terms of Sun signs, it will also apply to the Moon and everything else too. For now, it's enough to remember that each sign is a psychological process with a distinct goal, specific strategies for attaining it, and absolutely no guarantees about anything except for the existence of a few fundamental resources. Beyond that, we're on our own, free to experience the heights of creativity and joy or the depths of depravity, all based on decisions we make.

How does this relate to intimacy?

A Sun sign astrology book might inform us that all Arians require stimulation and adventure, and that therefore they should dutifully hook up with people of the other Fire signs—Sagittarians and Leos. But what if one particular Arian has her Moon in Virgo? Then we have a much more complicated situation—and a much more human one! Her solar Arian function—her everyday ego function—does require more intensity and variety of experience than average. But her lunar "soul" has a Virgoan spirit: her instincts (Moon) are a bit more cautious, grounded, and conservative, and also a lot more inclined to self-doubt, than we might guess from a Sun sign book. She could enjoy a rewarding casual friendship with a man who embodied all the pyrotechnics and color of Fire, but it is doubtful that he could ever touch her very deeply. Her Virgo Moon simply wouldn't trust him enough. For anyone to get through to her on that lunar *heart* level, he would first have to convince her that he could satisfy her Virgo needs. In other words, he would need to demonstrate responsibility and competence and prove to her that he could keep his promises.

She might, in her youth, fall madly in love with a free-spirited Sagittarian gypsy, only to have her heart broken when she realizes that he might never make a reliable commitment to her. His energetic charisma feeds her Sun, but it leaves her Moon starving.

She might rebound out of that situation and fall in love with a solid Taurean accountant—who might soon threaten to bore her to death with his predictability. He might be as solid, reasonable and faithful as a canine, and therefore a delight to her Virgo Moon. But then her Sun is left hungry.

Through an accumulation of experiences like these, our heroine eventually comes to realize that her intimacy needs are more subtly shaded than the "thou shalt marry a Leo" injunctions she received in Sun sign books. Eventually, as she matures, she comes to realize that any potential husband or long-term lover must touch her on both the solar and the lunar levels. He, in other words, must be as complicated an individual as she is.

So far we have limited our considerations to the Sun and the Moon. With the Sun alone, we divide humanity into a simple pattern of twelve types. When we add the Moon sign, the number of possible combinations leaps to 144. As we have just seen in our example, the power of the astrological symbols to describe our intimacy needs increases proportionately.

Eventually we need to add the rest of the planets, as well as aspects, houses, and the nodes of the Moon. By the time we get to that point, we'll be light years beyond any schematic typologies. We'll be talking about real people, with all their subtlety and uniqueness of character.

But that's tricky business and it's best to approach it one step at a time. For now let's suffice to add one more vegetable to the astrological stew.

The Ascendant

Like the Sun and the Moon, the Ascendant serves a distinct psychological purpose. We learned a little bit about it in Chapter Two. Let's go further now. The Ascendant helps us organize an outward, social personality. In a word, the Ascendant represents your *style*. The word "style" is accurate, but unfortunately it also conveys an air of insignificance or ultimate dismissability, and that's very misleading.

A shy kid is attempting to ask a girl to go out with him. He's had his eye on her for months. Finally he's gotten up the courage to approach her. Now that he's standing in front of her, he discovers that his courage is gone. Beads of sweat form on his forehead. He stares at his shoes. "There's a band playing in the park on Saturday . . . uh . . . maybe I'll see you there." He walks away from the girl without popping the question. It's a thoroughly agonizing experience for both of them.

This little tale is a cliché, of course. Still, if we take a closer look, it can teach us something about the Ascendant. At the deepest motivational level there is really nothing at all wrong with that young man. He likes the young woman. That's a good thing. They could perhaps share some experiences that would be important to both of them. His problem is purely one of style. *He is unable to translate his inward psychological reality into the outward requirements of life.* Technically, that's a superficial problem—that is, it's on the surface. It's also an emotional disaster.

The Ascendant interlocks all the complexities of our inner world with the relatively two-dimensional exigencies of external reality. If we make a strong response to it, we feel centered and at ease, readily feeding our deep psyche with a set of meaningful external experiences. We *have our act together*. If we make a weak response, then the opposite happens: we feel goofy and disconnected, and painfully self-conscious.

The woman in our earlier example is a solar Arian with her Moon in Virgo. Now let's carry our astrological analysis a step further. When she took her first breath, the sign Taurus was rising in the east. With that Ascendant, her social personality, for better or worse, radiates on a Taurean wavelength. We say "for better or worse," because she has a lot of freedom in determining how she's going to respond to those potentials. At best she'll present herself unpretentiously, in a disarming spirit of naturalness and an earthy tranquility. As she matures, she'll increasingly develop a mask (Ascendant) of quiet efficacy and easy warmth. She'll become the sort of person in front of whom you'll feel easy letting your hair down, putting your feet up, and speaking your mind without calculation. On the down side, we could imagine her slipping into a darker Taurean posture of stolidness, stubbornness, and predictability.

In intimacy she'll respond to a man whose style complements her own. That suggests that she might have difficulty in the long run with an "airy-fairy" or a self-appointed professor full of long-winded abstractions. That kind of man would be just too abstruse for her more concrete personality. Virgo, like Taurus, is an Earth sign, so despite her Fiery Sun, we have a woman in whom the earthy ideals of patience, realism, and the practical view predominate—but one who still draws her basic solar vitality from the Arian process of courage-seeking.

Adding the color of the Ascendant to our astrological palette radically expands the subtlety of our typology. As we have seen, there are twelve Sun sign categories and 144 possible Sun-Moon combinations. With the Ascendant we leap to 1,728 different patterns—and we are still only scratching the surface: we haven't brought in anything yet about the rest of the planets, nor the houses. Anyone who ever finds himself or herself using the twofold typology of introversion and extroversion (or good guys and bad guys) should think twice before accusing astrology of cubbyholing anyone!

One more point regarding the Ascendant: if one sign is rising in the east, then the sign directly opposite must be setting in the west at the same instant. This sign, called the *Descendant,* is also the cusp of the seventh house, which is the traditional house of marriage. Thus, in synastry the descending sign takes on extra significance. It represents a quality that complements or balances the tone of the Ascendant. Since the Descendant opposes the Ascendant, the essential quality of the interaction involves tension as well as attraction.

Think of the Descendant this way: the Ascendant, representing our style or our mask, is by its very nature a superficial symbol. This is not to diminish the significance of its role in the birthchart, only to indicate that its field of action is the *surface* of the personality. Such "streamlining" of the psyche is essential if we are to meet the functional requirements of daily life. But it comes at a cost. Much of what we actually are as human beings is left out of expression. A risk exists that we might become too identified with our masks and therefore shallow and rigid, caricatures of ourselves. Human consciousness, as reflected in astrological symbolism, seems to recognize this problem and make an effort to compensate for it. *We are drawn to people whose natures are opposite our own*—people, in other words, who have qualities like those symbolized by our descending sign. Typically, after the intoxication of the initial attraction, we experience an emotional tug-of-war with our partner as our characters seek to come into equilibrium. But that tug-of-war insures that neither one of us becomes a two-dimensional cartoon of our ascending sign, cocksure and empty.

The woman in our example has Taurus rising. The sign opposite Taurus is Scorpio, which is her Descendant. Here's how it works for her: with her Taurean Ascendant, there is a risk that she could become too flat and complacent in her outer expression, and that some of the more complex and shadowy dimensions of life could be denied—which of course would only give them more power in the long run. Put very simply, she could become too docile and "grounded" for her own good, while her tricky psychological ambiguities and hungers slowly inched toward the boiling point.

Enter the Descendant—or perhaps we should say "enter her soulmates."

With Scorpio on her seventh-house cusp, our protagonist is drawn in mutual attraction to individuals whose natures emphasize Scorpio qualities. These are people who like to delve into the murky areas of human consciousness, asking hard questions and breaking conventional social taboos in their interactions with her. They may upset her at times, but she needs them lest her life become too prosaic. Similarly, she might in turn help them by giving them a more "chicken soup" perspective on themselves, helping them laugh, relax, and perhaps take themselves a bit less seriously.

Despite the delicacy of the purpose it serves, the operation of the Descendant is largely unconscious and automatic. We simply *like* people who resonate with our seventh houses. We are drawn to them. We experience, initially at least, an easy comradeship with them, often spiced with romantic or sexual feelings. Only once the bonds have formed does the more subtle "combat" of balancing, deepening, and healing begin.

These, then, are the primary features of our astrological individuality: Sun, Moon, and the Ascendant/Descendant complex. A thorough grasp of all four functions guarantees a solid foundation in our understanding of how one person approaches the labyrinths of human love.

Before we consider the twelve signs in detail, let's recapitulate what we've covered so far.

* The Sun represents identity, self-image, and the more conscious or intentional dimensions of the personality.
* The Moon represents instinct, emotion, and the more unconscious and subjective dimensions of experience.
* The Ascendant symbolizes our outward style and the most ideal interlock between our psychological selves and outer reality.

41

* The Descendant represents a kind of person to whom we are drawn in an unconscious effort to balance our most characteristic blind spots or limitations.

These four functions are universal. They exist in everyone. But in each person they operate differently depending on which of the twelve signs are shaping them. In the pages that follow, we'll introduce the signs in detail, emphasizing their particular approach to questions of intimacy and love.

If you're a beginning astrologer, it's fine to think of these twelve descriptions in relation to Sun signs, but we hope that by now you're convinced that there's more to the picture than the solar ego! Always remember that while a given sign can shape one's identity (Sun), it can just as readily modify one's style (Ascendant) or cast its glow over the private landscape of our intimate inner life (Moon).

Real skill in astrology arises when we learn to keep these Sun-Moon-Ascendant distinctions clear. Conversely, the surest course to astrological chaos lies in putting all the key concepts you've memorized about Aries, Virgo, and Taurus into the mental Cuisinart, closing your eyes, and pressing the button.

The Twelve Signs

Knowing one's Sun sign is as simple as knowing one's birthday—almost. If you are born on February twenty-fifth, then any pop-astrology book will tell you that you're a Pisces. But if you're born on February twentieth, then you'll get mixed messages. One book says "Pisces" while another one tells you "Aquarius." There's a simple reason for that. The Sun does not enter a new sign on exactly the same day each year. No need for a complex explanation of that problem here. It's enough to point out that astrology is based on the true solar year, and that year is not precisely 365 days long. As a result, astrological events can't be lined up exactly with our calendars.

In the pages that follow, we explore each one of the twelve signs. For convenience, we also give the approximate date marking the entry of the Sun into each sign. If you don't know your Sun sign, you can find out below, unless you happen to be born right on any one of the specific dates we mention, or on the day before or the day after. In that case, don't trust us! To

42

learn your true Sun sign, you'll need to have an accurate birthchart. See the Appendix.

In any case, no matter what your birthday, to learn your Ascendant or your Moon sign, you definitely need a birthchart. If you know the date, time, and location of your birth, then there's nothing stopping you. If you don't already know yours or those of the people you love, we recommend that you get their charts cast. Just the chart alone, with no interpretation, is inexpensive or even free over the Internet. No sense flying on one engine. Again, see the Appendix.

Let's repeat: *nothing that follows is limited to Sun signs.* Our descriptions of the twelve basic astrological signs also apply to the Moon and the Ascendant. In fact, at the end of each section below, we'll make some distinctions among the Sun, Moon, and Ascendant in each of the twelve signs—if you are curious about your Aries Ascendant, for example, you can find a description of it here. In later chapters we also apply them to the rest of the planets. No matter what your Sun sign, we encourage you to learn about all twelve. As you'll discover later in the book, each one plays some kind of role in your birthchart.

One more note: if you or your partner has, say, a Gemini Moon, look at the whole Gemini section first, then skip down to the part about the Moon—we introduce the basic concepts first, then at the end of each section we fine-tune them for Sun, Moon, or Ascendant.

Aries the Ram
(March 21 through April 20)

Archetypes: The Pioneer, The Warrior, The Daredevil, The Survivor.

Developmental Aim: Consciously or unconsciously, any Arian astrological feature is striving toward the development of *courage.* To reach the full flower of its potential, that feature must sharpen its willpower, especially in the face of stress, obstacles, and the distractions which fear creates. Fearlessness is not the point. That's just a psychotic state in which we are out of touch with natural, self-preserving emotions. For Aries, the motto must be "feel the fear and do it anyway." Always, panic is the demon that guards the gate to the garden. The part of the soul that is defined by Arian energy has reached a point in its evolutionary journey where natural emotions of fear stand between it and the experiences it needs to have. The metaphysical implication is that the part of a person touched by Aries was scalded rather badly in a prior life. Something scared it, and now it's steeling itself to face the fear in a more warrior-like fashion—to "get back on the horse that threw it."

Strategies and Resources: To learn courage, we must intentionally expose ourselves to that which frightens or intimidates us. For Aries, that means accepting risk and seeking adventure. Swallow your fear, for example, and take that scuba diving class! You will learn more than how to dive. In facing your fear of deep water, you teach your unconscious self a lesson about its own strengths, and the next time you have to walk across a dark parking lot at two o'clock in the morning, the soul remembers that lesson and feels less afraid.

The Ram's resource, paradoxically, *is* courage. All that Arian bravery already exists in the person, but it must be invoked by a set of scary circumstances before the individual becomes fully conscious of it. "Until I actually had the experience of keeping my cool when I met that hammerhead shark forty feet down, I had no idea how brave I could be—or that bravery had nothing to do with not being afraid. I was petrified! But I did all the right things."

The Arian courage-gathering process doesn't always involve swimming in shark-infested waters. The process is not always so physical. The shark we must face might well be a human one: an obnoxious boss or a critical parent. The shark might even be cigarettes if we're trying to quit smoking, or a bowl of Breyer's Mint Chocolate Chip ice cream if we're trying to lose a few pounds. Whatever the nature of the shark, the Arian principle is the same: face enough sharks without flinching, and you've become a lot more courageous than you were.

Shadow: The dark side of the Ram lies in the misdirection of that fiery power. Perhaps a woman commits the Arian "cardinal sin" and allows fear to prevent her from fulfilling a dream. "I'd just *love* to take that scuba class with you, Jane, but I really don't have the money right now." Then the energy that should have gone into conquering her fear of deep water dissipates itself pointlessly and destructively in bursts of temper, silly arguments, and random passions.

Aries Sun in Love: With Sun in Aries, the individual is likely to be intense, adventurous in at least some sense of the word, and experience-oriented. In relationships, he or she needs robust contact and a certain amount of psychological arm wrestling with the partner. If a relationship shows symptoms of going to sleep, the Ram rocks the boat—maybe even

44

picks a fight. Remember that in love, as in every other part of life, Aries is learning courage, and its lover had better be ready to hold up his or her end of that bargain: the lover, in other words, must be brave enough to tussle head-to-head.

In matters of intimacy, with the Sun in Aries, there is likely to be a pronounced taste for directness and blunt honesty. Negatively, the possibility arises of pointless fireworks and purely symbolic arguments that needlessly damage both partners, often creating a caustic atmosphere of mistrust.

Aries Moon in Love: With the Moon in Aries, the logic of intimacy remains the same except that it is buried more deeply. You might not see it at first—and since the Moon tends to be more instinctual and unconscious, the individual in question might have no idea that he or she is carrying this much fiery energy. The greater the level of real trust and true intimacy the person is feeling, the more he or she reveals this innate spark. The same can be said for anger: the direct revelation of anger is an act of trust for the individual with an Aries Moon. He or she is learning emotional courage in particular—a willingness to share needs and fears and personal realities with the partner no matter how impolitic that might seem. Helping to make that process perhaps a little safer, there is also compelling, instinctive *loyalty* in the Aries Moon. On the dark side, we sometimes observe a distinctly irrational (lunar!) quality of touchiness, competitiveness or combativeness as the Arian wildfires burn out of control. That's especially likely if the person with this Moon is starving for adventure, passion, or the need for some extremity in life—and one early warning of that condition is that the individual becomes quiet and wistful after a film featuring a lot of edgy action. The Moon is always connected to domesticity, so there is a tendency toward a constant state of crisis in the home environment.

Aries Ascendant in Love: The Arian Ascendant suggests a developmental emphasis upon building a more direct and confrontive personal style. The shadows remain the same—misdirected temper and symbolic warfare—but now the process is closer to the surface. Many people with Aries rising come to learn, much to their shock, that their Arian "vibrations" frighten people, and that they must make an effort to reassure their partners that they are not as dangerous or angry as they seem. The whole process of "getting their act together" depends on their expressing themselves forthrightly and with unvarnished honesty. The planetary ruler of Aries is Mars, and as we'll be learning soon, Mars plays a particularly important role in love. The ruler of the Ascendant is always a tremendously

45

important force. The bottom line here is that if someone has Aries rising, you'll learn a lot more about how he or she functions in intimacy by paying close attention to all our remarks about his or her Mars in Chapter Five. That's doubly true if Mars falls in one of the "arc of intimacy" houses—see Chapter Six.

Taurus the Bull
(April 21 through May 21)

Archetypes: The Earth-Spirit, The Silent One, The Elf, The Solid Citizen, The Pagan, (Pick a specific "totem animal").

Developmental Aim: What does Taurus seek? Peace. Security. Gentleness. Ease. Naturalness. Simplicity. Silence. If you roll all those virtues into one fuzzy, sweet-smelling ball, you've grasped the developmental aim of the Bull. Any Taurean astrological feature, whether the person understands it or not, is embarked on a course with that mellow, timeless feeling at its logical end. That part of the soul has reached a point in its evolutionary journey where it really needs to calm down, and to regain contact with its body and its instinctive side. The metaphysical implication is that, prior to this lifetime, the soul effectively and bravely faced trauma. It learned what it needed to learn—but it was badly shaken in the process. There is now an evolutionary intention to recover stillness, peace, and simplicity.

Strategies and Resources: Taurus is instinctively attracted to anything (or anyone!) that offers steadiness, naturalness, reliability, and peace. The security the Bull seeks is an internal condition, not really an outward one. Taurus might reach its goal a thousand times faster sitting in the woods on a June morning than it ever would swallowing antacids on the New York Stock Exchange, however lucrative that course might be. Music soothes Taurus. So do reliable tools, tried-and-true friends, familiar landscapes. Planting a garden is a Taurean joy. Painting too. And building a bookcase out of fine oak. Or feeling the texture of a wonderful old violin.

The Taurean strategy is one of endless simplification. No existential melodramas. No exhausting "heavy personal changes" that don't really change anything—just a gradual paring away of everything non-essential in life until we are left with its essence: health, truth, love, beauty, and silence . . . and a reverence for them.

Shadow: The Bull's shadow lies in confusing inward peace with

46

external security. Taurus can become obsessed with stability at every outward level: financial, interpersonal, experiential. As a result, this sign can *bore itself to death,* becoming stubborn, materialistic, and fearful of breaking up routines. The Bull needs to be reminded that motion and change are two of the most characteristic qualities of life—and that one of the most universal features of death is stability.

Taurus Sun in Love: In affairs of the heart, the Taurus Sun seeks the same ends it pursues elsewhere: stability, solidness, reliability, a fidelity to instinct. The idea that such a person will always be practical in affairs of the heart goes too far. There is a sensual quality here, even a romantic one, so it would be misleading to get the idea that Taurus seeks a lover the same way one might buy a car—unless it has succumbed to the Shadow. The key astrological insight is to recognize that, in intimacy, the Bull is concerned with the long haul. Rarely will someone born with the Sun in this sign be taken in by mere glamour or the flimflam of glittery fantasy. There is generally a quality of down-to-earth reasonableness, and also dogged persistence in emotional situations. Hanging in there—the proverbial stubbornness of the Bull—can usher many a human bond through a stormy passage, allowing the relationship to be reborn in the quieter, deeper waters. Simple, physical touch is greatly emphasized in this sign, and much needed. We could say the same for concrete manifestations of the lover's affections: simple gifts, flowers, a bit of jewelry. Materialism is not the point; instead it's really about tangible demonstrations of the deeper inner reality of feeling.

Taurus Moon in Love: The Moon, being emotional, emphasizes the Bull's sensuality and its instinct for stability. Given half a chance, a Taurus Moon is simply *cuddly.* It has an elevated need to touch and be touched. Creature comforts figure prominently here, and a kind of earthy "chicken soup" realism about relationships and sexuality. If trust truly develops and the deeper lunar layers of the psyche are revealed, a man or woman with a Taurus Moon becomes quite unabashed about the body and its functions, and increasingly content with quiet. Because of the reflexive need for peace, there is a shadow-danger linked to the avoidance of natural processes of conflict—which can lead to a build-up of resentment or frustration, with the subsequent inevitable detonations down the road. Domestically, there is great comfort to be derived from the presence of animal-friends, plants, and ideally a natural environment.

Taurus Ascendant In Love: The Taurus Ascendant, being more external, exudes a disarming air of naturalness and honesty. Those qualities

47

alone are conducive to planting relationships on the solid ground of psychological and biological realism. Everything else being equal, a person with the Sign of the Bull rising appears to be comfortable in the body, physically "present," with an aura that pulls one closer. An easy feeling of familiarity tends to arise quickly with such a person. The planetary ruler of Taurus is Venus, and Venus of course plays a particularly important role in love. Since the ruler of the Ascendant is often simply called the ruler of the chart, you can count on its being a tremendously important planet for anyone with Taurus rising. The bottom line is that, for people with this Ascendant, a lot more can be learned about how they function in intimacy by paying close attention to all our remarks about his or her Venus in Chapter Five. That's doubly true if Venus falls in one of the "arc of intimacy" houses—see Chapter Six.

Gemini the Twins
(May 22 through June 21)

Archetypes: The Witness, The Perceiver, The Storyteller, The Journalist, The Communicator.

Developmental Aim: Gemini's ultimate evolutionary goal is the attainment of a sense of wonder. The Twins must learn to give the universe permission to be amazing, full of surprises, thick with miracles. *Confusion*—that's their aim, provided we think carefully about the word! "Confusion," in this sense, is a psychological condition in which what we have allowed ourselves to experience is a giant step ahead of what we have already figured out. From an evolutionary perspective, the implication is that any planet touched by Geminian energy has reached a point in its unfolding where it requires *shock*. It needs to stretch beyond its comfort zone in terms of its elemental description of reality. Its mantra must become, "Whatever I see, it's more than that." The metaphysical implication is that the part of a person impacted by Gemini, in a prior life, developed too much certainty, clarity, and "rightness"—and therefore got stuck.

Strategies and Resources: The central Geminian strategy is *experience* and lots of it. Curiosity, restlessness, a distaste for repetition and predictability: all these are the Twins' resources. So is a love of conversation. Pop astrology generally emphasizes the talkativeness of this sign. That quality is often observable, but more central to Gemini's work is its love of listening. Why? Simply because we usually learn more with our mouths closed than with them open.

Gemini is often described as a youthful sign. It's a pity to use that word since we then imply that open-mindedness, freshness of thought, and a willingness to be surprised are adolescent qualities. Those qualities shouldn't be limited to anyone's early years, especially if his or her Sun, Moon, or Ascendant lies in the sign of the Twins.

Shadow: The sheer rapidity of the Geminian process can be its downfall. Slickness and superficiality can result. So can overextension, nervousness, and a blithering, dithering style of living in which everything is in perpetual crisis. Working with this energy is like driving a Porsche down a mountain road at ninety miles an hour—you can probably do it, but only if your concentration is absolute. At that speed, life is not very forgiving. Stop, take a breath, and read the fine print: that's good advice for the Twins.

Gemini Sun in Love: As always, once we understand the basic developmental aims of a sign, an understanding of its relationship dynamics follows logically. At the evolutionary level, someone with the Sun in Gemini seeks wonder. He or she is driven by curiosity, and needs a lot of stimulation. The routine and the predictable have a deadening effect, stripping such an individual of solar vitality. It follows that any lover capable of holding the Twins' attention for long must offer more than solid, predictable middle-class virtues. Those virtues might be part of the package, but he or she had better offer the spice of exciting ideas, surprise, and wide-ranging interests as well. Pop astrology suggests that Gemini is fickle. Certainly that's a possibility. But recognize this so-called fickleness for what it is: the Twins' insatiable appetite for experience. One way of fulfilling that appetite is to maintain contact, sexual or otherwise, with a variety of fascinating people. Don't be misled by that comment: commitment in monogamous love is a Geminian option . . . with two provisos. First, the Twins must have access to many lively friends, all with the mate's blessing. Second, the lover must be willing and eager to contribute equally to a shared life of surprise, endless learning, and variety. The ideal marriage for Gemini would revolve around one rambling, 'til-death-do-us-part conversation—funny, profound, and endless.

Gemini Moon in Love: With the Moon in Gemini, the central, driving psychological need in intimacy is *communication*. Naturally, this must include serious conversations about feelings—but it also includes simple banter and verbal play. There, content is less important than *the simple feeling of connection that arises in dialog and shared attention.* Bonding is supported and sustained by fresh, joint experiences—the whirlwind trip to Japan . . . or the spontaneous late-night film. The Moon is always vulnerable to slipping beneath the radar-screen of conscious thought. When that happens, a person with a Gemini Moon might lose touch with these needs and drives. If intimate life becomes routine, the result is a mood of restlessness and undefinable discontent—and sometimes a vexing compulsion to chatter. The domestic environment around a Gemini Moon person tends toward sensory overload and some degree of chaos. They can be comfortable, even relaxed in such circumstances—and anyone trying to function under one roof with such an individual needs to be tolerant of tripping over the computer to go turn down the stereo in order to get to the phone.

Gemini Ascendant in Love: With Gemini rising, an individual radiates quickness, alertness, and generally good cheer. It's easy, from a lover's point of view, to lose sight of what such a person is actually feeling—or to underestimate the emotional intensity behind the words. As a tool for functioning in the social world, this Ascendant generally works splendidly. In the intimate, secret world of the couple, it's more of a challenge: the depths of the psyche tend to be eclipsed from view. If you were born with Gemini rising, practice making short, clear, concise statements from the heart, and follow them with silence: make space for your heart to be heard, in other words.

The planetary ruler of Gemini is Mercury, which makes Mercury the ruler of the chart in this case, further elevating its centrality to the psyche. The bottom line is that, if someone has Gemini rising, you'll learn a lot more about his or her intimacy profile by paying close attention to Mercury's sign and house, particularly if Mercury falls in one of the "arc of intimacy" houses—see Chapter Six.

Cancer the Crab
(June 22 through July 23)

Archetypes: The Mother, The Healer, The Sensitive, The Invisible Man (Woman), The Psychotherapist.

Developmental Aim: Perfect sensitivity to the inner realms of feeling and imagination—that's the Crab's goal. To understand that aim accurately,

50

we must recognize that this sensitivity ultimately applies not only to the Cancerian individual's own psyche, but also to his sensitivity toward other people as well. First: a healing of the Crab's own heart, an opening of the imagination, a deepening of the ability to *feel*. Then there is an extension of that process out into the world, as Cancer adopts a loving role of nurturance and support. From an evolutionary standpoint, anything in the birthchart touched by Cancerian energy has reached a point in the journey where it requires a tender, inward, indulgent process of self-healing in an environment of safety. If it succeeds in that, then it will also seek to foment healing in other beings. The metaphysical implication is that in a prior life, the part of a person touched by Cancer experienced a crippling *excess of sympathy and compassion*, which actually rendered it incapable of action, hobbled by hurt and fear. Thus, inner healing is naturally followed by healing actions toward others in this lifetime.

Strategies and Resources: Like his saltwater counterpart, the astrological Crab requires a shell. He is born fluent in the language of the deep Self: the language of feeling. In Cancer, the volume is turned all the way up on subjectivity and emotion. If this world were the Garden of Eden, that kind of vulnerability wouldn't present any problems. But the world isn't quite that gentle. The Crab must protect his inner processes, often hiding inside a shell of shyness or withdrawal while he gathers strength.

Radical self-protection is fine at first, but after a while Cancer must take courage and dare to shed the shell—dare truly to love and let itself *be loved*, that is. If he is brave enough to take that step, then, just like the saltwater crab, Cancer grows a second shell, a larger one, more suited to his more evolved dimensions. He now relates actively to the world, protecting himself within his new, more formidable shell: the role of the healer and the helper, the comforter, extending outwardly the very processes of delicate nurturance he first employed inwardly to explore the misty terrains of his own spirit.

Shadow: Both the Crab's shells present evolutionary dangers. If Cancer gets caught in the first shell—shyness—then typically he adopts a fearful, conservative posture in life, enduring a dull job, a silent marriage, a spirit bound and gagged. In the second shell—that of the nurturer—there lurks another shadow: the trap of continually being cast in the role of the forgiver, the protector, the psychotherapist. Those roles are natural and healthy ones for the Crab, until they become so automatic and so addictive that the multidimensional wholeness of the individual becomes invisible, lost behind the shell of mothering.

51

Cancer Sun in Love: "Defensiveness" is a word we must use with great caution when discussing a Cancer Sun. The scurrying ghost crab on an Atlantic beach—is she being defensive? Or would it be plain foolhardiness for her to shed her shell beneath the hovering eyes of the sea gull? *Sensitivity must defend itself.* The alternative is destruction. In romantic situations, if Cancer seems a bit guarded, it's only because she is playing for high stakes: her walls are strong, but once someone is allowed inside her shell, she's utterly vulnerable. So the Crab is cautious, extending her feelers into the other spirit, sounding him for dangers. One who would court the Crab must first convince her of his gentleness, his honesty, his capacity for tenderness and commitment, his willingness to nest with her. Until then, he'll see only shell: maybe ice, maybe aloof wisdom, maybe wit, maybe even "great sex." But never the Crab's soul.

Cancer Moon in Love: With the Moon in Cancer, the situation is trickier. Much then depends upon the Sun sign. The Cancer Moon seeks a safe shell to lurk behind, and the Sun often provides an excellent one. It might be quite a while before the lover is allowed to penetrate the extraordinarily tender base of emotion that arises when the planetary symbol of feeling (the Moon) interacts with this most emotional of the twelve signs. Until then, he or she experiences only the more outward features of the person's birthchart. With its predilection for instinctive behavior, the Cancer Moon is a natural healer and nurturer—and anyone with such a Moon needs to be particularly alert to the danger of confusing nurturing compassion with real intimacy. Such individuals can be magnets for wounded people who are ultimately incapable of returning their love in equal measure. That dynamic may look like over-abundant forgiveness and kindness, but in reality it's just a form of self-protection. Domestically, the Cancer Moon excels at creating a warm, embracing, "hobbit-hole" feeling in the home—and needs that kind of environment in order to restore its own feelings of wellbeing.

Cancer Ascendant in Love: With the sign of the Crab rising, the individual's *style* is Cancerian: in love, just "getting a foot in the door" is the hard part with such a person. As always with this Sign there is a natural, healthful, needful defensiveness. With reserve and circumspection, he or she will at first study you as if you were a potentially dangerous zoological specimen. Then, if you pass scrutiny, the floodgates of caring and tenderness will be opened—but only if you pass scrutiny. The planetary ruler of Cancer is the Moon. Since the ruler of the Ascendant is the ruler of the chart, you can always count on its being a tremendously important planet. The bottom line is that, if someone has Cancer rising, you'll learn a lot more about his or her intimacy profile by paying close attention to all our remarks about his or her Moon Sign elsewhere in this chapter. That's doubly true if the Moon falls in one of the "arc of intimacy" houses—see Chapter Six.

Leo the Lion
(July 24 through August 23)

Archetypes: The King (Queen), The Performer, The Clown, The Child, The Movie Star, The Aristocrat.

Developmental Aim: The lion's developmental aim is a warm, confident, self-expressive sense of *belonging* in the world. It is a sense of safety, but not of caution. The Lion's safety is based on a feeling of being totally accepted, spontaneously and uncritically, by everyone. The Leonine ideal is one of blissful, unpremeditated abandon. "Life, I love you! I celebrate you!" (Once we have a few miles on our existential odometers, we might add one more clause: "Life, I forgive you!") In a word, the evolutionary goal of the Lion is *joy.* The metaphysical implication is that the part of a person touched by Leo has been the victim of prior-life rejection or perhaps persecution, from which it is attempting to recover.

Strategies and Resources: Feeling good—it's easy to talk about, not always so easy to accomplish. For Leo, joy and spontaneity do not arise automatically. They must be attained through the use of very specific strategies. The fact that these strategies often arise unconsciously does not diminish their power.

Leo is a woman who has been lonely for a while, maybe hurt too. Now she's two weeks into a new relationship—and scared. She writes a poem about it, straight from her heart. Passionate. And revealing . . . maybe too revealing, considering the usual politics of an embryonic sexual bond. Should she show the poem to her lover? She takes the risk . . . and he responds. As he looks up from the poem, a tear runs down his face. They hug. For the rest of the evening, she feels more relaxed and spontaneous with that man than ever before.

That little tale contains in microcosmic form a clear description of Leo's evolutionary strategy: *learning to take the risk of personal creative self-expression.* If we reveal ourselves that way, and earn applause for it, then we instantly feel better, safer, more positive about our place in the world. Life feels friendlier to us, which in a nutshell is the Lion's goal.

53

Leo's resources? Creativity, a sense of drama, verve, a bigger-than-life presence: all the elements of an endearing, praise-gathering performance.

Shadow: What if the poem falls flat? Maybe the woman's lover says, "I've got some advice for you: don't write poetry." Maybe she clams up, never taking another risk with him. Maybe she whips herself into a frenzy of people-pleasing and performance, desperately pursuing her lover's affirmation, even at the price of falsifying herself. Down either road lies Leo's shadow. The first course, clamming up, usually leads eventually to haughtiness and egomania. Those Leo fires just can't be bottled up that way, not without emerging again in a twisted form. The second course—people-pleasing—inevitably produces a noisy brand of superficiality, the kind of brainless good vibes you expect in a soft drink commercial. The Lion is simply trying too hard.

So what's the answer? It's deceptively simple: *find a more appreciative audience.* To evolve, two pieces are necessary: the Lion must leave some tangible evidence of her inner self in the hands of the world, *and* that evidence must be appreciated. For the Leo's strategy to work, she must see to it that both conditions are satisfied: honest, creative, uncalculated self-expression and a positive reception for that self-expression. If either condition is unmet, then her strategy is mere bluster, accomplishing nothing.

Leo Sun in Love: Courtship is a natural activity for the Lion. Expressing ourselves—telling our personal story—is one of the essential processes of sexual bonding. So are the giving and receiving of praise. So is playfulness. And all of them are right up the alley of the Leo Sun. Roses, poetry, heartfelt talks, candlelight, mutual admiration: these are the coin of the realm for Leo in love.

Falling in love comes easily for Leo. What about *staying* in love? That's a possibility too, but only if the Lion continues to receive affirmation and active appreciation from his or her lover. Nobody likes the numbness of love gone stale. For a Leo Sun that numbness is fatal, unless it's cured immediately with a hefty dose of renewed courtship behavior. Solar vitality simply depends upon *attention*—attention received, of course . . . but also attention given. And to feel motivated to give that attention, the Leo Sun requires a certain theatricality in the partner: color, presence, style, and some pizzazz.

Leo Moon in Love: The Leo Moon still needs the same applause, but that need might remain invisible: an unexpressed emotion. Clap your hands for the Leo Moon, and you'll see a smile that can't help but remind you of sunrise on the open road. This one has the *soul of a performer*—it just might not show unless it's encouraged a bit. Underlying these observations is the notion that the Moon is always shy, regardless of what sign it occupies. The importance of a creative outlet can never be overestimated for Leo—and with the Moon in this Sign, the lover must be in Row One, Center, clapping hands, or there's a sulky sense of estrangement in the air. That creative outlet can be a carefully-crafted dinner or a new "look," as well as more obvious artistic expressions. Domestically, someone with a Leo Moon tends toward "bigness"—the home might not be palatial, but must still invoke healthy pride and dignity in those privileged to sit in it.

Leo Ascendant in Love: The Leo Ascendant can be misleading and hard to penetrate. Wearing the mask of the King (or Queen), the individual with Leo rising might not appear to need praise, support, or attention. Don't be fooled. There's hunger and a bit of insecurity behind that regal bearing. Feed it, and you'll pass the outer perimeters of that person's defenses. Starve it, and you'll go no further—all you will see is the air of a stone pharaoh: self-contained, unrevealing, and unresponsive. The planetary ruler of Leo is the Sun, which makes the Sun the ruler of the chart in this case, further elevating its centrality to the psyche. The bottom line is that, if someone has Leo rising, you'll learn a lot more about his or her intimacy profile by paying close attention to all our remarks about his or her Sun sign elsewhere in this chapter. Pay extra attention if the Sun falls in one of the "arc of intimacy" houses—see Chapter Six.

Virgo the Virgin
(August 24 through September 23)

Archetypes: The Servant, Martyr, The Perfectionist, The Analyst, The Critic, The Craftsperson.

Developmental Aim: Purity—that's the Virgin's goal. But don't be fooled by the word "Virgin." Virgo's purity has nothing to do with sexual inexperience, or with any other kind of inexperience for that matter. Virgo's aim is to attain the highest, most refined levels of her own potential. Her purity is a style of living and a quality of thought uncontaminated by anything less than the best truth she knows. In a word, the Virgin's aim is *perfection*. Reaching perfection is naturally not a reasonable human option, but *motion toward it* is the lifeblood of this sign. Any planet touched by Virgo energy has reached a point in its evolutionary journey where it is ready to roll up its sleeves, humbly face the reality of its own karmic predicament, seek counsel and guidance, and grow. The metaphysical implication is that the part of a person touched by Virgo, in a prior life, experienced a sense of stasis or stagnation—*soul-boredom*. Because of that condition, vague, undefinable feelings of guilt, and a driving, exacting restlessness both arise now.

Strategies and Resources: Virgo's most fundamental resource is a sense of the ideal. A sense of what *could be*. She is also blessed with a meticulous, scrupulously honest sense of *what is*. In the tension between those two—the ideal and the real—Virgo's growth is accelerated and directed. She has a restless, internal insurance policy against laziness and complacency. No matter what she attains, she wants more, and knows that more is possible. Relentlessly, and often with cunningly effective tactics, she transforms her personal reality into ever more perfect patterns.

To the medievals, Virgo was the sign of the Servant. Take heart: working as a stock clerk or a chambermaid is not the point. Service is a very effective evolutionary strategy. Virgo looks inward, finding some aspect of herself that can be polished brightly and offered to the world. She finds, in other words, the most nearly perfectible part of herself. Then she becomes radically identified with that virtue. In a sense she becomes a servant of that particular virtue. How? Simply by logging a lot of hours practicing it.

Perhaps a particular Virgo is a writer, for example. When she's writing, she feels that she is living out her best self. So she writes and writes, refining her style, always seeking to weave her words more economically and eloquently today than yesterday. Perhaps our Virgo writer is also inclined to gossip; definitely not the part of her character that she'd call her best self. Here's the crux of her strategy: *when she's writing, she doesn't have time to gossip.* That part of her character is starved. The better part is fed.

Don't be deceived by the apparent simplemindedness of this Virgoan strategy. It works. Given a lifetime, it can utterly transform a character, move it toward perfection. And perfection, as we've seen, is the Virgin's goal.

Shadow: "There's my ideal. That's what my life could look like . . . if I weren't weak, lazy, and crazy. Here, on the other hand, is who I am . . . God help me." Perfection is a harsh mistress, and the shadow she casts is *crippling, destructive self-criticism*. Virgo must learn self-acceptance and self-forgiveness. Otherwise, she falls into a bleak pattern of doubt, self-sabotage and self-limitation. And if she succumbs to that poison, she quickly falls prey to a second shadow: niggling negativity regarding anything and everything around her.

Virgo Sun in Love: In intimacy, the Virgo Sun prizes two qualities: grown-up realism and commitment to growth. She might not use those words, but let either quality disappear in her lover, and Virgo soon disappears along with it. Under the banner of realism, we would include virtues such as logic, clearheadedness, patience, competence, perhaps elements of ambition—all the qualities that help us live in the real world. A commitment to growth: under this Virgoan banner, we find honesty, a capacity to receive criticism gracefully and appreciatively, and a willingness to make concrete efforts to alter our bad habits.

For the Virgin's love to survive, the love itself must be constantly changing and growing. She responds to a lover who offers shared projects, new ideas to be explored in detail, plans for the future. She might fall for empty glamour once in her life, but it won't last long. With some experience behind her, she simply won't trust enough to love someone until the object of her affections has proven himself trustworthy.

On the dark side, Virgo's love of perfection can lead to nagging criticisms of the partner, criticisms that eventually erode the trust, spontaneity, and shared joy upon which love thrives. Similarly, the Virgo shadow of self-doubt can lead one into a self-destructive liaison with an insensitive, selfish, or authoritarian partner.

Virgo Moon in Love: The Moon is moody by nature, and when it's in Virgo the mood is one of chronic discontent. Clearly, that can easily correlate with Shadow perspectives: a worrisome, nagging, petty attitude that could drive anyone crazy in a week. But there's something precious here too: that chronic discontent can also translate into forward motion. Humble self-appraisal—and a willingness to improve. Solid insight and concrete support for the partner. The sense of building a life together, methodically, relentlessly, and effectively. Virgo is ruled by Mercury, and thus places a great emphasis on communication: intimacy with anyone with the Moon in this sign is dependent upon a free-flow of words. If the Virgo Moon begins truly to relax and trust, increasingly it is easy about revealing its self-doubts and second thoughts. On the domestic front, the Virgo Moon tends to run a tight ship—and probably needs some help remembering that home is a place for some merrily slothful rest and renewal too.

Virgo Ascendant in Love: Men or women with Virgo rising radiate competence and effectiveness. We tend to trust them quickly, and often find ourselves asking for their help or advice early in the relationship. There's something punctilious and precise about them, which often extends to they way they dress. With the strong Mercury signature in Virgo, they tend toward talkativeness. Often they are compelled to offer more detail than is necessary. Getting through the words and ideas, down to the level where their hearts are beating—that's the challenge. They center themselves through work and responsibility, so such men and women need unstinting support for their careers, and will often "do for" their partners when they're feeling inwardly insecure about the relationship.

The planetary ruler of Virgo is Mercury, which makes Mercury the ruler of the chart in this case. If someone has Virgo rising, you'll learn more about his or her intimacy profile by paying close attention to his or her Mercury's house and sign, particularly if that Mercury falls in one of the "arc of intimacy" houses—see Chapter Six.

Libra the Scales
(September 24 through October 23)

Archetypes: The Lover, The Artist, The Peacemaker, The Diplomat, The Counselor.

Developmental Aim: *Serenity*—that's Libra's aim. The Scales symbolize balance. Equilibrium. Underlying every healthy Libran action is the effort, conscious or unconscious, simply to *calm down*. Releasing tension, finding the middle ground, smoothing ruffled feathers, the Scales move step by step toward their goal: the attainment of unflappable peace. Any planet touched by Libran energy has, from the evolutionary perspective, reached a point in its journey at which it must restore peaceful equilibrium and harmony. The implication is that in a prior life-experience, something of an exhausting, shattering nature occurred, from which the soul is now recovering.

Strategies and Resources: A cynic has a rigid view of the world: "People are just looking out for themselves, no matter what kind of philosophical masks they hide behind." Faced with an act of pure altruistic charity, that cynic is first confused, then struggles to force that perception into his bitter view of life. So hooked is he on his dark picture of human motivation that charity makes him nervous and pushes him into a frenzy of rationalization as he tries to explain it away.

58

An idealist, on the other hand, may be determined to believe that every event, however agonizing, has a purpose and is ultimately a spiritual lesson. Faced with the brutal murder of a friend's daughter, this idealist feels a sense of strain very similar to what the cynic felt in the first instance. The effort to squeeze the murder into the more prosaic model of life doesn't work very well either. Once again, the muscles of the face become tense. The mind whirs into high-gear rationalization. And a feeling of struggle overwhelms the psyche.

Truth is always complex, always paradoxical. Any effort to cling to simplifications or to defend them against reality always results in stress. And stress is the antithesis of Libra's developmental aim. As a result, Libra is given a powerful resource: *a high tolerance for paradox and ambiguity*. The Scales weigh both sides of every issue. They seek the middle ground and find their balance there.

Beauty soothes us too. We are surprised by a lovely sunset. We sigh. We release tension. Cultivating the aesthetic side of life is therefore a Libran strategy, either passively as an appreciator or actively as a creator of art.

Interpersonal tensions—fights with our mate, for example—are extraordinarily stressful. Libra has a strategy in this area as well: *courtesy*. That can be a pale word. As we use it here, we don't mean the ability to discern which fork in the fancy restaurant is the salad fork! Courtesy is the ability to convey respect and affirmation toward another person at all times, to build and maintain a *bridge of rapport* between two beings. It is the ability to gauge our actions partly by a sense of how they impact upon another person, and Libra has that ability in abundance.

Shadow: The Libran shadow, as is the case with dark sides of all the signs, is nothing but a distortion of the Scales' normal strategies and resources. Libra's tolerance for ambiguity can be corrupted into mere wishy-washiness and indecision. The sign's aesthetic sensitivity can descend into glossy tackiness. Courtesy can collapse into shallow slickness and an inability to face real conflicts squarely. Paradoxically, all these perversions of the Libran nature lead directly to increased levels of tension. In other words, they do worse than merely subvert the healthy strategies; they work actively in the opposite direction.

Libra Sun in Love: To traditional astrologers, Libra is the sign of marriage. In a symbolic sense it's true. In Libra we find the principle of balance. Two very different entities try to enter into a state of equilibrium with each other—mutual understanding, fairness, and the creative, enriching collision of different perspectives. It's an effective symbol for the spirit of healthy relationship and commitment in general. Every sign is "about relationship" in some sense, but for no Sun sign is human intimacy such a fundamental evolutionary proving ground. Simply to feel fully alive, a person with the Sun in Libra needs the challenges, negotiations and pitfalls of human interaction. As nothing else does, those experiences accelerate that individual's growth and ultimately support his or her sanity. Still, because of its elevated level of empathy, the Libran Sun must remain alert to losing its own center and going into to orbit around another individual—a scenario which usually entails endless arbitration over fairness in trivial matters, all of them symbolic of the deeper rift, discussion of which is being systematically avoided.

Libra Moon in Love: In intimacy Libra requires courtesy and emotional delicacy from the partner. That is especially true of the Libran Moon, in which that delicate lunar sensitivity must be charmed to the surface. There is a refined sensibility here: coarse jokes and crude remarks just won't fly in Libran Moon airspace. For people with this Moon, intimacy is an intuitive art. To them, it seems natural and obvious that it must be approached with grace, with the senses open, with awareness of every move. Even simple cleanliness is a great help—the aesthetic sensitivity is extremely high with this Moon sign. On the Shadow-side of the equation, there's a need to beware of going too far in the direction of smoothing out love's inevitable wrinkles. The risk here lies in so thoroughly understanding and internalizing another person's viewpoint that the individual loses track of his or her own needs. Libra can create the appearance of blissful harmony in a relationship, only to realize his or her true individuality has been completely submerged behind a false mask of sweetness, patience, and acquiescence. On the domestic front, given half a chance the Libran Moon creates a serene, calming asylum of beauty. With comfortable resources, art and music flourish there. But even when scratching out a living, someone with the Moon in Libra puts the pale green candle in the indigo wine bottle and the Zen-like arrangement of dry leaves and branches in the vase on the January kitchen table.

Libran Ascendant in Love: With Libra rising, an individual radiates an attractive, we're-on-the-same-page quality—one that often leads others to exaggerate their sense of how much they have in common. There's a basic drive to establish and maintain a bridge of rapport with others. One word for this quality is *courtesy,* and that doesn't mean stiff, formulaic

60

appropriateness. Rather, it is the art of gracefully minimizing the inevitable frictions that arise whenever two human egos are put in the same small box. The planetary ruler of Libra is Venus, and Venus of course plays a particularly important role in love. Since the ruler of the Ascendant is often simply called the ruler of the chart, you can count on it being a tremendously important planet for anyone with this Ascendant—and that love and intimacy play a correspondingly more pressing role in the dynamics of the biography. The bottom line is that, if someone has Libra rising, you'll learn a lot more by paying close attention to all our remarks about his or her Venus in Chapter Five. That's even more true if Venus falls in one of the "arc of intimacy" houses—see Chapter Six.

Scorpio the Scorpion
(October 24 through November 22)

Archetypes: The Detective, The Hypnotist, The Sorcerer, The Psychologist, The Shaman.

Developmental Aim: Our ancestors clearly weren't aiming to comfort us when they named a sign of the Zodiac after a scorpion! Each one of us sits on a volcano, motivated by unconscious—or at least by unconsidered—psychological forces. Sexuality is an example of one of these forces. Ask a heterosexual eighteen-year-old football player to explain exactly why he is attracted to the cheerleaders. First, he looks at you as though you were crazy. Then he probably makes a joke. For most of us, that's enough. We simply accept those unconscious givens in our lives. For Scorpio, that's only the beginning. The digging must be deeper, and it quickly gets frightening. Down there in the inward layers of the psyche, like parasites on our basic instincts, are many twisted, wounded places—places where we just don't want to go. They warp our lives without our ever knowing exactly what is going on. For a planet touched by Scorpionic energy, the time has come to do that inward journey. Some deep, dark part of the soul must be retrieved from hell, brought to consciousness, and healed. The metaphysical implication is that in a prior life, the part of a person impacted by Scorpio experienced a dark night of the soul—and that going back into the dark to face, integrate, and ultimately heal that part is the intention.

Strategies and Resources: Penetrating, feeling-centered self-analysis is the fundamental Scorpionic evolutionary tactic. No sign peers with such unremitting intensity into the depths of the human psyche. No sign is less inclined toward internal repression and denial. In *The Inner Sky*, we spoke of Scorpio's "defective repressive mechanism." Instinctively there is a suspicion that more is going on than meets the eye. Probing, feeling, sensing the inner terrain, Scorpio grows wiser and deeper, more acutely aware of the dimly illuminated core of the human spirit . . . unless in the course of that inward journey it slips into the snares of the shadow.

To make that passage into the depths of the psyche safely, Scorpio must support this strategy of emotional self-analysis with two essential resources. Neither one arises automatically. Both must be cultivated intentionally. The first resource aims at standing back from oneself and gaining perspective. Scorpio must give up some its *reverence* for its own depth. It must learn to laugh at itself, to see the humorous side of its own intensity.

The second Scorpionic resource is *friends,* although "allies" might be a better term. These are people who help Scorpio maintain perspective. They help it laugh. They support a healthy, active interest in the outer world, offering fascinating alternatives to self-preoccupation. More importantly, these allies can dive right into the heart of the psyche with Scorpio, but still offer those resources that the Scorpion might lack: humor and a sense of the larger picture.

Shadow: The Scorpion's shadow is morbid introspection. Brooding. Moodiness. Heaviness. Those are the traps. That "defective repressive mechanism" gives Scorpio effective access to the unconscious. But it's a two-way street: the unconscious also has effective access to Scorpio. Without the two critical resources—perspective and friends—all the painful, confusing material in the deep psyche eventually erodes, dragging Scorpio downward into a swampy morass of dark emotions. A Scorpio person who follows that low road eventually hurts not only himself or herself. In the grip of the shadow, the Scorpion begins to sting others as well, pointlessly forcing them to "face themselves," insisting that they deal with all manner of painful psychological realities. Gentleness is sacrificed on the altar of truth. Pandora's box is opened . . . but no one knows how to close it or what to do with the demons that have been released.

Scorpio Sun in Love: Pop astrology suggests that Scorpio is the sexy sign. We've run a little survey on the subject and discovered that sex is actually rather popular with the other eleven Sun signs as well! This is one area where no sign has cornered the market. The idea that "Scorpio is sexy" is a distorted perception of a more fundamental astrological idea: Scorpio is the sign of *cathartic emotional intensity.* For anyone with the Sun in this sign, their elemental vitality and much of their sanity depends upon regular doses of it. The fact that our culture tends to associate those kinds of "deep encounter" feelings with sexuality doesn't mean that they can't be found through other avenues, or that sexuality cannot exist without them. There are plenty of people for whom sex is essentially "fun" and no complex psychological depths need to be invoked. But none of those people are healthy Scorpios!

Scorpio Moon in Love: With the Moon in Scorpio, the logic remains the same, except that the Scorpionic hungers are usually more buried, less immediately visible, and less rational. Such a person must get in tune with the Scorpion's way—doing the *work* of ever-deepening intimacy and honesty—or all his or her relationships will feel unsatisfying. In that case, there will be silent, simmering moodiness punctuated with horrific outbursts, often for vague or contrived reasons. Such an individual commutes to the Underworld, often quite unaware of the descent. From the lover's perspective, this can be scary: out of the blue, the partner's mood seems bleak, the soul faraway. To live with such a being, we must learn to respect that primeval Plutonian rhythm: when they are gone, they are gone. And when they return, they need you to look them right in the eye and *be there.* On the domestic front, living with someone with a Scorpio Moon involves a high tolerance for emotional nakedness.

Scorpio Ascendant in Love: My nose is two inches from your nose. My pupils are focused on your pupils. Suddenly we're both covered with goose bumps. I blurt out, "My God . . . you're a soul inside a body!" That's a Scorpio Ascendant in action. Whether or not we're lovers is immaterial. In intimacy, Scorpio rising requires a sense of *encounter.* A touching of spirits. A willingness always to cut deeper. Such a man or woman even looks that way: they wear the mask of the shaman or the mask of the witch, radiating penetrating intensity. If the Scorpion's lover is not a partner in growth, then all feelings—erotic ones included—quickly fade. In any case, we usually find an intimidating intensity. A penetrating gaze. But what's behind it? That depends upon the deeper structures of the birthchart. Often we find a person with this Ascendant who has a knack for getting into dramatic intimacies with extremely intense individuals—but doesn't know what to do with them once they've begun. As we've learned, the Ascendant relates to the *surface expression* of the character. In questions of ongoing love and sexuality, it plays an important role, but one not nearly so important as the role played by the Moon or the Sun.

One more point: the planetary ruler generally cited for Scorpio nowadays is Pluto. That works quite well in practice. But traditionally, Mars was the ruler of Scorpio, and that principle still holds water today. It's helpful in practice to think of anyone with Scorpio rising as having *two* planets ruling the Ascendant—and thus functioning as the co-rulers of the chart. In *Skymates*, however, we're paying particularly close attention to the Mars rulership of Scorpio, because of Mars's sexual significance. The bottom line is that if someone has Scorpio rising, you'll learn a lot more about how he or she functions in intimacy by paying close attention to all our remarks about his or her Mars sign in Chapter Five. That's doubly true if Mars falls in one of the "arc of intimacy" houses—see Chapter Six.

Sagittarius the Archer
(November 23 through December 21)

Archetypes: The Gypsy, The Pilgrim, The Explorer, The Anthropologist, The Philosopher, The Scholar.

Developmental Aim: Life, to Sagittarius, is above all else a *Quest*. The Archer is a seeker. Restless and relentless, a sense of endless searching motivates the inner logic of this sign. Exactly what is the Archer pursuing? Ultimately, it is a sense of life's quintessential *meaning*. As always in evolutionary astrology, this goal is not necessarily one of which the individual is aware. Many times the opposite is true. But conscious or not, the underlying developmental aim of the sign still drives the person and accounts for much of his or her behavior—behavior that otherwise might seem utterly incomprehensible and pointless. In the case of the Archer, we are recognizing a soul that has come to place in its evolutionary cycle where, above all, it requires an *immersion of the mind and senses in wide experience*. The bounds of the familiar must be shattered. The prosaic and stultifyingly provincial "tribal" view of reality must break through into a more universal perspective. The metaphysical implication is that in a prior life, in the part of a person impacted by Sagittarius, this evolutionary hunger was there, but pent up by limiting circumstances. Thus, there is now a compelling drive to "get out of jail"—and stay out.

Strategies and Resources: To find the meaning of life! Is that goal completely quixotic? For Sagittarius, that's not the question. The question is *what* life means, not *whether* it means anything. This is a primary Sagittarian resource: confidence that behind all the seeming randomness of our lives, there exists a great Pattern. How to find the key to that Pattern? Experience. Exploration. A willingness to break up the mind-deadening routines of daily existence. These are the Archer's strategies. Without considerable freedom, no such quest is possible. As a result, no sign is so chary of compromising its autonomy. Critics of Sagittarius might interpret this love of freedom as a *fear of commitment*. In individual cases that analysis might be accurate, but more broadly we must recognize that without freedom, the Archer withers. And it is a sad but seemingly inescapable fact that love is often very hard on freedom.

Shadow: But there is another side to love: it can enhance one's freedom and vastly enrich one's experience of the human condition. The meaning of life? Who knows? But most of humanity's great teachers have agreed that whatever life means, that meaning has something to do with love. The Archer's shadow lies in his possible avoidance of real caring—the kind of caring that only arises when we have truly thrown in our lot with another person, come what may. Sagittarius can skitter across the surface of life like a stone bouncing and careening across a frozen pond, and learn just about as much. As the song tells us, "Freedom's just another word for nothing left to lose."

The principles at stake here are broader than questions of intimacy and sexuality. Sagittarius can learn more about life's meaning by studying one excellent book than it ever would by skimming the first page of every volume in the Library of Congress. Breadth is a virtue, but so are intensity, commitment and focus, whether in love or in the library.

Sagittarius Sun in Love: In affairs of the heart, Sagittarius has a reputation for eloquent theorizing and poor performance. This dispiriting picture need not be the case, but to avoid unpleasant Sagittarian scenarios such as compulsive infidelity or a lonely pattern of superficial emotional contacts, the Archer needs to accept philosophically the idea that inevitably, even in the most vibrant of human bonds, there are dull patches—and that, on the other side of them, the psychic adventure of adult love can grow even richer. Ideas are powerful motivators for people with the Sun in Sagittarius, but those ideas must be convincing and stand the test of real experience. No empty-headed romantic posturing is going to hook the Archer for long, at least not long after that experience has been sampled and digested. Furthermore, for anyone with the Sun in this sign, freedom is a true evolutionary necessity. He or she must choose a partner who values freedom too—one who has his or her own separate interests and separate friends, one who is open to endless change, and most especially one who is relatively free of infantile jealousies and insecurities. If all these requirements are fulfilled, then the Archer may grasp an elemental Sagittarian secret: the quest is far richer and far deeper if it is shared.

Sagittarius Moon in Love: In intimacy, there is a paradox when the Moon lies in Sagittarius. The Moon has to do with our reigning needs, and Sagittarius has a *need not to have any needs,* at least ones that might make it dependent in any way upon another human being. This tension can underlie the ambivalence men and women with this Moon sign often display toward their partners: idealization mixed with distancing. Traditional culture attempts to stabilize marriage by exaggerating the interdependence between partners. Women, for example, are socialized into crippling incapacity in the face of malfunctioning mechanical objects. Men, on the other hand, are socialized into ignorance and helplessness in the face of their own nutritional needs. With the Archer's love of independence, people with this Moon cannot allow themselves to be caught in these snares. Even though they would rather have a colorful home life than the sort epitomized by 1950s television shows about the nuclear family, to avoid inflating their fear of entanglement, they must actively maintain the practical, daily living skills that underlie self-sufficiency. That way, commitment remains a choice rather than an odious, dangerous necessity. We emphasize the sensitivity of this issue for people with the Moon in this sign, since the Moon is more susceptible to the temptations of domestic life.

Sagittarian Ascendant in Love: When Sagittarius is rising, the individual generally radiates an expansive, robust, plucky attitude—the "Mask of the Gypsy." There's usually quick humor, a certain flair, and considerable generosity of spirit. Naturally, this can be a potent magnet for romantic and sexual attention, as well as simple social popularity. "Getting the act together" depends upon living a life that interlocks frequently with all that is novel and unexpected, and one which avoids habitual, mechanical predictability. There's much in this mask that legislates against the humdrum aspects of long-term intimacy. That perspective is realistic—but we must not take it too far. As we say with the Sun and Moon, the key with the Sagittarian Ascendant is not avoidance of commitment, but rather the avoidance of those *kinds* of commitments in which a promise of love becomes a metaphor for prison.

The planetary ruler of Sagittarius is Jupiter, which makes Jupiter the ruler of the chart in this case. If someone has Sagittarius rising, you'll learn more about his or her intimacy profile by paying close attention to Jupiter's sign and house, particularly if Jupiter falls in one of the "arc of intimacy" houses—see Chapter Six.

Capricorn the Sea-Goat
(December 22 through January 20)

Archetypes: The Hermit, The Father, The Prime Minister, The Authority, The Strategist, The Elder.

Developmental Aim: It's a truism that to be sane, we must be in touch with our feelings. But what if we were all simply in touch with our feelings, and nothing arose to balance them? Think of the mayhem: absenteeism, the rampant running of red lights, an epidemic of childishness, homicide . . .

Capricorn represents the other side of that coin. Not being out of touch with feelings, but rather the radical development of those virtues that balance our emotions: integrity, patience, character, personal honor, persistence, the ability to delay gratification, the capacity to resist temptation. Any planet conditioned by Capricorn energy has reached a point in its evolutionary journey at which it is making a great push toward excellence. It is full of "the fascination of what is difficult," to quote William Butler Yeats. The metaphysical implication is that the part of a person affected by Capricorn, in a prior life, experienced a sense of failure. Somehow the higher road was not taken, filling the soul with a sense of shame and guilt—and a steely resolution to get it right this time, whatever the cost.

Strategies and Resources: To grow, Capricorn must take on some great work, some endeavor that pushes him to the limits of his potential. He must struggle and persist, wrestling with demons both inwardly and outwardly. In simple astrology, Capricorn is often equated with ambition. It's true that the Sea-Goat's "great work" might unfold in the professional world, but other possibilities exist. Capricorn might take a small sailboat across a wide ocean. He or she might raise a healthy, happy family in a ghetto. Write a novel. Establish a homestead in the Montana outback. Master a musical instrument. The pivotal point with Capricorn is always to make one's actions reflect one's intentions rather than one's feelings, especially in circumstances where those feelings are full of trepidation, surrender, and frustration.

67

Shadow: To fulfill Capricorn's developmental aim, natural emotions must be controlled and directed. The horror is that they can be suppressed entirely. Subjected to extreme stress, the last of the Sea-Goat's functions to collapse is behavior. The surface. Even with the spark of life flickering out, Capricorn sticks to his course. Is that good news or bad? In any case, the danger is not so much that Capricorn might get out of touch with its feelings. It's more that *everyone else* might get out of touch with Capricorn's feelings. She can find herself locked into the role of the Authority, flawlessly running the show—and meanwhile withering in self-imposed solitary confinement. Down that road, we begin to observe an exaggerated tendency to control others. These control issues ultimately stem from fear—Capricorn's unnaturally-elevated terror of its own human needs, drives, and limits.

Capricorn Sun in Love: Simple commitment comes relatively easily to the Sea-Goat—promises are Capricorn's middle name. It's what to do within the context of intimate promises that might prove baffling. Capricorn must learn the *discipline of emotional self-expression*, if love is to be viable and satisfying. Capricorn must also learn *to ask for what it wants*. Otherwise a person with this Sun sign can get caught in a "responsible," ritualized pattern of relating, stoically enduring all the necessary disciplines of love without really reaping any of the benefits. Typically, Capricorn appreciates solid, reasonable virtues in a mate: dependability, self-sufficiency, a level head. Less obvious is the need to find a partner who also fills in some of the gaps in the Sea-Goat's own behavioral repertoire: someone with an easy emotional expressiveness, a certain sparkle. On the Shadow-side of the equation, if a Capricorn man or woman has gone too far down the cold road of absolute self-sufficiency and unremitting "adulthood," repressing their own natural needs and drives, then we find a messy phenomenon: attraction to individuals who embody the parts of themselves Capricorn has lost. That spells disaster because it creates a parent-child dynamic between the allegedly equal partners. And the poor Goat can make it a point of honor to endure that mistake forever.

Capricorn Moon in Love: With the Moon in this sign, there is a *mood* of solitude about the individual. That's not always the same as loneliness! Such people simply need more time alone than most of us. They also thrive emotionally on big, solitary projects that might daunt another person: building a house alone, writing a novel, earning a doctorate. There is an unconscious attitudinal assumption of everyone's ultimate aloneness. Thus, a person with the Moon in Capricorn must learn a set of alien skills—sharing skills—if love is to survive. Otherwise, the partner soon feels estranged and shut out. On the other hand, such a man or woman also requires a partner who won't be too profoundly shocked to discover that, while he may be well loved, he is ultimately not needed. As a sign, Capricorn is very much concerned with the practical realities of survival. With the Moon there, that concern becomes reflexive and instinctual, which can breed an exaggerated sense of caution, even fearfulness. At that point, the Shadow can take over and we observe a compulsion to *control everything*—life's natural risks, money, conversation, the home, and the partner himself or herself.

On the domestic front, a Capricorn Moon tends to prefer an organized, efficient and responsibly maintained environment, even though various projects and commitments may keep these people too busy to devote much time to housekeeping.

Capricorn Ascendant in Love: On the Ascendant, Capricorn can denote a street-smart outward style, efficient and cautious, with an instinctive understanding of the ways of the world. It can be urbane, even expansive—but there are a handful of aces pressed close to the Sea-Goat's vest, and a poker player's eyes coolly gauging the hands of everyone else around the table. For real love to evolve, this Ascendant must sooner or later become transparent enough to reveal the deeper material behind it. For some individuals that dropping will occur quickly, almost without effort, as soon as trust develops. For others it might never happen. What's behind the Capricorn Ascendant? Only one way to find out: look at the rest of the birthchart.

The planetary ruler of Capricorn is Saturn, which makes Saturn the ruler of the chart in this case. If someone has Capricorn rising, you'll learn more about his or her intimacy profile by paying close attention to Saturn's sign and house, particularly if Saturn falls in one of the "arc of intimacy" houses—see Chapter Six.

Aquarius the Water-Bearer
(January 21 through February 19)

Archetypes: The Genius, The Revolutionary, The Exile, The Scientist, The Truth Sayer.

Developmental Aim: A grandmother appears on the evening news. She's climbed Mount Everest. We marvel, quite rightly, at her courage. What we might not be so quick to realize is that ninety-eight percent of the courage it took to get her to the top of that mountain was already expended by the time she reached the foothills. Simply becoming *the kind of person* who would choose to climb Mount Everest—that's the heart of her accomplishment. Maybe her parents wanted her to marry the boy next door. Almost certainly, her peers pressured her into conventional styles of living: career, family, children. Society, in other words, put many "mountains" between her and Everest. Each one had to be scaled.

Not all of us have come into the world to climb mountains. Most of us, in fact, have poignant, spiritually valid experiences while leading relatively conventional lives. Conventionality is not a sin. But some of us have come to a point in the evolutionary journey of our souls where the experiences that feed our hearts are not the experiences our parents had in mind for us. These people are typically the ones whose birthcharts are touched in some central way by the sign Aquarius. Their developmental aim? In a word, it is the attainment of *individuality*. What feeds them happens to lie outside the framework of the tribe's expectations for them. The metaphysical implication is that in a prior lifetime they experienced the soul-splitting, dissociative trauma of being compelled to live a life that had no connection to their true selves.

Strategies and Resources: Aquarius must learn to break the rules. Throwing bricks through windows is not the point—that's closer to the Aquarian shadow, as we'll soon see. The heart of the process lies in becoming conscious of the way consensual group-think stands between us and our true natures. Aquarius must learn to recognize that society got us when we were very young and programmed us with a set of values and assumptions that might have little to do with our real needs or our true purpose in the world. We must sort out our real identity from all that mythology. We may speak of free spirits, but the truth is that most of the real human free spirits were eaten by saber-toothed tigers aeons ago. As a species, our survival has always depended upon our ability to band together. This far down the evolutionary road, our species is gregarious, social and tribal. Instinctively we seek membership in a group and are usually willing to dance to any tune to gain that membership. The tribe might not always be the fabled middle class. Many times people prefer membership in some subculture. Don't be fooled—that's still the tribal instinct.

The Aquarian strategy is to *override the tribal instinct*. "I am what I am. If you like me, that's delightful. If I bother you . . . well, that's interesting." That's the Water-Bearer's way.

Aquarius has resources to support its developmental strategy. The Water-Bearer is born with an instinctive distrust of patriarchal hierarchies. It tends to be a divergent thinker, drawn magnetically into areas of thought that arise outside the mainstream. It has an exile's mentality, the kind of clear, cold vision we expect of refugees in a new land—men and women who expect shock, and don't expect understanding.

Shadow: Symbolic rebellion is the Aquarian shadow. The grandmother who was supposed to climb Mount Everest instead succumbs to social pressure. She marries conventionally, pursues an "appropriate" career, dresses for success. What happens? *All those rebellious, independent Aquarian instincts are vented on irrelevant targets.* After a while, she starts insisting upon her God-given right to wear purple stockings to work. She refuses adamantly ever to speak to a certain neighbor again. Instead of defending her individuality and her right to have unique Aquarian experiences, she deflects that energy into the defense of pointless quirks. With her true individuality undeveloped, she increasingly hides behind mere eccentricities. People who try to get close to her quickly sense that she's "not there" somehow, despite her superficial self-assurance. They describe her as "aloof" or perhaps "cold," mistaking the hand of the Shadow—psychological *dissociation*—for her real individuality, now absent.

Aquarius Sun in Love: If the world were populated only by Aquarians, we might still have marriage, but it would look a lot different. For one thing, many happily married couples might choose to live on opposite sides of town. Or live in threes or fours. Or be of very different ages, or ethnicities. And these varied arrangements would be seen as perfectly normal and in tune with psychological reality: *people are all different, aren't they?* Individuation—and respect for it in others—is the heart of Aquarius. Navigating human sexuality is a knotty process, and society often tries to come to our rescue by providing us prefabricated scripts about how to handle it. Promiscuity is discouraged, or carefully directed into prescribed rite-of-passage rituals. Monogamy is generally supported, and where it's not supported, "safe" outlets are provided. Women are encouraged to nest. Men are encouraged to develop an unreasoning compulsion to earn money. All these themes have the effect of channeling sexuality in socially acceptable directions. We can critique that channeling, but we might also observe that it represents the accumulated wisdom of humanity regarding a very tricky subject. Flawed wisdom, certainly—but, so far, the best we've got. Committed love is so difficult that for most of us it's helpful to plug into those patterns to some extent, if only to help us keep our balance. Not so for the Water-Bearer. For Aquarius, everything must be questioned. Toss out the scripts. Flush the rule book. Make it up as we go along. *"Let's get married, and not live together!"*

Aquarius Moon in Love: Love can be hard on individuality, or it can support and enhance it. For anyone with an Aquarian Moon, everything depends upon making sure that coin lands heads up. How? First, before facing the risks and challenges of committed love, the man or woman with an Aquarian Moon must have a head start on his or her own individuation. For this reason, although marriage can be healthy and happy for Aquarians in general, *early* marriage tends to be stultifying and often short-lived. That's a particular risk for the Aquarian Moon, simply because the Moon thinks less than the Sun, and is therefore more susceptible to *rebelling* its way into complex romantic or sexual situations. In any case, breathing room is necessary for intimacy to prosper here. A kind of closeness that would feel natural for Scorpio or Cancer will seem claustrophobic for the Water-Bearer, unless the rest of the birthchart bends over backwards to say the opposite. For the Aquarian Moon, periods of separation—even just a few hours—are times of healing. Once individuation has taken hold, these people can be loving and fully present—but at earlier developmental stages, their partners will be frustrated by a certain perception of coldness, detachment, or distance: symptoms of the person simply not having come out into the world yet. And when they do come out, be ready for some surprises. In all cases, a partner must be selected who is willing to give the Aquarian Moon a lot of room to maneuver—people with markedly conventional expectations of their mates will ponder these individuals uncomprehendingly: their feelings just don't seem to "work right." The natural domestic scene for someone with an Aquarian Moon tends toward the exotic and the iconoclastic, with plenty of unexpected touches—and maybe a shock or two for grandma.

Aquarius Ascendant in Love: The standard analysis of an Aquarian Ascendant suggests a generalized friendliness and sociability, and also a certain coolness in more intimate situations. This perspective is often accurate in practice, but here's a more illuminating perspective. The *natural* outward style of such individuals is unique; they hear the proverbial different drummer. Thus, right from birth, the warping social pressure from family, peers, and culture is enormous on people with this Ascendant—they are pressured, threatened, bribed and cajoled into conforming. That translates, sometimes without their even knowing it, into keeping themselves secret behind a kind of hologram of a "normal, well-adjusted person." If those forces win, then we observe a surface appropriateness—and of course a certain distance when we try to get closer. They're just not there somehow. For these reasons, people with Aquarian Ascendants benefit enormously from having partners who are cheerleaders for their visionary wildness.

The planetary ruler of Aquarius is Uranus, which makes Uranus the ruler of the chart in this case. If someone has Aquarius rising, you'll learn a lot about his or her intimacy profile by paying close attention to Uranus's house and sign, particularly if Uranus falls in one of the "arc of intimacy" houses—see Chapter Six.

Pisces the Fishes
(February 20 through March 20)

Archetypes: The Mystic, The Dreamer, The Poet, The Seer, The Visionary, The Romantic Idealist.

Developmental Aim: Pisces is the last sign of the zodiac. In one sense it's the highest sign, although a far more practical statement is that in Pisces, the stakes are the highest. We win big or lose big. This is the sign of the great escape—not an escape from the world so much as from the tyranny of our own self-aggrandizing egos.

In the Fishes we become aware of the fact that ultimately *we are the consciousness that observes the personality* and expresses itself through it. We stand back. We experience ourselves as players in a vast drama. From that perspective our "normal" preoccupations with success and failure, gain and loss, pride and humiliation, all become unspeakably, inexpressibly funny. This distinctly Piscean humor is not biting or cynical. There is not a drop of sarcasm in it. It fills the heart with compassion.

Ultimately it is difficult to describe the Piscean developmental aim without drifting into mystical, religious language. That is simply the file in the great human card catalog where we've traditionally stored our information about the Fishes' experience.

Any planet touched by Pisces has reached a point in the evolutionary journey where the perceptions that feed it and accelerate its growth have nothing to do with belief or even with human reason. They are all in the category of direct, mystical contact with deeper dimensions of reality. The metaphysical implication is that in a prior life, the part of a person impacted by Pisces quietly developed considerable psychic or spiritual sensitivity, but

73

was unable to flesh out that sensitivity with appropriate experiences: the right soul-connections, contact with conscious teachers, sufficient meditative time. There is a compelling hunger for those things now.

Strategies and Resources: To attain the Piscean goal, we must experience ourselves as something more than name, rank and serial number. We must go beyond identifying with the part of ourselves plays a specific role in the human world. We can call this process "meditation." That's a perfectly good word—except that society has put a lot of salad dressing on it. By meditation, we do not mean to imply any particular system of beliefs. We are speaking of a brain-state: the raw, uninterpreted process of consciousness becoming aware of itself. Close your eyes, breathe deeply and slowly, and watch for the silent spaces in between your thoughts. Pop! Meditation. Nothing to it.

The trick lies in learning to string those silent spaces together until they form long, unbroken chains of pure awareness. If Pisces succeeds in accomplishing that, then the individual begins actually to experience himself or herself as consciousness, just as if one plays basketball constantly, one soon learns to experience himself as a set of physical reflexes.

Shadow: Pisces can twist this mystical urge or misunderstand how to go about fulfilling it, descending into mere escapism. Old-fashioned astrology books are full of injunctions about the Fishes' susceptibility to alcohol. Nowadays we must add to a few items to the list: the abuse of drugs, television, food, sex, sleep, novels, work, music, money, art, travel, shopping, hobbies, education, social activism, and religion. *Virtually anything we enjoy can be used in an escapist way.* The point is not to avoid pleasure, but rather to avoid the Piscean tendency to disappear into it.

Pisces Sun in Love: Unless it's gone down a dark road of self-numbing behavior, there is profound tenderness in the Pisces Sun. For no other sign does the romantic ideal of "touching souls" feel so palpably real. Thus, the only kind of bond that is likely to survive meaningfully for the Fishes is one with a spiritual basis. Like most clichés, the notion of a "spiritual relationship" can slip from our tongues without really passing through our brains. Two Piscean Presbyterians might sit together in church, have profoundly Presbyterian experiences, and still not have a spiritual relationship. Why? Simply because their spirits are not relating to each other! On the other hand, two atheists might sit together in silence before a campfire and drift off into a meditative state—"dreaming the fire," as the Swahili people put it. Still, they are aware of each other's presence, and appreciative

74

that they can share this magical space without comment and without the threat of either one's ego intruding. Those spirits are actively touching. They have entered an altered state of consciousness and still feel a sense of contact: Piscean paradise. Once such lovers have found each other, their bond must be fed with the kinds of input that support these high soul-touchings: silent time together, candlelight, quiet walks on the beach or in the forest, perhaps experiences in churches, temples, or even formal meditation groups. Given all that, the two lovers, connected on the Piscean wavelength, share something only the Fishes know: a sense of loving, dancing hilarity, a sense of the cosmic joke—and of the tides of magic between them . . . tides that could one day laugh at the frailty of death.

Pisces Moon in Love: Almost everything we just saw about the Piscean Sun applies to the Moon as well, but in a softer, more reflexive and intuitive way. At its best, the Pisces Moon is the repository of the highest human aspirations in terms of the soul-potential of Eros—a precious, temporary merging of spirits in the alchemical fires of conscious sexuality. But the Moon can be sleepy and subjective, especially in this most other-worldly of signs. It can also be self-sacrificial and given to martyrdom, drifting through the psychological and biological motions of relating. Learning to ask for what it wants, and learning actively to guide the partner toward entering these deeper territories of the spirit—these are essential intimate skills for anyone with a Piscean Moon. The sensitivity must be emboldened; the lover must take his or her own hunger seriously. They must learn not to give up too much. Domestically, the Moon in Pisces needs its home to have some of the attributes of a sacred temple: serenity, beauty, and hints of the next world. Anyone whose attitudes are radically removed from that aesthetic will simply prove too jangly a presence for the Piscean Moon, leading it to withdraw into dreamland.

Pisces Ascendant in Love: Wearing the mask of the master actor, a person born with Pisces rising can play many roles. Socially, there are many advantages to this Ascendant: it can fit seamlessly into almost any kind of situation, even very aggressive or chaotic ones that would fry the circuitry of a Pisces Moon or Sun. But in intimacy, anyone with Pisces rising must be wary of taking on too much of the coloration of the partner's expectations or style. They must be true to the core archetypes of the sign: the mystic and the visionary. Certain behaviors are natural to those archetypal fields: meditation, contemplation, creativity. If, as a result of time spent in a given partnership, those behaviors become less central to the shape of the life, then too much truth is being sacrificed on the altar of the "master actor." Too much truth has been surrendered. The "act must be gotten back together" by returning to the root action of the Fish: diving deeply into the ocean of consciousness.

The planetary ruler of Pisces is Neptune, which makes Neptune the ruler of the chart in this case. If someone has Pisces rising, you'll learn a lot about his or her intimacy profile by paying close attention to the sign and house of Neptune, particularly if Neptune falls in one of the "arc of intimacy" houses—see Chapter Six.

CHAPTER FIVE: LOVE AND WAR

The Sun, Moon, and Ascendant are astrology's *primal triad,* but mature love exists between two human *totalities.* Ultimately, all the planets are relevant to intimacy, just as the entire person is involved in a relationship. Two planets, however, are particularly important when considering our intimate behavior. It's time to meet Venus and Mars—the Goddess of Love and the God of War.

Since antiquity, traditional astrologers have equated Mars with "masculinity"—courage, initiative, assertiveness, and the power of the will. Venus has been associated with "femininity"—gentleness, relatedness, receptivity, and beauty.

But this chapter does not have a Venus section for women and a Mars section for men. In the modern world, both principles are increasingly active in, and accessible to, both sexes.

Venus symbolizes the capacity to form relationships, to create, to attract, and also what we find attractive. Venus is Eros, not just sexuality, but *relatedness:* the capacity to feel connected to someone or something. Have you ever fallen in love with a place, a house, a book or a painting? That was Eros, in the sense that you felt a connection. Something in that song or landscape seemed to speak to you personally, and you took pleasure in that feeling. Your Venus was buzzing then, much in the way that it does when you fall in love with another person. In human relationships, Venus represents the capacity to feel warmth, affection, liking and compassion, to identify deeply with someone, and to make his or her needs as important as our own. It is the more tender, feeling-oriented side of loving.

Mars represents drive, determination, and the impulses to protect ourselves and to seek what we desire. Astrologer Jeffrey Wolf Green says that Mars is our desire-nature. Mars in the birthchart works a lot like the adrenal glands in the body—our "flight or fight" mechanism. If your adrenals are low, you feel tired. If your Mars is low, you lack energy not only for relating, but for defending yourself and for going after what you want. The sign and house of Mars can show you *what you need to feed your elemental energy,* as well as where you need to assert yourself. Think of Mars, the warrior planet, as using both a sword and a shield. The sword helps us discriminate between what we want and what we don't want, and helps us pursue our goals. The shield protects us and defends us. Mars is related to our vital energies in general, our capacity for enthusiasm and willpower. And of course Mars is libido—our sexuality, the heat of the blood.

Sometimes we actively try to establish or refine a relationship, and other times we play a more passive role, letting the other person take the initiative. Mars shows how we reach out to the person who catches our eye. Venus reveals how we make ourselves attractive and hope to capture attention.

Let's return to a very important point about Venus: its sign and house can indicate what we find appealing in others, what makes us respond with a feeling of relatedness and connectedness. Astrologer Stephen Arroyo advises learning people's Venus signs when trying to please them. When it comes to Venus, all of us act on the principle that *like attracts like*. Someone who embodies the qualities of our Venus appeals to us, and we demonstrate our own Venusian qualities when trying to attract others.

That Venusian element of simply liking someone is critical, because a growing relationship, one with true evolutionary potential, challenges you to face the worst in yourself and to try to heal it. Relating can be joyful too, but it inevitably presses our buttons and brings out our dark side sometimes. For a relationship to thrive, sometimes we have to say hard truths to each other about those difficult aspects of our natures. It's threatening to hear such things. We have a natural Mars-reflex to defend ourselves against the perceived attack.

Enter Venus. Although it's never easy to hear painful truths about yourself, it's easier to hear them from someone you like, trust and find appealing. Also, if someone has been a jerk, it's easier to forgive him or her and move on if you deeply and genuinely *like* that person. Anyone who triggers a Venus-response in you has plenty of the exact qualities that most appeal to you. We're naturally vulnerable to such a person. He or she has the power to *disarm our defenses.*

That, of course, can be the theme of heartbreaking stories as easily as live-happily-ever-after ones.

Enter Mars. Mars is our warrior-function. Sometimes we have to send someone packing. Sometimes we do have to growl in a relationship, even a good one. Maybe we've been attacked unfairly. Also, regardless of how much you love your partner, it takes courage both to confront him or her with areas that need work—and to be confronted with them yourself. It takes energy too. Have you ever avoided a fight because you were just too tired? Finally, if you're going to change, you have to exert willpower and energy—Mars—to do so.

78

As you read the following descriptions of Mars and Venus in each element and sign, please keep in mind that each planet represents *only one* feature of a chart, and *no feature should be considered separately from the rest*. No one relates only from Venus or only from Mars. Context is everything. Think of these descriptive—and necessarily limited—paragraphs as guidelines to trigger your own interpretive process, and you won't lose sight of the chart as a whole. We'd also like to emphasize that since *Skymates* is a book about synastry, we're of course focusing on the specific dimensions of Mars and Venus that are most pertinent to relationships. There's more to both planets.

One more point: sexuality is a strange convergence zone of body, mind, and soul. The ancient, luminous spirit in you is fascinated by it—and so is the inner, primeval monkey. Our deepest soul-consciousness—and our most embarrassing, most human silliness—are both apparent in our sexuality. In the material that follows, we try to cover all those bases. We open each section with an italicized reference to the *actual evolutionary intention* underlying each Mars or Venus sign configuration—and then we explore the very human tools the soul has available and might use to fulfill its intent. You'll get, in other words, a taste of the sublime and a taste of the ridiculous! The deepest wisdom lies in seeing the way that those primate behavioral and characterological tools can serve the soul's evolutionary intention, all in one seamlessly integrated whole.

Venus Through The Twelve Signs

Venus in Aries. *The evolutionary intent is to establish relationships that help the person learn courage and develop the will. There is a soul-desire to learn how to express strong emotions, positive or negative, in the context of love. This is in reaction to soul-memories of deadening prior-life dynamics in which intimacy was eclipsed by unresolved, unexpressed anger.*

This Venus sign can bill itself as the *Warrior* or the *Amazon*, and charge through life with a pioneering spirit that seems to survive all blows, even to thrive on them. "Look how gutsy I am. I'm not just a date; I'm an adventure." Venus in Aries may throw out a romantic challenge, daring you to win his or her hand. "Hit me with your best shot." This Venus sign appreciates independence, spunkiness, directness and courage. These people are risk-takers. They like feeling potent, have a taste for healthy competition

79

and enjoy winning. Marilyn Monroe and Elizabeth Taylor, two of the most courted, pursued women of all time, have Venus in Aries, as do Robert Downey, Jr. and Harlan Ellison. So does Jack Nicholson, whose longtime companion Anjelica Houston says, "He makes my blood boil."

Venus in Taurus. *The evolutionary intent is to develop lasting bonds that help one maintain calm, simplicity and an easy connection with one's instinctive side. There is a soul-desire to experience naturalness in the sexual arena, in reaction to stiff, formal, or undesired prior life sexual relations.*

Venus in Taurus attracts through emphasizing the physical, body-centered nature of Earth. They appeal to your senses. They radiate touchability; they're cuddly. "Look how easy it is to be with me," their aura seems to say. "Look how soothing my company could be for you." Venus in Taurus is drawn to Earth Mother/Earth Father qualities in someone. They tend to like the outdoors and those who are comfortable there, and who are comfortable in their bodies. Most of all they prefer simplicity and naturalness, and dislike unnecessary histrionics. John Wayne, hero of many back-to-the-land Westerns, had Venus in Taurus. Marlon Brando exemplified the earthy attractiveness of Venus in Taurus. Musicians Alanis Morissette, David Byrne and Billy Joel have Venus in Taurus.

Venus in Gemini. *The evolutionary intent is to form relationships that help develop one's open-mindedness and ability to perceive without judging. There is a kid-in-the-candy-store quality here, based on prior-life experiences of celibacy or sexual monotony.*

Venus in Gemini seems to believe that the way to your heart is through stimulating your brain and thrilling your senses. This Venus sign can be the original Good Conversationalist, a raconteur who can keep you enthralled with stories about the lectures attended, authors read, events experienced. "I'm intelligent, but not a pedant," says Venus in Gemini. "I'll never be boring; we'll always have something to do—and then we can discuss it!" They like verbal byplay; they flirt well. The eighteenth century institution of the salon, where great minds of the day could meet at the home of an intelligent hostess, was probably created by someone with Venus in Gemini. These people are observant and friendly, interested in almost everything and disposed to talk to almost anyone, unless the rest of the birthchart suggests a taste for solitude. They like people with an enormous variety of interests and a ravening curiosity. Bob Dylan and William Shakespeare have Venus

80

in Gemini, as do Georgio Armani and Naomi Campbell, along with Harrison Ford and Uma Thurman.

Venus in Cancer. *The evolutionary intent is to form relationships that help develop and heal one's inner world of feelings. These relationships must be as safe as possible, involving profound, lasting commitments by gentle, nurturing partners—in stark contrast to prior-life dynamics in which the soul was driven to take refuge within a psychic shell.*

Venus in Cancer attracts by showing how protective, tender, and healing it can be. People with this Venus sign seem to telegraph, "Come to me, you who are weary and heavy laden, and I will give you rest." They radiate the promise of helping you find and nourish your domestic, psychological, or archetypal roots. They provide a home base where you can feel secure. Venus in Cancer likes people who are gentle and nurturing, and feels safe enough to open up only after such people have proven themselves for a while. With that basic need met—and only then—we could add that Venus in Cancer is also drawn to people who are fanciful, who would be good copilots for their own flights of imagination. Judy Garland had Venus in Cancer and drew on it in her characterization of home-loving Dorothy, "the small and meek." Carl Jung had Venus in Cancer, assisting him in the exploration of his clients' personal myths. Garrison Keillor has Venus in Cancer; no wonder he tells stories about the little town of Lake Woebegon! Gene Roddenberry, creator of Star Trek, had Venus in Cancer; so do Wynona Judd and Stevie Nicks.

Venus in Leo. *The evolutionary intent is to establish relationships that help the person learn about joy, spontaneity, and a celebration of the Self as a path to growth. The implication is that there is a strong soul-desire to use love as a method for healing an ancient pain based on rejection, betrayal, persecution, or judgment.*

Outwardly, these people can clown their way into your heart or impress you with their noble ways and sweeping gestures. Venus in Leo demonstrates how dramatic and colorful he or she is, how generous, creative, entertaining, and worthy of respect. Leo is ruled by the Sun: Venus in Leo people are attracted to those with a lot of (solar!) presence and charisma. They will do their best to shine for you, and they want you to shine, too. A Leo archetype is The King or Queen. Think about the courtship style of a good sovereign who wants to rule wisely and well over a happy, productive country, and also about what sort of person would make a fine royal consort, and you'll go a long way toward understanding the outer trappings of this Venus sign.

81

Underlying everything is the desire to create an atmosphere of complete spontaneity and guaranteed mutual approval—that's the only incubator in which the soul-healing can occur. P. T. Barnum had Venus in Leo; so did Coco Chanel. Musician and performer extraordinaire, Ian Anderson, has Venus in Leo; so do David Copperfield, Madonna, and Whitney Houston.

Venus in Virgo. *The evolutionary intent is to form relationships that emphasize an almost militant focus on growth and active mutual helpfulness, in reaction to prior-life dynamics involving the feeling of being enslaved within stalled, static, hopeless marital situations.*

This Venus sign appeals by informing you how much better life could be if you were together. Venus in Virgo shows how much attention he or she pays to details, how willing he or she is to make improvements. "See how honest I am, and how eager to make this relationship all it could be." They want to make themselves indispensable to you. Mercury rules Virgo, and these people generally both have and appreciate Mercurial wit, critical abilities and discrimination. They are drawn to people who are devoted to their work, who have a gift for fine craftsmanship, and who are very serious about personal growth. Consummate jazz artist John Coltrane had Venus in Virgo; so does director Pedro Almodovar. Poet and mythological historian Robert Graves, lyricist and singer John Lennon, and comediennes Lily Tomlin and Jane Curtin all have Venus in Virgo, showing this placement's potential for verbal creativity.

Venus in Libra. *The evolutionary intent is to form relationships that help develop one's ability to relate in sophisticated, romantic, courteous ways, with a constant focus on empathetic alertness toward each other. There is a strong reaction against prior-life experiences of sexual crassness or crudity in a partner.*

These people attempt to charm you with their social graces, their love of peace, harmony, and beauty, and their aesthetic sensibilities. This Venus sign demonstrates how ethical and *fair* it is, how much it loves justice and hates wrangling and bigotry, and therefore how sweet your life together could be. Venus in Libra is drawn to people who are creative, sensitive, warm, empathetic, tactful, and fair themselves. The mental quality of Air tends toward idealism in Libra, and sometimes to an attachment to the appearance of harmony at all costs, if the rest of the chart isn't that of a scrapper. Oscar Wilde, a playwright who wrote polished and urbane high-society comedies, had Venus in Libra, as do supermodel Claudia Schiffer, actress Kate Capshaw, and singer-songwriter Kenny Rogers.

82

Venus in Scorpio. *The evolutionary intent is to form relationships that help develop one's ability to be deeply and nakedly human together, and to make a non-judgmental space for catharsis in one's self and one's partner. There is a soul-desire to experience radical honesty, thereby re-establishing the ability to trust which was damaged by intimate lies and deceptions experienced in a prior life.*

This Venus placement exudes mystery, power, and sexuality. Through the Sorcerer archetype, they invite you to explore the psychic dimensions of intimate relating. Venus in Scorpio offers primal, transformative *intensity*: sexually, emotionally, or psychologically. They can come across as very seductive, since something about them seems to simmer with the promise of volcanic emotions—and to invite yours. This Venus sign likes people who are capable of radical honesty, intensity and fervor, who don't flee from emotionally cathartic experiences. They also like people with an aura of the unknown, the hidden, the occult. Tina Turner has Venus in Scorpio, and Mick Jagger has said about her, "Standing next to her (on stage) is the hottest place in the world!" Bruce Springsteen, another electrifying performer, has Venus in Scorpio, as does Monty Python alumnus John Cleese. Mystery writer Agatha Christie had this Venus sign; so did surrealistic artist Salvador Dali.

Venus in Sagittarius. *The evolutionary intent is to establish relationships that will help the person widen his or her perspective on the world, and to restore broken faith and pagan delight in love. There is a reaction against prior-life dynamics involving repressive sexual restraint, intimate boredom, and relationships which were more settled for than cherished.*

This Venus sign's complex approach to the art of attraction can be grasped through a consideration of its archetypes: the Gypsy, the Scholar, the Philosopher, the Explorer, and the Anthropologist. The Gypsy and the Explorer might say, "See how daring and carefree I am. Kick over your traces and go to Europe with me." The Scholar or Philosopher tantalize you with glimpses of the accumulated wisdom of the ages. The Anthropologist waltzes you through a spellbinding collection of human types, a dowry of fascinating friends and acquaintances. Venus in Sagittarius appreciates easy-going, tolerant, humorous people with a robust appetite for experience, adventure and variety, and people who stand up for their principles. They want a relationship they can truly relish, one that adds to the color and variety of their lives. Guitarists extraordinaire Jimi Hendrix and Jimmy Page have Venus in Sagittarius, as do political activists Jane Fonda and Joan Baez, and actors Derek Jacobi, Ruth Gordon and Robert Duvall.

Venus in Capricorn. *The evolutionary intent is to form grown-up relationships based on integrity, commitment, and maturity, in reaction to prior-life dynamics involving failure and abandonment that were driven essentially by the immaturity of one or both partners.*

These people arouse your interest with Capricornian strategy and efficiency. They project an aura of reserve, fascinating you with still waters that run deep. They have a taste for solitude and don't respond well to overly dependent people. Venus in Capricorn appreciates a sense of responsibility, practicality, maturity, self-containment and integrity, and are drawn to people who give the impression that they could become a Wise Elder in their later years. Saturn, ruler of manifestation in the world of form, rules Capricorn, and this Venus sign can be attracted to those with some mastery of the material world, status, or reputation. Unless the rest of the chart strongly suggests otherwise, this Venus sign is usually not horrified at the idea of commitment, regardless of current cultural mores. Actors James Dean and Anthony Hopkins have Venus in Capricorn, as do writers Louisa May Alcott, Robert Bly and Toni Morrison.

Venus in Aquarius. *The evolutionary intent is to form relationships that support individuality and guarantee personal freedom. There is a reaction against feelings of being sexually used but not really "seen" in a prior life, perhaps connected with sexual unions that were not freely chosen. Often, the trauma associated with that karmic dynamic was severe enough that there may be some present-life dissociation in sexual situations.*

This Venus sign broadcasts its originality, independence, and open-mindedness in order to attract. "I have revolutionary ideas and insight that can liberate you," their aura seems to say. "And you can be completely yourself around me." Venus in Aquarius people try to demonstrate their clarity of thought, their attachment to speaking the truth, and their quality of genius, and they are drawn to those free-spirited qualities in others. These people seek to make themselves worthy of attention by being different, by not fitting in, and by questioning the world around them in general, and sometimes that world's relating customs in particular. This Venus sign both needs and will give a great deal of space, sometimes to the point of seeming overly detached. Unless the rest of the birthchart indicates otherwise, Venus in Aquarius prefers people who are free-spirited, open-minded, non-possessive and highly individual, people who break rules and challenge

84

conventions. Feminists Simone de Beauvoir, Gloria Steinem, and Erica Jong have Venus in Aquarius, along with existentialist playwright Edward Albee, writers Umberto Eco and Carlos Castaneda, and actress Ellen Degeneres.

Venus in Pisces. *The evolutionary intent is to form relationships that function first and foremost as a bond between consciousnesses, integrating the sexual with the spiritual. This is in response to damaging prior-life dynamics involving some mixture of three hurtful realities: partners with narrowly utilitarian and biological perspectives on the erotic; prior-life monastic vows of celibacy; and grievous bereavement.*

This Venus sign attracts through the Neptune-ruled archetypes: the Mystic, the Poet, the Dreamer, and the Seer. They want you to notice the pure, untrammeled Spirit looking out through their flesh-and-blood eyes. They seem to offer a romantic escape from the dreary "real world" into another realm. In that idealized, Venus-in-Pisces place, a place of awareness, fantasy, and illusion, consciousness reigns supreme—not personality with its social security numbers and shopping lists. Venus in Pisces appreciates people with a similar visionary or otherworldly quality, in or out of church, temple, mosque, or ashram. "Renew your spirit with me. Listen to my CDs, play Dungeons and Dragons with me, or let's just watch the Moon on the water. Your innermost Self can breathe in my presence, and I won't chase it away with bright lights and harsh questions." Mythologist Joseph Campbell had Venus in Pisces, as does Mikhail Baryshnikov. Edgar Allan Poe and Elizabeth Barrett Browning had Venus in Pisces, along with Francis Ford Coppola, Michael Caine and Drew Barrymore.

Mars Through The Twelve Signs

Mars in Aries. *The evolutionary intent is to learn to apply one's sexual will with courage and directness. There is a soul-desire to reclaim unabashed Eros, and to resolve karmic anger linked either to the repression of natural sexual desires or to sexual humiliation.*

Ardent and impetuous, the Warrior-archetype Mars person may appreciate a battle to win your heart. Passion and directness are tactics here, unless the rest of the birthchart is very mild. This Mars sign can be exceptionally protective. Competition energizes Mars in Aries. It likes adventures, challenges, the thrill of the chase, and almost any relational situation that tests its will. The energy of Mars in Aries thrives on feeling powerful and victorious. A steady diet of defeat, or a lack of exciting and

85

self-chosen challenges, will deplete this Mars sign. Rocker Pete Townshend has Mars in Aries, and his song titles show it: "Gonna Get Ya," "Rough Boys," and "I Am an Animal." Clint Eastwood has Mars in Aries, and draws upon it for his roles in Westerns. ("Go ahead, make my day.") Elisabeth Kubler-Ross, who pioneered work with the dying, has Mars in Aries. "Riverdancer" Michael Flatley has Mars in Aries, along with rocker John Fogerty and poet Nikki Giovanni.

Mars in Taurus. *The evolutionary intent is to apply one's sexual will toward the development of connectedness to the world of nature and to one's instinctive side. There is a soul-desire to restore the natural freedom of erotic self-expression to the physical body, implying prior life experiences in which sexuality became stilted or was viewed as a shameful expression of our animal natures.*

This Mars sign can style itself as a good provider, and not only financially. It includes the sensual—all five senses, plus your toes and your nose. Mars in Taurus looks out for your physical comfort and well-being, whether it's by putting fine food on the table, helping you balance your checkbook, rubbing your shoulders, or wearing your favorite cologne. They want to lull you and relax you. They'll enlist Mother Nature on their side, taking you to the zoo in the spring or walking you through the honeysuckle on a summer's evening. This is a very physical, hedonistic placement for Mars, and a determined one. Feeling in touch with one's body and with the world of nature feeds the energy of Mars in Taurus, while ignoring one's instinctive side and spending too much time indoors depletes it. Dancing partners Rudolf Nureyev and Margot Fonteyn both have Mars in Taurus; so do Mick Jagger, Paula Adbul and Jamie Lee Curtis.

Mars in Gemini. *The evolutionary intent is to apply the sexual will towards the development of radical alertness, pure perception, and above all the free exchange of ideas. Erotically, there is often a hunger for diversity in reaction to prior life dynamics of "dutiful" sexual functioning, complicated by prior life trauma related to sexual damage sustained—and silenced—at an early age. Unaddressed, that can manifest as childish sexual attitudes and behaviors.*

This Mars sign will dazzle you with wit, brilliance, and precocity. Mars in Gemini will ask to see your poetry and take you to every rare book store in town. They read your favorite novel and loan you theirs, so that you can discuss the books together. Mars in Gemini wants to expand and deepen the communication between you. Hungry for shared new experiences, they might

86

suggest a trip to the state fair, the circus, or the Third World. They tell you stories; they camp out on your answering machine or your email in-box. All this activity is meant to open a fascinating intimate dialogue with you and persuade you to continue it. This Mars sign is energized by ideas, debate, well-crafted language, unanswered questions, new experiences and wonder. It is depleted by boredom, certainty, and prejudices. Writers F. Scott Fitzgerald, Robertson Davies and Erica Jong all have Mars in Gemini; so do Neil Armstrong, David Duchovny, Aretha Franklin and Steve Martin.

Mars in Cancer. *The evolutionary intent is to create a safe environment for the comforting and healing of the deepest expression of human sexuality, which is the capacity truly to bond with a partner. Prior life dynamics led to fear and mistrust: a sense that sexuality will spin out of control and pain will be created. There is a soul-desire to find the courage to trust again.*

Outwardly, this Mars sign sets out to prove how utterly nurtured you could be, how your every emotional need could be met, by this relationship. Mars in Cancer people offer protection, security, and a nest where they will soothe and heal all your frazzled nerves, and their aura says that they would wrestle tigers to keep that nest safe. They provide emotional support and understanding, and an active, sensitive participant in your inner life. Inwardly, it is hoping that you return those favors! This Mars sign is energized by time to do inner work, having someone or something to nurture in a healthy way, and the use of imagination. It's depleted by invasiveness, lack of respect for its sensitivity, people who consistently take advantage of its nurturing qualities, and by having no place or time to retreat. Humphrey Bogart, who excelled at playing tough, crabby men with soft hearts under their hard shells, had Mars in Cancer, as does actor/director Kenneth Branagh. William Shakespeare and Lord Byron, a Romantic poet, had Mars in Cancer, along with singer Ray Charles and food writer M.F.K. Fisher.

Mars in Leo. *The evolutionary intent is to learn to express Eros with creativity, unabashed self-confidence, and verve in response to prior-life experiences involving circumstances of inhibition, repression, and public shaming—a delicate process involving the restoration to the sexual nature of elements of healthy selfishness and natural pride.*

Mars in Leo excels at "courtly love," and understands the drama and theater of courtship better than any other Mars sign. These people pay attention to stage settings and props: the right restaurant, the right gesture, the right gift. They can be truly noble, warm, honest, loyal, encouraging, and generous with their time and affection. Creativity, playfulness, humor, praise, and being a leader in an area that matters to the Mars in Leo person will all energize people with this placement, while a lack of fun and constant negativity will deplete them. Some very well-loved entertainers have Mars in Leo: Robert Redford, Bruce Springsteen, and Frank Sinatra. Robert Graves, famous for his love poetry and studies of the archetypal Great Goddess, had Mars in Leo. This Mars sign is also shared by poet William Blake, singer Cher, and actress Jodie Foster.

Mars in Virgo. *The evolutionary intent is towards the development of personally meaningful competencies which are applied in service toward the partner. Driving this behavior is a soul-desire to resolve relational or sexual guilt from the karmic past. That guilt may have come from actual wrong-doing, or from the general shaming of sexuality under the repressive culture of the patriarchy.*

This Mars sign seems to say, "Look how much I could help you. A relationship with me is like being an amoeba in a zoologist's growth medium; you're guaranteed to go through some changes. Don't you want to be all you can be?" Mars in Virgo challenges you to perfect your interpersonal skills as you would perfect artistic skills, with attention to technique and detail. It offers to help you in every dimension of your life, from your soul's evolution to getting your car to the repairman in rush hour traffic. To the end of establishing a perfect relationship, these people can minutely scrutinize your life and offer suggestions for improvement. They are energized by helping you, even when you would prefer they didn't or when their help comes across as hectoring and criticism. Ernest Hemingway had Mars in Virgo. Dedicated dancer Mikhail Baryshnikov has Mars in Virgo, along with actors Ben Affleck, Bruce Boxleitner and Matt Damon. Ruth Ginsberg and Indira Gandhi also share this Mars sign.

Mars in Libra. *The evolutionary intent is to apply the will toward effectively bridging those gaps between self and other which are created by repressed anger. In a nutshell, there is a soul-desire to learn the art of healthy intimate conflict, based upon prior-life dynamics in which such conflict was either suppressed behind "appropriateness," or too dangerous to risk because of the partner's violent reactions.*

Mars in Libra will insist how well it understands you (the Counselor), and how peaceful and harmonious (the Peacemaker) your life could be if only you would surrender to this relationship (the Lover). The Artist wants to take your picture or buy you becoming clothes. The Lover uses romanticism, tenderness and sensitivity. The Counselor and Diplomat listen to you and advise you. The hook is that once you've taken the bait, the deeper reality is revealed—it's conflict that actually energizes this Mars placement. At its best, that can be honest, healthy explorations of the places where the tectonic plates of two distinct individualities grind. Even if it goes down the darker road, Mars in Libra is ultimately depleted by isolation, needless wrangling, hostility, injustice and ugliness. Romantic poet Percy Bysshe Shelley, and former Beatle John Lennon had Mars in Libra. Writer Jorge Luis Borges and director Ingmar Bergman have Mars in Libra, as do musician Peter Gabriel, singers Phobe Snow and Whitney Houston, and actress Alicia Silverstone.

Mars in Scorpio. *The evolutionary intent is to apply the will to a relentless, wrenchingly honest, shared process of self-examination, revelation and transformation. There is a reaction to a prior-life dynamic of sexual deceit, and a soul-desire to re-establish trust on the basis of the truth, the whole truth, and nothing but the truth.*

This Mars sign floods you with a tidal wave of passion, or fixes you with a penetrating gaze. These people can almost hypnotize you with their intensity. They offer fulfillment on a sexual, emotional, and transpersonal level. "This relationship will change both of us profoundly. I'm ready for it; are you? Let me tell you why I think you're frightened." Mars in Scorpio makes a point of its honesty, its ability to deal with touchy issues, its desire to share its depths with you. These people tell you about their hospice work, take you to a psychology lecture or a seance, or simply to their house for dinner and soul-revealing, mesmerizing conversation until three in the morning. Mars in Scorpio is energized by passion, intensity, profound closeness and the exploration of taboos. It is depleted by shallowness, and by situations that make it feel that it can show only the most superficial two or three percent of its nature. Author Henry Miller, passionate in every sense of the word, had this Mars sign. So do occultist Carlos Castaneda, writers Ray Bradbury and J.A. Jance, and musicians k.d. lang and Kurt Cobain.

Mars in Sagittarius. *Always with Sagittarius, the evolutionary intent involves applying one's will ethically and in accord with natural law. At the same time, there is a soul-desire for the freedom to experience erotic excitement, and probably some degree of erotic diversity. The tension between those opposing drives reflects an unresolved prior-life dynamic, for which the soul now intends a resolution culminating in lofty, profoundly erotic and freely-chosen commitment.*

Mars in Sagittarius uses styles of pursuit which reflect the archetypes of this sign. The Scholar asks you to expand your mind at a poetry reading or a documentary. The Philosopher or Anthropologist invites you to stretch beyond the known and the familiar, as do the Gypsy and the Explorer. All promise adventures: experiential, romantic, or sexual. Mars in Sagittarius impresses you with its inquiring mind, idealism, ethics, and visionary qualities. This Mars sign is energized by travel, causes, humor, and interesting new ideas and experiences. Confinement, too much routine, unethical situations, and insularity deplete it. Outspoken rock star Janis Joplin had Mars in Sagittarius. French poet Arthur Rimbaud, who claimed that a poet had to make himself a seer by overwhelming all his senses with experience, had Mars in Sagittarius. Other members of this Mars sign include ethnobotanist Terence McKenna, actresses Meg Ryan, Faye Dunaway and Tracey Ullman, and designer Pierre Cardin.

Mars in Capricorn. *The evolutionary intent is to apply the will towards self-control, integrity and meaningful accomplishments, which lead to the attainment of a position in life where effective protection, sustenance, and defense can be offered to the beloved. This intent is in response to perceived feelings of failure in that area in a prior life, which have left the scent of shame in their wake.*

This sign is the master strategist, using the savvy and cool-headed efficiency of the Prime Minister or Executive archetypes to get you to "join the company." After having expended Herculean effort to establish themselves in the world, they will give practical, demonstrable, tangible reasons to convince you that your best interests lie with them. These people may not be fountains of emotion, although much depends on the rest of the chart. They consider their responsible actions towards you as more important in the long run than demonstrativeness. This Mars sign is energized by meaningful accomplishments, often in the form of long term projects, and by a certain amount of solitude. It is depleted by never having any time alone, and by choosing the wrong mountains to climb. David Bowie, who's lasted a long time in the music world through changing styles, has Mars in Capricorn; so does Icelandic rocker Björk. Marlon Brando drew on his Capricorn Mars for his portrayal of the Godfather. Writers Jane Austen and Shirley Jackson also share this Mars sign.

Mars in Aquarius. *The evolutionary intent is to apply the will to claiming one's right to be spontaneously, even rebelliously oneself, sexually and otherwise. There is a reaction against prior-life dynamics involving sexual* *"rules," often including the monastic rule of sexual abstinence. It may also be connected with prior-life sexual coercion, where social pressures led to an unsatisfying and ultimately dishonest sexual union.*

Like Mars in Gemini, this Mars sign can come across as an intellectual, but in Aquarius the tone is different, implying something akin to, "I am a genius, and everyone will recognize it eventually. Stay with me and you'll get the truth, and infinite freedom to be yourself. Now, what are you going to do with it?" The Individual and the Truth-sayer intrigue you with originality and a unique viewpoint on the world. The Rebel and the Exile offer to break your chains and provide you with a nonrestrictive, individuality-enhancing lifestyle. The Reformer enlists in your favorite causes, or gets you interested in his or hers. Mars in Aquarius can also present itself as the (Mad) Scientist, and propose a trip to a science fiction convention or the Air and Space Museum. This Mars sign is energized by the freedom of heart, mind, spirit and speech, by breaking rules, questioning authority, or exploring some cutting-edge interest. It is depleted by restriction, being a slave to convention, and by petty tyrants. Civil rights activist W. E. B. Du Bois, botanist Luther Burbank, and writer J. D. Salinger have Mars in Aquarius. Writers Anne McCaffrey and Gabriel Garcia Marquez share this Mars sign, along with musician Dave Brubeck, astronaut Frank Borman and actress Bridget Fonda.

Mars in Pisces. *The evolutionary intent here involves a deep paradox: to find the strength, will and courage to surrender. There is a soul-desire to experience the fusion of erotic and spiritual passions, in response to their fission in prior lifetimes, when there was exhausting oscillation between celibate commitment to a spiritual path and surrender to compelling sexual desire.*

This Mars sign pursues you under the banner of the Spiritual Warrior. It's a crusade, and your heart is the Holy Grail. They want to touch your soul, gently, with their bare hands. They weave spells of enchantment and illusion. Since they can't slay dragons for you, they write you poetry, take you to fantasy movies, and in general do everything possible to aid and abet your exploration of other realities and states of awareness, whether those realities are spiritual or artistic. This Mars sign is energized by meditation or other constructive altered-state experiences, and by devotion to a spiritual ideal. Mars in Pisces is depleted by never taking any time for meditative, day-dreaming sorts of states, by harshness, and by lack of compassion. Bob Dylan has Mars in Pisces in the tenth house, and in many ways he's become a public symbol of this configuration. Read his lyrics or some of his song titles, reflecting Piscean fantasy: "Blowin' in the Wind;" "Mr. Tambourine Man;" "You Angel You." Magician and master illusionist David Copperfield has Mars in Pisces, along with musicians Miles Davis and Emmylou Harris, tennis star Martina Navratilova, writer Jane Brody and designer Oleg Cassini.

Venus and Mars in the Birthchart

Venus and Mars in the signs are far from the only indicators of how a person will choose to relate. We can't emphasize strongly enough how important it is to consider the chart as a whole. Venus and Mars draw their true meaning for each individual from that larger context.

Suppose a timid librarian has seven planets in Libra—but Mars in Aries too. That Mars in Aries will not turn her into a sexual Zorro! In this extremely Libran chart, Mars in Aries might translate into her always applying forceful energy (Mars) *to keep the peace*—serving a Libran intention, in other words. Perhaps she would always be brave enough (Aries) to take the lead in kissing and making up. Her courtship style may be more active than what we typically see in a woman with so much Libran energy; she might, courteously, approach a man with tickets to an event she knows interests him, but in an adept Libran way that makes it easy for him to refuse without embarrassment to either of them. Her courtship style will not be as insistent as is usual with Aries—she won't leave urgent invitations on his answering machine or camp out on his doorstep.

After you consider Venus and Mars as indicators both of relating styles, and of the evolutionary intent behind those styles, then look beyond these planets and consider them in the context of the chart as a whole. If you can remember that, you are doing fine.

Charts are not made up only of planets. Our next step is to examine the houses that possess special significance for intimacy, in Chapter Six.

CHAPTER SIX: THE ARC OF INTIMACY

When you first look at a birthchart, you see twelve prominent "pie slices." Those are the *houses.* Physically, they are an artificial, human-made construct: twelve sections of space above and below the birthplace's horizon, six houses above it and six below. See Figure Three on page 94. A planet's position in the houses tells us whether that planet was rising, setting, or somewhere in between. But that's not all.

We learned in Chapter Two that houses symbolize *territories,* internal or external, that can be entered and explored. Planets, you will recall, answer the question **what:** what part of the mind we are considering. Signs answer the questions **how** and **why:** what motivates that part of the mind; how it behaves. Houses answer the question **where:** in what arena of someone's life we can see that sign-planet combination in action. Signs are the *psychological fabric* of the psyche; houses are the *circumstances* of one's life. We "are" our signs, but we "do" our houses. If you need any of these concepts reviewed in greater detail, please see Chapter Two.

Houses show where the action is! Houses reveal *where someone's life happens.* They are experiential; a separate, specific life drama unfolds in each one. The scripts vary and include "Developing a Social Persona;" "Establishing a Public Identity;" and "Planning the Future," to mention only three. There are twelve of these ongoing dramas active in everyone's life, but in individuals some are more emphasized than others. Think of it this way: your birthchart is like a TV set with twelve soap operas in perpetual broadcast, but a few are your favorites and get more attention from you.

Five houses in particular form a mini-series pertinent to relationships. Houses four, five, six, seven, and eight constitute an **arc of intimacy** in the birthchart. Each of these houses can be considered a special dimension of the relationship-forming process. Each is a stage in that process, containing its own potential hazards and stepping-stones, and each builds upon the preceding house or houses within the arc. Each house must be mastered if we are not to suffer a repeating cycle of frustrations. You learn to sit before you crawl, crawl before you stand, and stand before you walk. The arc of intimacy represents another sort of developmental sequence in the growth of relationships.

Briefly, house four emphasizes the need to understand the psychodynamics of our childhood, lest we blindly repeat them with our partner. It's also very much connected with our sense of *home.* House five

FIGURE THREE

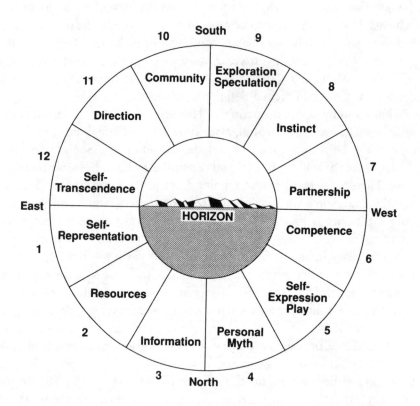

emphasizes playful, self-renewing romantic activity—and those mysterious people who suddenly go off like bombs in our hearts and then disappear from our radar screens. House six focuses on issues of responsibility, humility, and self-sacrifice, essential to the survival of any relationship—and also to the importance of getting appropriate guidance when we need it. House seven highlights issues of commitment and trust, and simple *liking*. House eight is sexual and rooted in the unconscious—issues of "chemistry" and "electricity," and how to sustain them in the long haul, arise there. At least sexually, the eighth house holds our deepest soulmates.

We'll examine the houses in this arc one at a time in Chapters Seven through Eleven. At the end of each of those chapters, we'll give some examples of how planets and signs might behave in a particular house.

95

CHAPTER SEVEN:
THE ARC OF INTIMACY—THE FOURTH HOUSE

The Fourth House

Traditional Name: House of the Home
Corresponding Sign: Cancer
Associated Planet: Moon
Terrain: The roots of the psyche; hearth, home, clan or tribe
Evolutionary Process: Understanding how the roots of the psyche were affected by one's family of origin and upbringing. With that understanding, forming a healthy home of one's own.
Abort Sequence: Unconsciously repeating the psychodynamics of one's childhood in one's adult relationships. Serious difficulty in making a true home with a partner. Rootlessness; homelessness.

The fourth house is profoundly related to hearth and home and, as such, is the most underestimated relationship house in modern synastry. It reflects relationships where we have entered a state of *radical, no-exit commitment.* We don't really trigger it inside ourselves relationship-wise until we have moved in together under one roof and begun to share our belongings, our money, our routines, our daily lives. In many ways, the fourth house is the true house of marriage, simply because it is the house of the home. When we cross the threshold of the fourth house, we cross a line that goes beyond loving and trusting and making love after the fashion of new lovers. We are actually saying, "Here I make my clan, my home, my *stand.*" That is the Holy Grail in terms of a committed relationship, and the fourth house captures that feeling.

In modern astrological practice there is a tendency to view the fourth house more psychologically—it's the inner self, and our family-of-origin issues. Those interpretations are quite valid both for astrology in general and for synastry. But they leave out a lot that's precious.

Around the Industrial Revolution, the paradigm of the *clan* began to break down. People began to lose their sense of absolutely permanent, "bonded" relationships. That's about when the study of psychology arose. The two events coincided, synchronistically, quite closely in time. That's probably because where a set of bonded, trusted, familiar and committed relationships should be, there is now a hole in most of us, and thus a sense of isolation, grief, and insecurity. We are now dealing with the fact that we have lost something. It was precious and most of us don't even remember what it was. But we know that we are hurting. When people go into therapy, much of what they talk about are fourth house issues, even in a very concrete sense. What happened to me in my family; what is happening to me in my current family; where is my family now? These are all fourth house questions.

This psychotherapeutic imagery dovetails completely with the image of the fourth house as a relationship house, because *in order to form your own healthy clan, you need to understand what happened to you in your clan of origin.* Does that mean what happened to you with the family who raised you in this life, or in some previous one? It's really not necessary to know the answer to that question, since understanding and resolving your relationship with your family now can only help to heal any previous karma, with them or with others. Let's just add that a significant part of our deepest karma often tends to be with our closest relatives.

Whether the parenting we got was healthy or less than ideal, it is a psychological truism that we are drawn to partners who (later!) remind us of our parents. Something inside us is drawn to the familiar, whether good or bad, *simply because it seems familiar.* We may look for someone who reminds us of a beloved parent—"I Want A Girl Just Like the Girl Who Married Dear Old Dad." Or we may be drawn to someone who resembles a disastrous parent, so that we get another crack at "fixing" Mom or Dad and finally getting enough love from him or her. Psychologically, probably the dumbest thing that's ever been said is, "once burned, twice smart."

In relationships, it's more like, "once burned, burned again"—until we do some inner work and inner healing. That's one reason why we need to be fully aware of our own fourth house energies—the energies around our own roots. Otherwise we're unconsciously looking for our partner to replicate those energies for us. Furthermore, we need to be aware of our own specific soul-needs in terms of an appropriate hearth and home, which might be different from the atmosphere of our original home.

How do we get there? A certain amount of life experience definitely helps, which is probably why statisticians observe that the single best predictor of a lasting marriage is the age at which the partners married. Teenage couples are far more likely to divorce. Maturity helps—but so does a careful consideration of the energies connected to our fourth house. It can provide a lot of insight in two important areas: the nature of any distortions that may have been introduced into our psyches by how we were treated as children, and what sort of hearth best serves our evolutionary needs now.

When you get the fourth house right, you are much more likely to find someone with whom you feel comfortable and at home. You live together easily. You have a profound sense of familiarity with one another. You feel like you have known the person for a long time. There is a clan feeling, a tribal feeling, a warm, soulful feeling of stable connection.

That feeling is at the heart of committed relationships. For a deep sense of the *rightness* of staying together as conscious adults, we need to have successfully navigated the fourth house.

Sun in the Fourth House

The evolutionary intention here involves cultivating a quality of inwardness and introspection in your character, perhaps even some guardedness. This is potentially a touchy subject because, while you do need to make sure you don't become so deeply enmeshed in your own subjective, internal life that no one can relate to you, you feed your solar vitality with that kind of private internal dialog. Without it, your energy would be sapped. This may be a reaction to a karmic pattern involving too much time in the public eye or public life, where that you felt you had no privacy and needed to calculate the impact of every word. Or you may be simply carrying forward soul-memories of lifetimes defined by authoritative roles of clan leadership. You possess a profound understanding of the mind, and, partly as a result of that, a deep capacity for commitment to a home or family. No one who really understands you is going to be too quick to interpret those parts of your character in terms of shyness or withdrawal from intimacy, although you'll hear that from a few self-appointed psychologists.

You get along most easily with other people who have a similarly inward orientation, those who have found a parallel kind of *silence* inside themselves. Such people are thus not inclined to be judgmental about your lack of some requisite extroversion. What a social butterfly might perceive as unreachability on your part, a deeper, quieter soul might see as refreshing sensitivity.

Key qualities in a clan member: Ability to honor the need for introspection; the gift of silence; openness to making a commitment to a place; prioritizing of home-life above all other worldly considerations.

Under thy roof one shall not be: intrusive.

Moon in the Fourth House

The Moon is the natural ruler of the fourth house, so the evolutionary intention here centers around the two elemental fourth house drives: quietly immersing one's self in the psychological depths and making a lasting home. In prior lives, there may have been uprooting experiences of exile, or you may be simply carrying forward soul-memories of domesticity, deep clan identification, and a profound sense of your place on the land. In any case, solitary self-exploration nourishes you. Without "down-time," you grow vague, distant, and unavailable. Paradoxically, that might create an impression of emotionlessness or shallowness. Your sense of security derives from having a sense of deep roots—solid walls between yourself and the world, and a warm hearth inside them . . . which means more than a fireplace! That warmth is basically human: committed, stable relationships with old familiar friends, domestic joys, nurturing behaviors, and a bottomless sense of reverence for the land, for family—and probably for your ancestors.
Key quality in a clan member: emotional availability.
Under thy roof one shall not be: cold.

Mercury in the Fourth House

The evolutionary intent here is to create a home whose spirit is something like a salon, where people come together to exchange fresh ideas and perspectives. There may be a reaction against a karmic history of feeling bored, stifled, silenced or censored by your clan. Or you may be carrying forward soul-memories of vigorous intellectual home-environments. While there is clearly more to home life than discussion groups, you would do well to make sure that anyone with whom you might consider living would be amenable in principle to such gatherings from time to time. These events are perhaps not so important in and of themselves, but they do provide a splendid barometer regarding the larger issues of your needs for a stimulating home life, as reflected in your natal Mercury.
Key qualities in a clan member: curiosity; communicativeness; energy.
Under thy roof one shall not be: closed-minded; unresponsive.

Venus in the Fourth House

Your gracious, aesthetic Venusian energies are strong and deeply rooted, although perhaps not immediately noticeable on first meeting. You are the type of person who grows on someone. Some of that derives from the fact that you are not very quick to trust, and we promise we are not defining that as a problem! With Venus in the traditional house of the hearth, one evolutionary intent is to learn to appreciate privacy and "down time" with a mate. Another is to create a healing domestic atmosphere of beauty, harmony, and civilization in the best sense of the word. Nesting is important to you. So are quiet hours spent with family or with trusted, probably creative and cultured, friends of long standing. This may arise as a reaction against a karmic pattern involving a lack of affection or graciousness—or perhaps simple crudity—among your clan. That, or you may running on the happy momentum of successful domesticity. Whatever relating patterns, healthy or otherwise, that you learned in your present family of origin can remain a powerful influence upon your relating behavior. Therefore, you would be wise to make some effort to understand what those early patterns might have been, and whether they are helpful to you now. They may have been simply loving—or they may have involved the darker side of Venus, which boils down to false smiles, manipulation, and reality hidden behind a pleasing facade. With that work done, you are capable of making a deep and lasting bond, almost sacred in its reverence, to a mate and a home, and to establish a real haven there.

Key qualities in a clan member: good relating skills; aesthetic sensitivity; grace.

Under thy roof one shall not be: boorish.

Mars in the Fourth House

The fiery energy of Mars is associated with your deepest, innermost core. Peel away the layers of your onion, and sooner or later you arrive at your fundamental resiliency of nature. You are the pluperfect *survivor*. The evolutionary intent here resolves around claiming your essential strength, courage and ability to survive. There may be a karmic history of not being sufficiently assertive either with members of your clan, or in order to protect them—or you may be simply carrying forward soul-memories of righteous war in defense of home and hearth. In either case, there are soul-memories of attacks upon the home, land, and loved ones. You are learning to be fervently protective of your home and the creatures with whom you share it

101

now. The downside is that anything in this part of the birthchart, while it is very basic to a person's essence, is also often hard to ferret out. Mix that with the fact that Mars is the planet of anger, and we can see how you are susceptible to holding rage inside yourself, building up explosiveness behind a veneer of silence. You don't have to be that way, but avoiding the pattern takes effort—and the help of a partner who is willing to get a little scalded from time to time as you find your balance in this difficult area.
Key qualities in a clan member: strength; fierce loyalty; robustness; a sense of adventure.
Under thy roof one shall not be: cowardly.

Jupiter in the Fourth House

With the cosmic Santa Claus in your fourth house, the evolutionary intent is to establish a hearth whose atmosphere is magnanimous, generous, expansive and tolerant. If you imagine a mythic regent sitting on a golden throne, laughing, surrounded by musicians and courtiers, celebrating the abundance of the kingdom, you begin to sense the archetype that underlies your ideal home and hearth. The karmic patterning here implies either an ongoing "inner seed image" of blessedness and joy in terms of home—or a reaction against a prior-life clan where a fundamental sense of lack and perhaps puritanical restriction prevailed. Now there's a desire for abundant life in general, with a specific focus on the home and the land upon which it sits. Spend money on it, polish it, lavish love on it, be proud of it, and merrily throw open the doors to your dear and precious intentional family.
Key qualities in a clan member: optimism; generosity; humor; lack of pettiness.
Under thy roof one shall not be: chronically negative; abstemious.

Saturn in the Fourth House

Your evolutionary intent is to experience earnest, thoughtful attitudes and behaviors toward the responsibilities of home life. In the karmic past, one of two scenarios probably applied: either you or your mate may have balked at the deep promises to each other that are implicit in any two souls agreeing to become "one house," with all the archetypal mysteries that sacrament implies. Or there were compelling and arduous external circumstances which erased the possibility of domestic stability and happiness: poverty, political

102

repression, famine. It is not unlikely that you had some experiences in your family of origin, reflecting the prior life experience, that have made you hesitant or cautious about accepting that level of vulnerability ever again. Your natural partner is one who is custom-designed to help you get over that fear: reliable, trustworthy, mature, and grounded.

Key qualities in a clan member: integrity; maturity; competence.
Under thy roof one shall not be: immature, unrealistic, or frivolously self-indulgent.

Uranus in the Fourth House

The evolutionary intention here revolves around creating a home that supports individuality rather than repressing it. This placement strongly implies a karmic past where your clan misunderstood you or squelched you, where you did not fit in and might even have experienced the traumas of censure and exile. Deep inside, you are a very singular individual, and as you resolve the karmic wound, your uniqueness will be increasingly reflected in your highly individualized choice of home, style of decoration, and probably lifestyle. There is no moral law that says one can't have a computer in the kitchen, or turn the living room into a recording studio or an airplane hangar . . . and if a person doubts that principle for a second, he or she is probably not someone with whom it would be easy for you share a domicile!

Key qualities in a clan member: independence; unconventionality; immunity to social pressure.
Under thy roof one shall not be: domineering, dull, or blindly conventional.

Neptune in the Fourth House

The evolutionary intent is the creation of a hearth that nurtures the more sensitive, mystical, meditative, spiritual dimensions of life. You may be reacting against a karmic past where your clan mitigated against those qualities in you, or simply carrying forward soul-memories of monastic life. You are a very sensitive individual, and that sensitivity must be honored in your domestic lifestyle. Positively, you may need soft music wafting through the rooms, indirect lighting, or the presence of holy icons. Negatively, you are easily jangled by disharmonious influences in your domestic environment: noise, unpleasant odors no one else notices, bad attitudes on the part of

household members. The high, ethereal feeling one gets walking into certain churches or temples is the vibration of your natural haven in this world.
Key qualities in a clan member: sensitivity, openness to mysticism.
Under thy roof one shall not be: atheistic, rigidly linear, or unsupportive of meditative states of awareness.

Pluto in the Fourth House

The evolutionary intent here revolves around the establishment of a home base where intensity, "processing," and profound self-expression are honored. There may be a reaction to unresolved prior-life dynamics connected to a wound, physical or emotional, that involved your clan, and that contributes to a need for absolute psychological honesty about the dynamics in your hearth now. At your core, you are a dark, stormy individual, eager for truth and realness. Those qualities must be reflected in your home life, or you'll likely become brooding, even whiny. There must be an agreement in your clan that nobody is ever perfectly warm and bright, that we all have darker, shadowy sides, and that home is a place where there should be no need for making a secret about any of that.
Key Qualities in a clan member: intensity, willingness to engage in deep analyses of oneself and other people; honesty.
Under thy roof one shall not be: superficial, dishonest, or a psychological lightweight.

South Node in the Fourth House: Your past karma has much to do with the powerful impact of family, hearth and clan upon you. The nature of the south node's sign and planetary aspects describe the psychological tone and qualities of the influence. It's reasonable to assume that some of that tribal influence was good for you and your development, but that from the present perspective you were too bound and defined by it. Whether the impact of your clan upon you was predominantly healthy or more challenging, it is virtually certain that unless you examine your family of origin's influence very carefully, you are much more likely than the average person to live out those patterns again in your relationships and your home today. (The nodes are not planets, so we have no "key qualities" listed for them.)

North Node in the Fourth House: The north node shows up in the house where we have had the least experience in the karmic past, and therefore where we are the most ignorant—which is not the same thing as stupid! The establishment of a hearth is one of the experiences you have had the least. Why? Your south node is in the tenth house, implying that you've been very much defined by a more public role. Details emerge through a consideration of the signs and planetary aspects involved, but essentially we recognize a person who, in the past, was swept into a vivid outward *persona* that precluded true intimacy, not to mention simple peace and quiet. Although prioritizing home and clan can feel awkward for you, it will also be one of the best actions you could possibly undertake to facilitate your own growth. The sign of the north node, and any planets in the fourth house, will describe the nature of the hearth you should build. (The Nodes are not planets, so we have no "key qualities" listed for them.)

CHAPTER EIGHT:
THE ARC OF INTIMACY—THE FIFTH HOUSE

The Fifth House

Traditional Names: House of Children; House of Love Affairs
Corresponding Sign: Leo
Associated Planet: Sun
Terrain: The need for pleasure and release, creative self-expression, falling in love, playfulness.
Evolutionary Process: Sharing one's history with an interesting stranger. Self-renewal through spontaneity, pleasures, relaxation. Willingness to be enchanted by another; openness to falling in love.
Abort Sequence: Inability to initiate contact with people or to respond. Rigidity, control, iciness, inability to play. Addiction to constant newness and excitement in relationships; refusal to accept routine or boredom.

Welcome to the house of love affairs—that's one of its traditional names. Step right this way into the house of pleasures, another of those names. Enjoy yourself. Play all you like in the house of creative self-expression, but if you get stuck here, you could wind up an adult lost in the house of children.

This is the house of falling in love, of romance, where the sparks first start flying. This is the house of the first date or the second or the third. The early stages of a love affair are ruled by the fifth house. Let's add that it's also the house of "falling in like;" friendships begin in the fifth house, too.

What happens in those early stages? Without fail, we trade our life stories. We're fascinated by the other person, his or her novelty and mystery. "Tell me the epic, the drama, the saga of you. Tell me about yourself." And of course: "Now listen to everything about *me*."

If we're smart, we'll pay attention to what those stories really reveal about our new love. How well does he understand his family's impact on him? What has she actually *learned* from her previous relationships? It can be hard to remember to keep our eyes peeled for such clues, because we are feeling so giddy, smitten, and besotted. We make our first connections to our partners here. We rediscover, through someone else's marveling eyes, how interesting we are, how colorful. We play. The other person seems endlessly perfect, and couples delight in every new discovery they make about each

107

other. The fifth house stage of a union is full of excitement, fresh, wondrously new, and feels like manna from heaven to our egos. Nature seems to use this trick to get us to take the enormous, terrifying leap into opening our hearts and our bodies to another person.

Planetary energies in your fifth house indicate what qualities you need to have present in the other person at the beginning of a love affair, as an indication that the relationship could possibly last. The fifth house is "first base;" if a person can't get that far, the rest of the bases are irrelevant.

Let's add that the fifth house also refers to the *renewal* of relationship. What do you and your mate need to do when you've been too busy for quality time together for a very long time, and then you finally get a date night? For one couple it might be dinner at a fine restaurant, a movie, dancing. For another, it might be a long rambling walk. Or time spent sharing a cherished hobby. Or a day in bed. Everyone—and every couple—is different.

Whether we're speaking of old relationships or new ones, another evolutionary intent of the fifth house is connecting to someone who can help us feel joy and help us play. Think about what your state of mind would be if you worked too hard all the time and never took vacations. Grouchy, right? Tight, sour and embittered. We all get that way—and we all have an organic, evolutionary need to correct it through fun, renewing pleasure, and plain, Dionysian ecstasy. Playmates help! Remember that the Sun is naturally associated with the fifth house, and that the Sun represents your core vitality. For everyone, fifth house activities—creative self-expression, play and relaxation—help feed that solar vitality.

How can the fifth house go wrong? We may not learn how to relax and have fun. But to learn the language of love, you must start with the language of the fifth house, even if seven of your planets lie in solitary Capricorn, and you feel awkward about expressing your romantic fifth-house Venus.

Another possible malfunction of the fifth house can be the refusal to leave it. Some people crave the thrills of the early stages of intimacy and become hooked on telling their stories, addicted to the enraptured attention of a first-time listener. Others are uncomfortable about having their faults subjected to the scrutiny of a post-fifth-house relationship, once the glow of apparent perfection has faded. Some people have a low tolerance for anything or anyone who has become at all routine, and they avoid the sameness or responsibility inherent in longer term intimacy. Such a person may take a quick peek at the sixth house (responsibility, humility and working on the relationship), become frightened, and run back to the fifth house, which has become his or her prison.

Let's take a giant step deeper, right to the heart of the evolutionary meaning of the fifth house, at least in terms of intimacy. Sometimes relationships begin fast and quickly grow intense. Sometimes, even before we've traded life stories, something about this person feels familiar or compelling right away. We often even say the words, *"I feel as if I've known you before."*

Not all our relationships are lifelong. Not all are meant to be. That doesn't necessarily mean that the briefer ones are inconsequential. Not all karmic debts are huge, but karma is karma, however great or small, and sooner or later it will be resolved. In other words, sometimes our business with a person doesn't take a lifetime, yet it's important for a week, for a season, for a year. Maybe it's as simple as a conversation. Perhaps that professor visiting your department for a semester taught you how to play the flute a few lifetimes ago, and you never thanked her properly. On the scale of karmic debt, this one isn't heavy, but again, sooner or later karmic scales will be balanced. You may be taking an inordinate number of long lunches with this professor now, and most of what you talk about is your common interest in music. Nothing sexual or romantic may be in the air, *but an exchange of energy is happening that is resolving that karmic debt between you.*

If your fifth house is emphasized, then this lifetime is one in which you are focusing on settling some of your karmic debts with other people. *That resolution and release of unresolved, prior-life relationships is one of the central evolutionary intents of the fifth house.* This doesn't mean bad karma and it doesn't mean good karma. It simply indicates that you have a lot of business to finish with a lot of people this time around. In the case of the visiting professor, you may resolve it in the semester when she's teaching in your department, and not feel any need to stay in touch once the semester is over. It's important to stay open to the possibility of working through something relatively quickly and moving on. Again, the aim with fifth house relationships is ultimately to finish them.

Not all fifth house relationships are sexual by any means, but if hormones are involved, once you've gotten past their initial intensity, listen to your intuition. Take your time. Don't cling to something that seems to have come to a natural end, and don't push something away that seems to want to develop further. Above all, listen to your gut. Here's how: start by reminding yourself that all relationships become difficult sooner or later—that's only natural because they represent our evolutionary work. Then, looking at this strangely-familiar stranger sitting across the table from you, ask yourself: if I went down the road with this person, what would our challenges be? Don't silently assassinate the person's character, but look at him or her as coldly and objectively as you can. Maybe, for example, you realize that he would ultimately be just a little too lightweight for you. Maybe you get the feeling that you could never really trust her to be faithful to you. There is an excellent chance that you are correctly seeing an available future, but far more magically what you are also doing is *remembering what actually happened between you in a prior life.* You've just moved into a deeper state of consciousness, gotten past the old, shared drama, and broken the karmic pattern. What do you do next? You split the check, shake hands, say a friendly goodbye, and go home.

What if the fifth house isn't active in your natal chart, but is being emphasized by transit or progression? Be alert to the logic we've outlined above—it may apply during that period of your life, even though the issue is of a low enough voltage that it didn't appear as an elemental part of your soul-intent in the birthchart.

Let's add that by agreeing to be the parent of another being, we not only offer that being a great gift, we also enter into a very complex, emotionally-charged relationship. In a sense, the aim of that relationship is to finish it—by seeing the child launched successfully and independently into adulthood. Thus, we recognize the outlines of the dynamic we've just described in this traditional house of children. Karmically, the parent-child relationship is complex and varied. With a strong fifth house, there may very well be a soul-intention to resolve a prior-life relationship that way.

Is the fifth a shallow house? Are the shorter-lived fifth house relationships minor and inconsequential? Absolutely not. Finishing our business with other human beings is serious, honorable, and necessary. It is profoundly healing, at this stage in our collective cultural evolution, never to trivialize these short-term relationships.

Sun in the Fifth House

You're in the house of pleasure in this lifetime, for an excellent reason. God kicked you off the end of the cosmic diving board and said, "Have a good time!" That sounds silly, but it's actually very serious. Due to unresolved pain from prior life experiences, you've become toughened. The evolutionary intent here centers around *softening and renewing yourself* through the enjoyment of self-expression, style, and the sheer playfulness in your character. You probably possess some real artistic talent, whether or not you've discovered it. Underlying that, you have a deep, pervading need to be seen and noticed. While you do need to guard against becoming too demanding of others' attention or simply against taking up too much psychic space, we must also respect a few legitimate facts: you heal your spirit with that kind of self-expressive performance and playfulness. Without it, your solar energy would be sapped. You possess a genuine calling toward *offering tangible evidence of your inner, creative processes to the world.* No one who really loves or even understands you is going to be too quick to interpret those parts of your character in terms of egocentricity, showboating, or childishness. You may be reacting against a karmic history of suppression of your creativity, or alleviating some great karmic sorrow that is best healed by joy and recreation. There is also a significant karmic pattern of unfinished business with people, from which can come a deep need for exploration and resolution, if possible, of those relationships now.

To launch a relationship or to renew it, you most need: play, creativity, self-expression, and friends or partners with whom you can take turns being the audience.

Your romantic feelings and capacity for joy are most swiftly diminished by: judgmentalness about your lack of some requisite self-effacement.

Recognize those soulmates with whom you need to finish business by watching for their: need to dominate you.

Moon in the Fifth House

The Moon is the Great Mother, and her evolutionary intent always revolves around healing and nurturing. You do that by honoring your greatest emotional needs: your drive to express yourself creatively, your hunger to be heard and noticed, and, rather delightfully, your simple desire to have a memorably good time. You are a natural performer, able to track intuitively the mood of a room, and thus rivet people's attention and create an atmosphere. Your emotional wellbeing is enhanced enormously if you honor this gift by developing it and expressing it. Failing that, you could catastrophically attempt to make up the joy deficit in ways that could ultimately hurt you—excesses or poor judgment in terms of food, alcohol,

111

recreational drugs, and of course sexuality. Let's add that one of the Moon's greatest joys lies in mothering. That could mean literally that the joys of having children are relevant to your evolution. But it means more: when you bring soothing sustenance to another being, you're also bringing joy to yourself. That might take the form of cooking, or writing a poem for someone you love, or simply listening to a friend's pain. However we look at you, we must recognize that you are a true pagan in the best sense of the word—alive, a little wild, and ready to drink the cup of existence to its proverbial dregs. And you need to do that. Something was still bleeding inside you when you were born.

To launch a relationship or to renew it, you most need: imagination, nurturing, tenderness, and friends or partners with whom you can share your innermost feelings.

Your romantic feelings and capacity for joy are most swiftly diminished by: insensitivity; emotional aggression.

Recognize those soulmates with whom you need to finish business by watching for their: tendency either to become dependent on you, or to need you to become dependent on them.

Mercury in the Fifth House

The evolutionary intent is to relish your self-expressive or creative communication style, get your "voice" heard, and to create relationships which involve active mental rapport. You appreciate perceptiveness, curiosity, and mental stimulation and exchange, and are willing to provide plenty of it in turn. If there is a need to resolve some old karma with people, they will be individuals for whom communication is also paramount, both in the relationship and across the board. But with them, you also get the sense that they are hiding their hearts behind all the talk. Your true "playmates" in this lifetime are rarely if ever bored, and lead active mental lives. They can stay up into the wee hours just talking with you, years and years into the relationship. Your natural mate doesn't have to be an intellectual, but should be curious about the world, and enjoy exploring it and comparing notes about it with you.

To launch a relationship or to renew it, you most need: wit; mental rapport; shared interests.

Your romantic feelings and capacity for joy are most swiftly diminished by: lack of curiosity; stony silence; a resolution to be bored.

Recognize those soulmates with whom you need to finish business by watching for their: intellectualizing their feelings; immaturity; glibness.

Venus in the Fifth House

Traditionally the house of children, the fifth house actually refers to all our various creative products: kids maybe—but also any art or decoration we undertake, the way we present ourselves to the world, and our general capacity to draw attention to ourselves and our inner processes. The evolutionary intent here is to experience renewal and delight through exploring your qualities of verve, style, through the joys of conscious eroticism, and, above all, through artistic creativity. The people with whom you have unfinished business are likely to be charming, and quite possibly creative, elegant and refined—and slick. You are drawn to "playmates" who possess the same qualities, minus the slickness. Such people can romance you—and expect the same in return—until you're both forgetting where you left your teeth.

To launch a relationship or to renew it, you most need: grace, harmony and attention to the aesthetics of self-presentation.

Your romantic feelings and capacity for joy are most swiftly diminished by: crudity, coarseness, tackiness.

Recognize those soulmates with whom you need to finish business by watching for their: apparent perfection, and / or messy, multi-faceted relationship histories.

Mars in the Fifth House

Fulfilling the evolutionary intent involves the enthusiastic, robust release of life-force through play, creativity, and general hellraising. People with this configuration are often drawn to some kind of participant sport, although we intend the word "sport" widely. It could be baseball, but it could just as easily be something without winners and losers, such as hiking, horseback riding, even playing in a rock and roll band—basically anything that's physical, fun, and makes you sweaty! Underlying this is a karmic history of having to suppress or restrain all of your naturally abundant physical or sexual energy. There's a compensatory, even angry, need to release it now—although you might fear doing so in proportion to how much this part of you was held back. If you have unfinished business with people, they are likely to be passionate, robust individuals with vigorous appetites.

To launch a relationship or to renew it, you most need: adrenalin; heat; intensity; physical activity.

Your romantic feelings and capacity for joy are most swiftly diminished by: passivity; timidity; lack of directness and engagement.

Recognize those soulmates with whom you need to finish business by watching for their: unresolved anger.

Jupiter in the Fifth House

The evolutionary intent is exuberant, and connected with the renewal of faith in life. It depends on playfulness, expansiveness, tolerance and an open-minded, forward-thinking attitude. Life is short—eat dessert first! There is a reaction here against prior-life experiences in which natural human appetites were suppressed or shamed. Perhaps you were a horny celibate, as Ram Dass once put it. While you must of course be wary of over-the-top excess, it also behooves you to be equally wary of people or beliefs which create an opposition of spirit and flesh. The relationships you most relish will add to the abundance of your life and widen your experiences—make life more colorful, in other words. You provide plenty of flair for a partner, too. Any true "playmate" of yours is likely to be robust, expansive, inclusive and funny. Such a person is also fundamentally an optimist, and lives faithfully at the level of principle—but those principles, while loving and non-exploitive, are elementally pagan. A larger-than-life quality can figure here; Jupiter types do everything big and want everything to assume almost mythical importance.

To launch a relationship or to renew it, you most need: an open, questing spirit; an appreciation of fun.

Your romantic feelings and capacity for joy are most swiftly diminished by: pettiness; small-mindedness; puritanism.

Recognize those soulmates with whom you need to finish business by watching for their: promising more than they can deliver.

Saturn in the Fifth House

The evolutionary intent is to take quiet satisfaction in meaningful accomplishment. An illustration would be learning to play classical piano.

114

Compare the good feeling of playing Chopin well with the good feeling of raising drunken hell with a bunch of strangers at a tropical resort—God may be there in both, but the first one is your aim! The tools you've brought into the world for the job are discipline, focus, and a certain amount of healthy reserve. You don't give your heart away. Your natural "playmates" are self-sufficient, realistic, reliable adults, people who are not fearful of commitment, but not quick about it either. They are serious souls, neither clingy nor dependent. They may sometimes err on the side of not discussing feelings enough, but that's a skill that can be learned. With age and experience, such a person may become not only strong, but truly wise.

To launch a relationship or to renew it, you most need: maturity; respect for your serious side.

Your romantic feelings and capacity for joy are most swiftly diminished by: irresponsibility; chronic silliness.

Recognize those soulmates with whom you need to finish business by watching for their: coldness; fear; inability to open up.

Uranus in the Fifth House

The evolutionary intent is the zestful enjoyment of innovation, independence, and self-determination, in love, life and creativity. Possibly from a karmic history of having been misunderstood or "type-cast," there is a driving desire to be treated as a unique human being, not according to anyone's formula or preconceived notions. You benefit enormously from having a creative or artistic outlet in which you cultivate an absolute lack of concern with your reviews. For you, the process of individuation is bound to the process of expressing your creative imagination. Your natural "playmates" are free spirits, non-conforming souls, those for whom a relationship helps people become more truly themselves. They want a lot of space and give it, too. The beings with whom you need to finish business may have a lot of the same qualities, but there is always something ultimately unreachable and detached about them. In both cases, gaining access to these people will probably involve your behaving in ways that raise a few eyebrows.

To launch a relationship or to renew it, you most need: freedom; individuality; the unexpected.

Your romantic feelings and capacity for joy are most swiftly diminished by: mindless conformity; predictability; concern with the opinions of others.

115

Recognize those soulmates with whom you need to finish business by watching for their: ultimate inability to commit to anything except their own autonomy.

Neptune in the Fifth House

The evolutionary intent is the accessing of other dimensions beyond our three dimensional one, both through your formidable creative imagination and through intimacy. It is important for you to learn to *enjoy* meditation, to let it be natural and spontaneous. This is in reaction to overly disciplinarian spiritual work in prior lifetimes. In relationship, you seem to possess a mysterious elixir that is one third romance, one third mysticism, and one third vague, undefinable longing. It follows that you are drawn, wisely or foolishly, to creatures of similarly gentle and slightly arcane inclinations, people who know that the human retina is at least as erogenous as human genitals. Together, in unspoken ways, you share the joys of connection, made more poignant by that unspeakable sorrow, that undefinable longing for some lost world, that Neptunian people feel so deeply in their souls. Your true "playmates" here want nothing from you except your presence. The ones with whom the drama needs to end will suck you dry if you let them.

To launch a relationship or to renew it, you most need: a sense of mystery, magic, and otherworldliness.

Your romantic feelings and capacity for joy are most swiftly diminished by: cold-hearted pragmatism.

Recognize those soulmates with whom you need to finish business by watching for their: escapism; neediness; "lost soul" syndrome.

Pluto in the Fifth House

Even though this is the house of fun, as always with Pluto the evolutionary intent involves a journey down into the dark. What wounded your capacity to relax, trust, and feel good about being alive? There's an answer. You'll probably find clues in your childhood, but the deeper realities are karmic. The cure lies in expressing yourself emotionally, with your full psychological depth and perceptiveness. The intent is to *turn the pain into art*, in some sense—and "art" is really too narrow a word to embrace all the possibilities. Your "playmates" thus possess a lot of intensity, honesty and realness. They are a naturally receptive audience for what you need to put on

116

the table. They'll initiate a difficult intimate conversation. They're not afraid to explore taboo areas of life: sexuality, death and dying, the occult, the deep unconscious. The ones with whom you need to finish business are capable of giving you real insight into yourself, but they can't receive insight into themselves from you.

To launch a relationship or to renew it, you most need: passion, depth, honesty, and intensity.

Your romantic feelings and capacity for joy are most swiftly diminished by: emotional dishonesty and lack of psychological courage.

Recognize those soulmates with whom you need to finish business by watching for their: defensiveness when confronted; need to play the role of your psychologist. (Since the nodes are not planets, we are not describing your soulmates here.)

South Node in the Fifth House

In your karmic past, you've spent a great deal of time developing your capacities for creative self-expression, and enjoying a wide range of pleasures. You may have even gotten into trouble in terms of excesses in general. You've spent a lot of time exploring relationships, possibly with a primarily youthful or romantic quality. The nature of the creativity, possible "debauchery," and relationships can be shown by the sign and aspects of the node. Because you are very accustomed to fifth house behavior, and because we all have a tendency to repeat that which is familiar, you may find it difficult to move beyond the fifth house in the arc of intimacy. To counteract this tendency, strive to think constructively about where a relationship could go in the future.

North Node in the Fifth House

Karmically, you have spent the least amount of time in fifth house behaviors. Therefore, creative self-expression, relaxation and courtship are all relatively unfamiliar territory for you, as if your past lives had been spent in an endless eleventh house committee meeting. Try to let go of an old habit of scheduling every minute with productive behavior. Try to be *less* strategic in your orientation. Stop and smell the roses, so to speak. Even though they may feel very foreign to you, your growth is most fed by learning how to play, how to express yourself creatively and spontaneously, and being willing

117

to explore interesting new relationships. (Since the nodes are not planets, we are not describing your soulmates here.)

CHAPTER NINE:
THE ARC OF INTIMACY—THE SIXTH HOUSE

The Sixth House

Traditional Name: House of Servants
Corresponding Sign: Virgo
Associated Planet: Mercury
Terrain: Humble self-appraisal; realism; acceptance of imperfection in oneself and others; healthy mentoring relationships.
Evolutionary process: Acceptance of teaching, role-modeling, and mentors; acceptance of responsibility for the relationship; tolerance of each other's faults; the recognition that no one is perfect; humility.
Abort Sequence: Dominant-subordinate patterns; one partner's contributing far more than the other to the relationship; refusal to accept responsibility or compromise; criticism, belittling or sabotaging each other. Underdevelopment of a function that needed mentoring.

At the sixth house cusp, we are attempting to cross the line into adult reality. We are invited to accept a series of difficult facts about life. Many people come to this cusp and turn back, dispirited. But in turning back, they return to an adolescent stage of consciousness: self-indulgent, unrealistic, given to whining complaint and a sense of being a victim. In the sixth house, we are invited to recognize that there has been one common denominator in everything that has ever gone wrong in our lives: *ourselves*. We are the problem. We are impossible, crazy, selfish—you name it. If anyone ever consented to love us, we should get on our knees before them in gratitude and amazement.

Hear how unfashionable those words sound! As a culture, we're not very good at the sixth house right now. This is the house of *humility*. Not humiliation—that's sixth house shadow material. But humility: which is another word for honesty. And honestly, we're all messes. Another way to say the same thing is that we're all evolving souls in a meaningful universe—prettier words, but think about them: we're evolving souls because we *need* to evolve. We're not done yet. We're not "right" yet.

Live with anyone for a year or two, and you begin to see these unflattering truths with great precision—regarding him or her! But in the sixth house, we need to look in the mirror. If we do that, two miracles occur.

119

First, we begin truly to work on ourselves, because no problem is ever solved until it is recognized. Second, *we learn to accept the flaws in the other person as well.* We stop looking for the perfect relationship, and feeling angry when we don't have it. We reject that futility. We lose our self-importance.

Only in so doing can we turn the key in the lock that bars the seventh and eighth houses—the true marriage houses. Without this sixth house humility, we just can't get there. We spend our lives longing for perfection, in one of three possible mental conditions: feeling frustrated and trapped with a partner, "dating," or plain lonely.

It's hard work—so hard that no one can do it alone. That brings us to the lost heart of the sixth house. This is the house of *mentors.* We find our teachers here. There is an ancient art to being human. How can we expect a child to know it? How can we expect anyone to know it without initiation into a lineage of consciousness?

The nearest you'll likely come to reading about the sixth house described in this way by traditional astrology books is in their references to "uncles and aunts." In most cultures, they play very specific teaching and initiating roles in the lives of their nieces and nephews. We've lost that nowadays, but perhaps we're re-inventing it. In any case, in your sixth house you'll see precise descriptions of your mentors and the lessons you need to learn from them. Since this is a book about synastry, we'll focus on the lessons that are most pertinent to making committed relationships work.

Underlying all this is one simple, ancient truth: nobody can be expected to succeed at anything as difficult as human love without a little guidance! In a more enlightened world, we could just go ahead and call this a form of sex education.

Sun in the Sixth House

Your natural mentors are solar people. They're colorful, and they take up some space. What they are teaching you is that you have a right to exist. You have a right to ask for what you need. That you cannot possibly be in an intimate relationship without revealing yourself—intimately. That means with your ego showing sometimes, warts and all. You have an attachment to hiding behind your supportiveness and your sense of duty. You don't need to be so "good." Truth is, this behavior creates a reaction of anger in you, and an unspoken sense of superiority. Release that, and intimacy becomes

120

possible for you.

Humbly recognize that: You hide your heart behind supportiveness.
Seek mentors who: shine.

Moon in the Sixth House

Your natural mentors are lunar people. They're nurturing and feeling-oriented, and they receive you into themselves. What they are teaching you is emotional receptivity—how to be vulnerable and to show it, and how to elicit that behavior in others. The issue here revolves around creating a warm, nobody-here-but-us-chickens vibration, where supportiveness is naturally given generously and expected without fear or forethought. Be wary of your tendency toward slavery. Be wary of expressing love only through action. Be conscious of intimate expression through eye contact, touch, body language.

Humbly recognize that: you fear being seen; you fear being defenseless.
Seek mentors who: radiate an aura of emotional presence and availability.

Mercury in the Sixth House

Your natural mentors are verbal people, natural storytellers and raconteurs. They are quick, animated and curious, and excellent listeners. What is passing from their cells into yours is, above all, this ability truly to *listen* to your partners, and also the ability to invoke communicativeness in another person. Recognize that clarity, skill with words, and effective argument can actually legislate against the two-way-street of real connection.

Humbly recognize that: you need some help with intimate dialog.
Seek mentors who: fill you with the desire to tell them everything.

Venus in the Sixth House

Your natural mentors are gracious and romantic, radiating an aura of civility. Because you need to learn it, they are teaching you the sophisticated arts of love—how to keep magic alive, how to present yourself seductively and alluringly, how to broach difficult subjects with effective diplomacy, how to get what you want. Civilization has brought us long lives—and thus problems we have no instinctual basis for solving, such as keeping love vibrant beyond the half-life of hormones in the blood stream. Seek mentors

121

in these delicate arts.

Humbly recognize that: lasting sexual love is an art and a craft you don't fully grasp.

Seek mentors who: have magnetic personalities.

Mars in the Sixth House

Your natural mentors are fierce, robust, sexual and vibrant. They're in-your-face kinds of people, whom others tend to love or hate. They're here to help you express your passions effectively. Some of that involves conveying skills to you regarding the appropriate release of anger. Some of it is connected with putting your sexual needs frankly and clearly on the table. A lot of it boils down to your natural right to be difficult sometimes—lest you contain your passions so long they finally break the dam and drown the village.

Humbly recognize that: you tend to eclipse your "hotter" side.

Seek mentors who: are fiery, passionate, and direct.

Jupiter in the Sixth House

Your natural mentors believe in themselves—and in you, too. They are natural "kings" and "queens," creating an aura of expansiveness, easy laughter and hope wherever they go. They expect the best from you and for you, and their faith in you is contagious: you might catch it! And that is the point. Your sense of your own worth needs a booster shot, as does your willingness to drink the proverbial cup of life to the dregs.

Humbly recognize that: you are attached to humility; you settle for too little.

Seek mentors who: make everyone around them feel better about who they are.

Saturn in the Sixth House

Your natural mentors are serious, accomplished, and grounded. They have demonstrated that they are capable of great works. They share certain positive qualities with you: a sense of responsibility, self-discipline, a willingness to do the scut work that underlies almost any worthy existential accomplishment. But they've hitched those energies to something worthy of their highest vision. They've avoided mechanical slavery and mere "goodness and maturity." Maybe they can inspire you to do the same.

Humbly recognize that: the slave archetype is trying to eat your soul, masquerading as virtue.

Seek mentors who: have accomplished something that fills you with awe and admiration.

Uranus in the Sixth House

Your natural mentors are zany wild men and wild women. They are divergent thinkers—troublemakers, from some perspectives. Geniuses, revolutionaries, paradigm shifters from another perspective. They've gotten where they are in life by taking chances. They've been unwilling to compromise, even when logic and reason might have suggested they should. And they've survived. Emphatically, they'd never imply that they expect you to follow in their footsteps! They expect you to create your own footsteps, hopefully ones that have never been seen on this earth before.

Humbly recognize that: the wild man or wild woman in you is an underachiever.

Seek mentors who: annoy figures of authority.

Neptune in the Sixth House

Your natural mentors are mystical, visionary and sensitive. Many of them are truly psychic. Many make their living with either their imagination or their wisdom, or both. They recognize that, on the psychic plane, you are a diamond in the rough—wide open, in some ways, but in need of steadying, training, "technical support." You've got some deep mystical gifts, but you don't know how to handle them. Because your sensitivity is also a form of vulnerability, it will damage you unless you find teachers who can convey to you how to handle it.

Humbly recognize that: you have a set of gifts that could hurt you if not well-managed.

Seek mentors who: quietly radiate a closeness to the spirit-world.

Pluto in the Sixth House

Your natural mentors are intense, deep, almost shamanic. Shallow people flee them, and then betray their fearful motives in their need to discredit

123

them. Lying to them while meeting their eyes is nearly impossible, as is resisting the impulse to tell them the truth. What they are conveying from their cells to yours is a sense of the *legitimacy* of being in the world that way. You've been shamed and put down—successfully—for having some of those same qualities.

Humbly recognize that: your own natural intensity is underrepresented in your outward persona.

Seek mentors who: look into your eyes, not just at them.

South Node in the Sixth House

In the karmic past, you've been an apprentice or perhaps a disciple, under a master. More details would emerge through an analysis of the node's sign and planetary aspects, but the bottom line is that now it's time for you to let go of that role, trust what you know, and start paying more attention to your own inner guidance and less attention to the approval or disapproval of authorities. (Since the nodes are not planets, we are not describing your mentors here.)

North Node in the Sixth House

Service to others, perhaps the mentoring of others, is elemental to your evolutionary intention for this incarnation. You've been "on the mountaintop" long enough. It's time to recognize that you are becoming self-absorbed. The only effective balance for that tendency lies in focusing your attention skillfully and generously on the needs of others. (Since the nodes are not planets, we are not describing your mentors here.)

CHAPTER TEN:
THE ARC OF INTIMACY—THE SEVENTH HOUSE

The Seventh House

Traditional name: House of Marriage
Corresponding Sign: Libra
Associated Planet: Venus
Terrain: Commitment, intimacy, trust. Identification with others. Partnership, cooperation, healthy interdependency.
Evolutionary Process: Establishment of long-term, committed relationships. Equal, flexible sharing of duties and pleasures of the relationship. Day-by-day attentiveness to the relationship and each person's changing needs.
Abort Sequence: No firm commitment from one or both partners. Mistrust, guardedness, lack of intimacy. Unequally shared responsibilities and benefits. Rigid role-division. Selfishness, self-absorption. Loss of one's identity in the partner. Polarization, stagnation.

For the first time in the arc of intimacy, we move above the horizon as we pass from the sixth house into the seventh. That passage from the subjective to the objective areas of the chart carries symbolic meaning: to make an adult commitment, we must lose our egocentricity. We must become aware of other people, sensitive to their differences. In the house of "the other," the house of the "not-self," we must recognize that other people are not replicas of ourselves—nor should they be. That realization—"this person is different from me"—leads to a question: what might he or she have that I might lack? What does he or she know that I don't know? How could my life be enriched by this person? We recognize that someone who embodies our seventh house qualities seems, in some mysterious way, to complete us.

In the fourth house, we recognize the early childhood influences that most affected us, and what we need to feel "of one hearth" with someone. In the fifth house, we experience the magic of attraction, the headiness of romance—and we meet some people who are the tempting embodiments of our favorite mistakes. In the sixth house we are humbled, as each partner realizes that no one is perfect, and that most of us could have used some guidance along the way. In the seventh house, having accepted our own shortcomings and those of our partners, we accept our need to *grow beyond our natural human egocentricity through the input of another person.* We discover our blind spots in the sixth, and we seek partners to help us overcome those blind spots in the seventh.

We always feel pulled by someone who represents our seventh house qualities, and it's quite normal that we do. In a healthy response to this house, we identify with the other person, who is exhibiting traits that we already possess to some extent, but that we need to develop further. Our seventh house partner functions as a role model for those traits, bringing them out in us, encouraging us to express them more. Without this type of identification, we can't sustain a seventh house relationship. However, there is a difference between *liking* certain characteristics in a partner, and *thinking that we don't possess any of them ourselves*, and therefore demanding that the partner make up for our perceived lack. *But the partner is the role model, not the supplier.* Signs and planets in your seventh house paint a picture of the person who beckons you with that promise of wholeness, but you must remember that it is *your* seventh house, and its signs and planets belong to you, not to someone else. You will be drawn to those qualities in another, but your seventh house is not a gaping hole in your chart that cannot be filled except by another human being. If you feel that way, then you are no longer identifying. You are projecting.

Here's an example of projection. Susan can't understand why she's always getting involved with men who aren't willing to make a commitment, who insist on "space" and autonomy. She likes freewheeling, zany men who keep her in stitches but never want to stick around. What's going on? Hint number one: Susan is an Aquarian, working on developing independence and individuality. Hint number two: Susan has Uranus in Leo in her seventh house.

Projection is what happens when, usually unconsciously, we take one of our own positive or negative characteristics that we find difficult to express and place it on another person who acts it out for us. Once Susan starts to take back her projections and express her individuality, she will feel more whole and complete.

This ability to identify with someone else, without losing your own identity, is essential to a seventh house relationship. To make a successful passage through this house, we must develop empathy, sympathy, understanding, and the capacity to put ourselves in someone else's shoes—and to remember which shoes belong to us. In other words, we must learn to make a clear distinction between Self and Other. We must lose our self-centeredness and be sensitive to another person—his fears, her needs,

126

and where they correspond to and vary from our own. We must agree to make rational, fair *compromises* about our differing hopes and dreams. We must take frequent inventory of the relationship, allowing it to change as each partner changes. We must acknowledge what each person can offer the other in the journey toward wholeness.

This house has also been called the house of open enemies—an interesting name, in view of the fact that we can project qualities we *dislike* in ourselves, just as much as those we like. The seventh house partner is someone in whom we meet our match, who pushes us to the limits of our growth, who makes us respond as deeply as we are capable.

How do we achieve such a partnership? We once heard a couple promise to "love, honor, cherish and negotiate." That really says it all. With these partners, we're committed to the long haul. We accept them as they are, not as we want them to be, nor as some echo of our parents. We respect differences. We try not to polarize over personality issues—"You're crazy and I'm sane; you're spiritual and I'm worldly; you feel and I think." That kind of split is a classic seventh house danger signal.

Seventh house intimacy is a slow-blooming flower, unfolding over time, nurtured by equality, healthy compromise, interdependency, trust and commitment.

One note before we begin: in what follows, you'll see a lot of emphasis on committed sexual intimacy. That's the place where our seventh house themes emerge most vividly. It's important to remember that these themes are also pertinent to non-sexual bonds—you and your best friend, for example. Please make that translation where appropriate.

Sun in the Seventh House

A central evolutionary intent is to develop empathy, caring, affection—and the ability to negotiate and make healthy compromises. Supporting that intent is a destiny pattern that is profoundly influenced by the impact of other people—which basically means that you will simultaneously change and be changed by a handful of human beings with whom you interact, and that the full creative flowering of your destiny depends on those alchemical interactions. While you do need to flow with others and let yourself be affected by them, you must also guard against simply going into orbit around them. At times you can be so tuned in to others' needs that you don't fully state your own. Perhaps in reaction to that trait, at other times you may blindly insist on your own point of view. Never lose sight of a few central psychological facts about yourself: you feed your spirit with mutuality and sharing, and the exercise of the skills connected with it. Without it, your solar energy is sapped, and you are diverted from a crucial evolutionary path. You get along most easily with other people who have a similarly consensual, partnering, democratic orientation. What a less empathetic person might perceive as a need for approval on your part, a more relationship-oriented soul might see as caring, kindness, consensuality, and sensitivity.

To commit fully, you need: Full reciprocity with someone with a well-integrated ego function and the capacity to negotiate. The ability to state your own needs and to compromise where appropriate.

Your trust is weakened by: Instability in the partner, evasiveness, or repeated attempts to dominate.

Moon in the Seventh House

The evolutionary intent is to form profound, mutually nurturing emotional connections with others. This is not about extroversion; it is about vulnerable, heart-felt bonding, with deep people, one at a time. You may be overcoming a karmic pattern of emotional isolation. To support that evolutionary intent, you are able to empathize with a wide range of different human types, and inclined toward supportive, caring behaviors, which incidentally makes you a natural counselor. Your emotional wellbeing is enhanced enormously if you're living in partnership. Friends are important here, but the essence of the matter is the ongoing business of two people creating a life together. To such a union, you bring sensitivity, commitment, loyalty, and a touching concern for the emotional and physical wellbeing of the partner. The downside? You need to be careful that your own direction in life doesn't get eclipsed by the needs or demands—real or perceived—of the significant other.

To commit fully, you need: in both yourself and your partner, the ability to share all emotions, not just the "acceptable" ones, and also tenderness and nurturing qualities.

Your trust is weakened by: insensitivity toward your feelings, or dismissal of your feelings.

Mercury in the Seventh House

The evolutionary intent is to establish vigorous, eager, stimulating communication in all your close relationships, perhaps to resolve a karmic pattern of not feeling truly heard, feeling bored, or not fully met on the intellectual plane. At one level, you are skilled here—you have an elevated ability to frame words in a way seemingly custom-designed for the listener. On a deeper level, the key for the longevity of your commitments lies in maintaining *interest* in them. That in turn depends partly on your willingness to listen freshly, to expect surprises, and above all never to finish other people's sentences for them. That may seem to be a minor breach of etiquette, but with Mercury in the seventh house, it's a far more serious one than it seems. If you do that, you've stopped truly listening, and have begun to imagine that you know what your partner is going to say. Right or wrong, that's the beginning of a kind of self-created mental boredom, which quickly kills the very roots of love for anyone with the planet of language in the house of marriage. Implicit in all this is the notion that the only suitable kind of partner for you is one who is curious, open, and committed to being a little smarter than he or she was yesterday.

To commit fully, you need: excellent mental rapport and two-way communication with a partner; an engaged intellect in the partner.

Your trust is weakened by: boredom, and not feeling heard.

Venus in the Seventh House

The evolutionary intent is to co-create an experience of intimacy in which grace, sophistication, and warm mutual respect are central. This is partly in response to a karmic pattern of relationships lacking in courtesy and finesse. Aesthetic sensibilities may be strong in you and are appreciated in a mate. Reciprocity and a fine-tuned social awareness are also important. However, because the seventh is the house of everything which we perceive as *not* part of ourselves, at least initially, you may feel that you lack all of those attractive Venusian characteristics. If that feeling remains, to make up for your perceived shortcomings, you may unconsciously seek an enchanting, creative, drop-dead gorgeous god or goddess for a partner—and be profoundly insecure about your ability to hold such a prize. The more that you develop and recognize Venusian poise, attractiveness and refinement within yourself, the more likely you are to draw someone who shares them.

To commit fully, you need: courtesy, respect, loftiness of intention in the partner, and graciousness in both your partner and yourself.
Your trust is weakened by: crassness, nastiness, insensitivity

Mars in the Seventh House

The evolutionary intent is include bring fiery energy and directness into your relationships. To that end, you bring tremendous drive and forthrightness to the process of building and sustaining them. One simple, evolutionary truth: you are here learning how to fight. And that doesn't mean just yelling—it's about honest, constructive efforts to bring real conflicts out in the open where they can either be resolved or accepted. You are reacting against a karmic pattern of either a significant failure of nerve in past relationships, or violence in them. Although you may be demanding, intense and blunt at times, you're also capable of impressive loyalty and devotion. You are drawn to assertive, gutsy individuals who can stay in the ring with you. More than you probably know, you thrive on passion—and if it seems to be diminishing, you will instinctively stir the pot somehow . . . tease, initiate sex, pick a fight, anything to get the blood flowing in your veins again.
To commit fully, you need: courage and energy in both partners.
Your trust is weakened by: fearfulness, "niceness," and passivity.

Jupiter in the Seventh House

The evolutionary intent is to make generosity, expansiveness, high-minded philosophy—and your own high expectations—a cardinal motif in all your close relationships. At one level, you are inclined to be extremely supportive of a mate, with a positive attitude and a tendency to rise above pettiness. On a deeper level, an evolutionary key for you lies in understanding that, for you, a relationship must constantly be heading toward an Ideal for it to feel alive. This is a delicate and demanding point, given human frailty. Basically, what you want is something bigger than life, something so wonderful and so perfect that it's never really existed here on earth, at least not in the context of the mundane realities of two human beings sorting out a household. That drive can go either way: on the down side, you can simply be too idealistic, and therefore never satisfied, and pulled toward a tendency to criticize, which you emphatically despise! The good news is that, if the idealism is tempered

130

with forgiveness, humor, and humility, you could hold up your end of a truly world-class romance. One bottom line: you need a mate who believes in you more than you believe in yourself.

To commit fully, you need: a sense of infinite possibility; a prince among men; a queen among women.

Your trust is weakened by: narrow-mindedness, niggling criticism, or a lack of ethics in the partner.

Saturn in the Seventh House

This configuration has received more than its fair share of bad astrological press. Traditionally, Saturn is a "malefic" planet, suggesting coldness, estrangement, and mere dutifulness where love should go. That dark prophecy will only come true if you fail to honor the real evolutionary intent of the ringed planet in this house: how to take a vow so seriously that the earth shakes when you speak the words. Saturn is about deep commitment, something of which you are quite capable. It also implies a serious, devoted, sober and honorable attitude toward intimate relationships, and need for a partner who is *equally reliable and committed.* Probing a little more deeply, you may have some knotty karmic issues to resolve around really *trusting* anyone. The Great Work of your lifetime is the recovery of your ability to trust. You cannot accomplish that alone—you need the help of someone, unsurprisingly, who is trustworthy. If someone lets you down in a fundamental way, *and* if you don't address the issue with him or her, your own heart will never again be fully touched . . . mostly because it will never again be revealed.

To commit fully, you need: fully adult responsibility, integrity and realism in yourself and your partner.

Your trust is weakened by: immaturity, neediness, irresponsibility.

Uranus in the Seventh House

Traditionally, this configuration is associated with a pattern of sudden disruptions and changes in one's intimate life. The real evolutionary intent is much deeper, and potentially a lot more satisfying. Wherever Uranus lies, the challenge is one of *individuation*—which basically means thinking for one's self. If your intimate life is going to work, that's exactly what you must do: the normal claustrophobias of conventional intimacy don't fit your nature.

You require more space and freedom than most of us do. Typically, even the sorts of partners who seem right for people with this configuration really aren't so right after all. You must mature sufficiently and get to know yourself well enough to sort out your real feelings from all the social pressures and cultural programming that try to eclipse your own natural instincts about your true partners. It's only when you succumb to that kind of programming that you find yourself saddled with an inappropriate choice of partners—the very mistake that triggers the fortune-teller's prediction about your instability. So throw away the script and create the rules of love anew from the ground up.

To commit fully, you need: a resolution from both yourself and your partner to overcome social pressures regarding your choice of mate and your style of relationship.

Your trust is weakened by: possessiveness, attempts to control you, unconsidered conventionality, or too much concern about the opinions of people outside the couple.

Neptune in the Seventh House

At the high end of the spectrum, the evolutionary intent is to establish relationships that have a *truly* spiritual basis. At the low end, this configuration can be associated with simple disillusionment and heartbreak, usually as a result of what appear to be dumb choices on your part. You are wired for a profound kind of psychic intimacy: relationships so connected that half the conversations have no audible words in them! Anyone who seems to be of that particular mystical tribe— soulful, sensitive people—is going to be at least somewhat appealing to you. That's where glory and trouble enter through the same door. You may fall in love with a beautiful soul, only to realize later that the soul was walking around inside a personality with serious flaws: gross irresponsibility, addiction, mental disorders. The key is to realize that your original perception of beauty was *totally accurate, just incomplete.* The general shape of the answer that really works is that, while you definitely need a relationship with a spiritual basis, you also need to train yourself to concentrate on a mundane checklist of practical, common sense concerns about a person before leaping into trust, vulnerability, and sexual mysticism.

132

To commit fully, you need: a spiritual dimension to your life and to your partner's life, but not such a "flight into light" that you lose your ability to function in the world.

Your trust is weakened by: lack of compassion, and an inability to admit the possibility that true reality is deeper and more mysterious than the three dimensional, day-to-day reality where most of us live most of the time.

Pluto in the Seventh House

Wherever Pluto lies, we are carrying some very hurt places. For you, that means there are issues about deep trust and a significant probability that in your intimate life, in both past lives and the present, you have had more than your fair share of heartbreak, betrayal, and painful contact with the more abusive side of human nature. The psychoanalytical, emotionally cathartic process of getting at those wounds and the events that created them is the evolutionary intent of this placement. That process is also an absolutely essential prerequisite for present-tense intimacy really working for you. The good news is that is an operation for which you're most admirably wired. You are an individual who brings a probing, questioning, delving quality to bear upon anyone with whom you become close. While there is nothing inherently wrong with that, and while it must be seen as a natural result of your simply being very scared and very hurt at some level, it is also important for you to keep some balance and perspective: to learn to lighten up a bit, to give a worthy partner with a good track record the benefit of the doubt, and generally to let old wars be over. Your natural partners are people unafraid of going into those dark places with you. They are honest, intense—and expect the same.

To commit fully, you need: intensity, passion, gut-level honesty and the ability to "process" deeply, in both yourself and your partner.

Your trust is weakened by: a refusal to go through catharsis, and lack of psychological perceptiveness.

South Node in the Seventh House:

In the karmic past, you have spent a great deal of time in intimate relationships. The good news is you have probably acquired some real relating skills. The bad news is that you may have developed some reflexes about putting another person's needs ahead of your own, or always seeking consensus before you act, even when it's not necessary. Strive to be conscious of any such pattern and not to repeat it. Some of your sensitivity toward others derives from unresolved karmic patterns where your survival or wellbeing depended upon your responsiveness to another person who had power over you. This has created in you elements of what a psychotherapist would call co-dependency: a danger of going into orbit around another person's defenses or issues. (The nodes are not planets, so we haven't written anything about what builds commitment or weakens trust here.)

North Node in the Seventh House

Intimacy is the arena of human existence with which you are the least familiar. Forming a true "I-thou" relationship will feel strange to you from the sheer newness of the situation, and you and your partner would both do well to be patient with you. Yet intimacy is the alchemical process that will most help you grow toward wholeness, so don't be afraid to begin it. The origins of this dilemma lie in the karmic past during lifetimes in which "the buck stopped with you"—you were in leadership roles in which true sharing was simply ineffective and inappropriate. (The nodes are not planets, so we haven't written anything about what builds commitment or weakens trust here.)

CHAPTER ELEVEN:
THE ARC OF INTIMACY—THE EIGHTH HOUSE

The Eighth House

Traditional Name: House of Death
Corresponding Sign: Scorpio
Associated Planets: Pluto, Mars
Terrain: Sexual bonding
Evolutionary Process: Imprinting on another person, sexually, mentally, emotionally. Acceptance of feelings arising from instinctive levels of consciousness. Honesty, psychological nakedness. Healing of karmic wounds that may impede these processes.
Abort Sequence: Sexual dysfunction. Lack of depth, relationship feels like friends but not lovers. Avoidance of psychologically charged issues.

Until now in the arc of intimacy, we might have been discussing how you get along with your best friend. But to arrive at the eighth house, we cross the line into sexuality. This is the house of the *instincts*, of motivations whose roots run deeper than our conscious minds: sexuality, death, and the "occult," or whatever notions we have about survival after death.

Volcanic stuff.

Now those seventh house partnership bonds of trust are truly tested. Now we abandon logic and rationality and simply feel: is this my mate? On a gut level, with every cell in my body, with all my reflexes, clear down to the reptile part of my brain, have I imprinted on this person? And *vice versa*?

Sex is part of this bond. More than physical sex is necessary to form it, but physical sex is essential for its creation and sustenance. Sexuality and bonding are multilevel processes, and physical sex is only one factor in them.

Planets and signs in the eighth house show the qualities you need in a mate to maintain this degree of instinctual connection, through your multi-dimensional, mind-body-spirit sexual circuitry. They also show the origins of the issues in you that could bring you to the psychotherapist's door—the karmic wounds you may have endured in this intimate department. The eighth house energies that you need in a mate will help you heal those eighth house wounds.

If your Moon falls in your eighth house, for example, your mate must have certain lunar qualities: imagination, sensitivity, tenderness, intuition.

135

Imagine that you've been dating someone for a relatively short period of time, and you discover that this person is sexy, intelligent, gutsy, and amusing, but he or she simply lacks depth. If you have an eighth house Moon, the thrill is gone, and it won't return. You may continue to *like* the person, certainly, but he or she is a bad bet for a life mate.

Healthy sexuality involves releasing and accepting overwhelming feelings. Sometimes this is easy and joyful; other times it's painful and embarrassing, but in any case, acknowledging all the emotions aroused by the partner is essential to the formation and continuation of the bond.

You are at a party. Your mate spends the entire evening huddled in a corner with someone attractive. Whether you casually inquire about their conversation or have a glorious fight in the car on the way home, you are bound to have had some twinges originating from your eighth house. *What if your mate abandons you?* The ancient primate in you knows that such abandonment means lessened chances of survival. Its hackles rise, growling, "Kill the interloper!" If you're a card-carrying New Age citizen, you may be mortified at this reaction, but mortified or not, it's better to deal with it, gently or directly according to your style, than to repress it.

The surest way never to feel crazy is never to surrender in sexual love. You may still *be* crazy, but you won't be nearly so confronted by it.

Your personal psychological issues are also triggered by your partner. Your reaction to that conversation at the party, for example, might also be rooted in childhood desertion by one of your parents (remember the fourth house!). If you don't face those emotions, you can pour salt on that early wound, never seeing its connection to your present insecurities. But if you broach the subject with your mate, who knows your life story (remember the fifth house!), he or she might gently point out that your reaction has some roots in your personal history. With sixth house *shared humility* and seventh house *trust*, you can go down into the hell-worlds of the eighth house together, retrieve the lost parts of your souls—and come away laughing at the feebleness of death and its paper-tiger surrogates.

Sun in the Eighth House

The evolutionary intention here centers on the transformation and purification of ego-consciousness, values, and self-imagery through an immersion in radical honesty and commitment. All rough edges and unresolved issues must be exposed and smoothed in the alchemical process of compassionate psychological confrontation. Implicit here is a reference to a reaction against unresolved, prior-life issues involving oppressive conformity to "tribal" patterns of rationalization and denial. The partner must be willing to face darkness and woundedness humbly and truthfully, both in the Self and the Other.

Key Quality in Partner: Intensity.
Turn-off: Avoidance; denial; shallowness.

Moon in the Eighth House

The evolutionary intention here centers on healing the capacity to form an instinctual mating-bond in which an emotional sense of home arises. Integrating deep domestic familiarity with sexuality is part of the intent. Having children is not necessarily the aim, but finding the place in us that *could* do that and want that is central. A reaction exists here to prior-life dynamics involving a lack of "rootedness," or perhaps the social shaming associated with "barrenness." The partner must be open to the full acceptance of the realities of life-long commitment.

Key Quality in Partner: Radical, monogamous commitment; sensitivity.
Turn-off: "Peter Pan" syndrome (in either gender).

Mercury in the Eighth House

The evolutionary intention here centers on healing the capacity to *communicate,* both in terms of speaking one's feelings and in terms of truly listening to the other person. The karmic patterning implies a strong reaction against boredom and mental tyranny in a prior-life bond. The partner must be open and eager regarding communication and learning, and typically will be a curious, exploratory kind of person, always embracing mind-stretching experiences, never threatened by receiving knowledge or information from you.

Key Quality in Partner: Intelligence; curiosity; willingness to speak, listen, and learn.
Turn-off: Emotional silence; rigidity; unwillingness to learn.

137

Venus in the Eighth House

The evolutionary intention here centers on healing pre-existing soul-damage linked to materialistic, crass or purely biological views of sexuality. There is strong desire for loftiness, grace, and easy dignity in the intimate arena. Simple *courtesy* is essential. The partner must be civilized, sensitive, and graceful, willing to continue courtship behavior for the length of the relationship. Great comfort and benefit comes to the relationship through exposure to art and artists.
Key Quality in Partner: Grace.
Turn-off: Crassness and vulgarity.

Mars in the Eighth House

The evolutionary intention here connects with the notion of reclaiming unabashed passion, perhaps as a result of prior-life sexual shaming, rape or repression. This intention includes the recognition that the price of *sustained passion* lies partly in a willingness to deal honestly, promptly, and directly with anger—and a humble recognition that sexual relationships will sometimes invoke long-buried soul-rage that has nothing to do with the present partner. Thus implicit in this configuration is the soul desire to master the art of *intimate conflict,* which includes finding a truthful balance between self-scrutiny and psychological scrutiny of the mate. The partner must be truthful, loyal, passionate—and unafraid of your passion in both the physical and energetic meanings of the word.
Key Quality in Partner: Courage and passion.
Turn-off: Word-mincing "niceness."

Jupiter in the Eighth House

The evolutionary intention here centers on healing the capacity to *believe in love,* and to trust enough to take those ultimate leaps of faith: interpersonal commitment and sexual surrender. There is a powerful reaction to unresolved prior-life dynamics linked with an overly dutiful marriage and sexuality in which one merely "settled for" a mate, with all the attendant, damaging self-repression. A strong intention exists to reclaim spontaneity, abundance, and joy in the intimate arena. The natural partner is therefore

138

generous, big-spirited, supportive, generally entertaining—and would probably feel like a real catch.

Key Quality in Partner: Supportiveness, generosity in assessing the Other, "bigness" of spirit.

Turn-off: Stinginess, control-issues, shaming.

Saturn in the Eighth House

The evolutionary intention here pivots on recovering the *capacity to trust.* There is evidence of prior-life *betrayal, bereavement,* or *abandonment,* leaving the individual with fear, a sense of impending doom regarding love, and inner layers of protective emotional self-containment. There is a resultant vulnerability either to emotional isolation or, more insidiously, to bonding with people who *symbolize these fears.* The natural partner is simply trustworthy; a person of high integrity, patience and maturity, capable of making and keeping adult vows in the long haul, thus inviting this soul in from the cold.

Key Quality in Partner: Integrity; trustworthiness.

Turn-off: Immaturity; self-indulgence, weakness.

Uranus in the Eighth House

The evolutionary intention here centers on claiming freedom and individuality *within the context of commitment.* This implies prior-life suppression, "enslavement," and confinement regarding the natural right to choose one's own mate or sexual partners. Perhaps this correlates with oppressive vows of celibacy in the past, or with some form of frustrating and unsatisfactory arranged marriage. The natural partner is tolerant and supportive regarding human differences, not unnaturally jealous, and eager to support freedom, the need for space, and individuation in you.

Key Quality in Partner: Respect for autonomy.

Turn-off: Insecurity, control issues, possessiveness.

Neptune in the Eighth House

The evolutionary intention here pivots on the desire to experience *sacred sexuality,* which is to say, direct contact between souls in the context of sexual bonding. Thus, the physical eyes become the most pressing erogenous zone, and sexual excitement is unsustainable without the experience of psychic and spiritual linking. There is a prior-life implication of a splitting of spirit and flesh, which strangely can result either from monastic vows of celibacy or from psychic adaptation to the realities of prostitution—the latter to be understood literally, but also as some form of loveless, essentially involuntary marriage. The natural partner is sensitive and open to spirituality in some form, although there is no need for symmetry in the belief-systems. He or she naturally integrates tenderness and "merging" feelings with sexuality.

Key Quality in Partner: Psychic and spiritual sensitivity.

Turn-off: A materialized, overly-biological view of sexuality.

Pluto in the Eighth House

The evolutionary intention here involves surrendering to a shared process of mutual healing. Beasts must be faced, and that facing must be shared. The implication is that there exists a deep and fundamental wound to the soul in general which manifest in the sexuality specifically. There is a powerful reaction to unresolved prior-life dynamics of suffering and numbness connected with sexual violence, war, or grievous and unnatural bereavement. The outward tone of this wound is angry; its interior is depression. The natural partner in this healing work is not unduly afraid of intensity and the processing of issues, and is committed to honest self-expression however sensitive the subject.

Key Quality in Partner: Humble, undefensive psychological self-analysis; penetrating and unflinching analysis of the other person.

Turn-off: Shallowness, rationalization, denial, inordinate fear of the darker side of human nature.

South Node in the Eighth House

Here, the karmic past is one in which much time was spent in eighth house processes. You've grown accustomed to unending, unbroken intensity. The sign and aspects of the node reveal the details, but probably you've seen the realities we associate with apocalypse: war, famine, plague. You may possibly have received shamanic or occult initiations. You've come away from those experiences with an innate wisdom about them, but your growth is no longer fostered there. You need more normalcy now. You would do well

140

to avoid the more soap-operatic side of the eighth house. How? Cry and process when you have to, and aim for stability, serenity, and "chicken soup" the rest of the time. (The nodes are not planets, so we are not discussing the qualities of a partner for this placement.)

North Node in the Eighth House

The eighth house terrain is that with which you are the least familiar, so unless there's a whole lot suggesting the opposite in your natal chart, venturing into "the dark" can feel frightening or unnatural for you. We need to understand this reality compassionately and respectfully. Your second house south node suggests lifetimes in which either the practical pressures of survival were fierce or in which "you paid too much for your money." In both scenarios, attention is naturally directed away from the psychological interior. Now, foreign though those passionate depths are to you, your soul needs them like the desert needs rain. (The nodes are not planets, so we are not discussing the qualities of a partner for this placement.)

CHAPTER TWELVE: HOW BIRTHCHARTS INTERACT

No matter how different two people might be, if we put them both in the pressure cooker and close the lid, they'll work out a pattern of relation. It may be joyful. It may be mutually destructive. But a pattern will appear—and no matter who they are, that pattern can be analyzed through a study of the interplay between their birthcharts.

The first step is to observe how the planets in one birthchart impact upon the planets in the other chart. There are many techniques for accomplishing that, and we'll be exploring all of them. But the core of the process doesn't lie in mastery of the technicalities. Far more centrally, it has to do with getting a sense of the human wholeness represented by each of the birthcharts. After that, we apply common sense, imagination, and a willingness to plug astrology into that wonderful library of personal experience you carry in your head.

If a mouse and a cat are locked up together, what happens? In the world of animals the answer is obvious. But in the world of men and women the patterns are more subtle. Maybe the "mouse" still gets eaten, but maybe not. Perhaps the "cat" adopts a posture of benign authority, content merely to display its teeth rather than actually using them. Perhaps we get a distinctly *nice* mouse. Many stories are possible, and none of them are difficult to imagine.

Cats and mice are familiar characters. Once Mars and the Moon are just as familiar, you'll be an astrologer.

A man has a very prominent Mars at the beginning of the sign Aries. It lies in his first house in a conjunction with his Sun. For purposes of generating a story, we might liken that Mars to a cat—he's a hunter-type: competitive, willful, and passionate. Maybe his partner has her Moon in early Libra. She's a milder, more vulnerable kind of person: potentially a "nice mouse," at least in relation to his fierce Mars placement.

What happens? No way to know exactly. Like the rest of us, those people can do as they please. Astrology describes many behavioral options for them. Trying to guess the one they will pick is not the astrologer's work. But translating Mars and the Moon to "cat" and "mouse" starts the interpretive ball rolling.

In the previous section of the book we went into great detail about how to understand the *individual* from an astrological perspective. Once you've accomplished that, much of synastry takes care of itself, at least if you are willing to rely heavily on your old friends: common sense, imagination, and your own human experience.

That man's Arian Mars and his wife's Libran Moon form an *opposition* aspect to each other, suggestive of tension (please see Chapter Two if you're fuzzy about aspects). But if you actually need to calculate that aspect before you sense tension between this particular cat and mouse, you probably also need a blow with a two-by-four to help you awaken in the morning! If you've really understood the individual birthcharts, the tension leaps out.

Hesitant? Don't feel dumb! This is one of those places where the great advantage of speaking aloud about astrological symbols becomes clear. If you had sat down with those two people to explore their relationship from an astrological perspective, you naturally would have dwelt on the brusque ferocity of the man's mask as you expressed your thoughts about his Mars. For similar reasons you would have also expanded upon the delicate sensibilities and profound relationship needs of the woman's Libran Moon. With all those words hanging in the air, the potential clash between the two configurations would be inescapably obvious, even if you didn't know a thing about how to calculate aspects between charts.

Still, these *interaspects*—aspects formed between the planets of one chart and those of another—are the workhorses of synastry. Why? Simply because not all interactions between birthcharts are quite as evident as the particular "cat" and "mouse" scenario we've been considering. Some are far more subtle. Without any knowledge of interaspects, you'd still pick up the broadest interactive themes without any difficulty. And if you were able to give warm, wise human advice about how they could handle those broad themes more lovingly, you'd be a fine astrologer. The advantage of understanding interaspects is that they telegraph *all* the interactive patterns to you, even the more subtle ones you might otherwise miss.

144

The term "interaspects," by the way, was coined by astrologers Ken and Joan Negus. Joan is gone now, but we suspect she'll live on in astrology's future history through that simple, workhorse word.

Too much technique, not enough human reality: that's probably the astrologer's riskiest pitfall. Be careful you don't get lost in the labyrinths of theory. Interaspects are powerful, but they can also be a one-way ticket into that labyrinth. Later in this chapter and all through the next one we'll explore them, but first things first: our initial step is to absorb both birthcharts, summarize them inwardly as feelings, then compare them intuitively on that gut level. What do we get? Cats and mice. Dreamers and realists. Homebodies and gypsies. That's the level where the magic happens. That's the level where astrology becomes human.

Here's the practical principle: *carry your synastry analysis as far as you possibly can on the basis of the "feel" of each birthchart, then further refine your understanding through interaspects.*

In harmony with our guiding principle, we'll use a few specific examples to flesh out this idea of getting the feel of various kinds of astrological interactions before we dive into the more technical side of interaspect work.

Saturn In Love

Saturn can be a symbol of blockage—a feeling that often arises in ongoing intimacy. It represents what we *refuse to experience*. More deeply, Saturn symbolizes an area where we are challenged to overcome our blockages through the application of positive Saturn virtues: self-discipline, patience, determination. But those virtues never arise automatically, personally or in relationships. We have to work toward them. And if we don't work, then the blockage remains, usually protected within a steel casing of stubbornness, controlling behavior, and self-righteousness.

Two lovers might have Saturn in Fire signs. No single astrological feature can safely be interpreted in isolation from the rest of the birthchart, but abstractly Saturn in Fire suggests a shared blockage (Saturn) in terms of assertiveness, tolerance of risk, and the expression of anger (Fire). Since the blockage is shared, there is harmony here:

145

He: "The O'Rileys called and asked if we'd like to go shark-wrestling with them this weekend. Care to go?"

She: (emphatically) "Are you crazy?!"

He: "I was hoping you'd say that."

So far, so good. But like most kinds of astrological harmony, there are dangers here too. In this couple, their hesitation to take risks could lead to a deadening collusion in which all possibility of newness and change was systematically eliminated from their relationship, collapsing everything into ritual and predictability. Once again, that's not their fate, it's just a danger that comes with this particular kind of harmony.

In a little while we'll learn that the harmony between those two Fire-sign Saturns is connected to the fact that they make a trine aspect to each other. We might miss that technical linkage in our preliminary, intuitive analysis of the two birthcharts. No problem. When we calculate the interaspects, we'll pick it up then. Interaspects, in other words, are a wonderful safety net. Still, like most tightrope walkers, your first priority should be staying on the tightrope.

Jodie Forrest may someday write a horror novel relating her early safaris into the darker reaches of Steven Forrest's apartment. *Tales of Mildew* is the working title. Steve has Saturn in Virgo on his Midheaven, and one of his blockages is connected with the distinctly Virgoan process of housekeeping. He feels he was born for greater things. (Presented with that announcement, Jodie pointed out that she was, too!)

On the other hand, in those salad days of their relationship, Steve experienced great frustration with what he perceived to be Jodie's lack of natural enthusiasm for life's adventures: scrambling up steep and slippery cliff faces, hiking out into the snowy woods with the wind howling, sleeping ingloriously in a mud puddle amid otherwise glorious natural circumstances. Jodie's Saturn lies in Sagittarius—the sign of exploration and robust engagement with experience. That's where *her* blockages lie.

Clearly, there is friction between these Saturns. Steve's Saturn blockage bothers Jodie and Jodie's Saturn blockage bothers Steve. So what happens? Divorce is one option. But so is adult compromise. Since their marriage, Steve has become a (somewhat) more industrious housekeeper and Jodie has

146

become a (somewhat) more adventuresome explorer. To make their marriage work, each had to respond to Saturn's call for self-discipline and determined effort. Otherwise, the blockages would have remained unchallenged and unmodified—and the rigid high-jinx prophecies of the fortune-tellers would have been right on the money.

If you start with a clear understanding of Saturn in Virgo and Saturn in Sagittarius, then the friction between them is rather obvious, provided you obey the cardinal rule of synastry and remember to *feel* the ideas as you think them or say them. And again, if you missed the connection intuitively, no problem. You'd see it when you actually calculated the interaspects and discovered that Steve's Saturn squares Jodie's Saturn: the ninety degree aspect of *friction*.

How To Recognize Interaspects

Now that we've put interaspects in their place, let's look at them carefully. They are a powerful tool, and you would have to be a very intuitive astrologer indeed to do high quality synastry interpretations without their help. Much of the rest of this chapter revolves around some fairly dry, technical procedures. Absorb them, and you'll be in position to penetrate the collision-zone of two souls.

Many neophyte astrologers are daunted by the prospect of picking out these geometrical angles around the birthchart. There's no need for the hesitancy. Once you get off on the right foot, aspects are not hard to grasp. The trick is to begin with a crystal-clear mental photograph of the wheel of signs—the Zodiac itself. Once you have that, everything else falls into place.

Aspects are geometrical angles formed between planets in various signs. Each angle suggests a different *pattern of relationship*—friction, harmony, tension. (Look at Table Four in Chapter Two on page 18 for a summary of all the major aspects.) Are there minor aspects? Yes, and they work too, but we find that so much vital information can be derived from the major ones that to keep the focus of the interpretation—and to keep the sheer amount of data to a minimum—we stick with the major ones.

Let's consider the birthcharts of F. Scott Fitzgerald and Zelda Fitzgerald on pages 149 and 150. We'll be using them in a synastry interpretation later in the book, so we won't go into much detail about them here. As we would suspect, their destinies were linked by many powerful interaspects.

Zelda Fitzgerald's Sun lies in early Leo. F. Scott Fitzgerald's Moon lies in early Taurus. Is there an interaspect between them? To find out, refer to your mental photograph of the wheel of signs. Leo and Taurus make a right angle to each other—one glance at the zodiac tells you that. Immediately you know that her Sun and his Moon are in a square aspect.

What if her Sun is in early Leo but his Moon had been in early Cancer? Is there an interaspect? These two signs are adjacent, so the two planets are separated by about thirty degrees: the width of one complete sign, in other words. Once again, look at Table Four in Chapter Two on page 18. No major aspect exists between planets separated by thirty degrees, so in this case, there would have been no interaspect.

Here's a methodical way of proceeding. Pick a planet in Zelda's birthchart, say her Mars, which lies in the middle of Gemini, in a conjunction with Scott's Pluto, his Neptune and his Mars, also in the middle of Gemini. Count *one sign* on either side of Gemini, and you'll come to Taurus and Cancer. Scott has planets in Taurus. Is there an interaspect with Zelda's Mars in Gemini? No, because counting one sign in either direction only moves us thirty degrees, and thirty degrees is not a major aspect. (It is a minor aspect called a semisextile, but again, we don't need to be concerned with minor aspects here. The major ones give us plenty to think about.)

Now count *two signs* on either side of Zelda's Mars. You'll come to Aries and Leo. Two signs' separation means a sextile aspect, and if Scott has planets in the middle of either of those signs, they are linked to Zelda's Mars through that interaspect. Does he have planets there? Nothing lies in Aries, but he has Jupiter and the south node in Leo. Do they form the sextile with Zelda's Mars?

Scott's south node certainly does; it is five degrees away from an exact sixty degree sextile. That's called a five degree *orb*.

Scott's Jupiter, on the other hand, is eleven degrees away from an exact sixty degree sextile. Many astrologers would feel that an orb of eleven

FIGURE FOUR

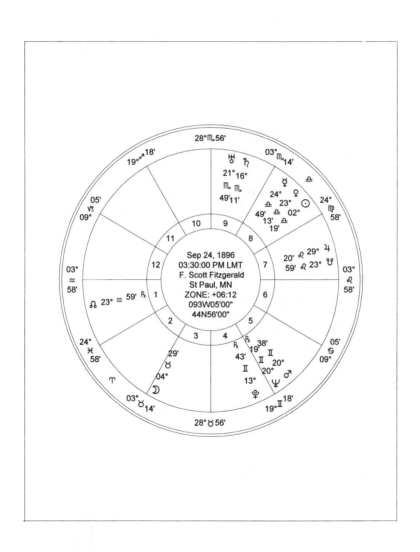

FIGURE FIVE

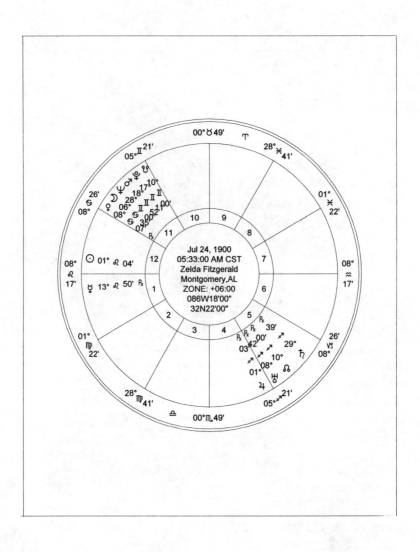

degrees is too wide for an aspect to be felt, but especially for the purposes of synastry, we feel that a sextile does exist between Scott's Jupiter and Zelda's Mars. It is not so powerful as it would be with a one degree orb instead of an eleven degree orb, but it is definitely there. Our friend and colleague, Robert Hand, in translating ancient astrological texts, has discovered that the standard practice of our ancestors for centuries and centuries was to use "whole sign aspects." Aspects were calculated between whole signs rather than between specific degrees of them—everything in Gemini was sextile everything in Leo. With the proviso that the tighter the orb, the more powerful the aspect, we heartily recommend paying attention to this practice in all synastry work.

Similarly, counting *three signs* brings us to the square.

Four signs means a trine interaspect.

Five signs is another minor aspect called the quincunx or the inconjunct, and we can safely ignore it for our purposes in this book.

Finally, counting *six signs* brings us to the opposition.

Remember to count both clockwise and counterclockwise around the chart. Aspects work in both directions!

This may seem like a lot to juggle, but the essential reasoning is simple. For whole sign aspects, the type we are using here, just count the signs separating the planets to determine whether an aspect exists. The tighter (the smaller) the orb, the more powerful the aspect.

Why do whole sign aspects work? Probably because aspects are very connected to the four astrological elements: Fire, Earth, Air, and Water. Every Fire sign, for example, trines the other two Fire signs. That is, they tend to get along fairly harmoniously, sharing the common goals and temperament of the fiery element. Communality and overlap are really the key concepts, and even though the astrological tradition implies that signs sharing an element will "like" each other, it's a little more complicated than that. Will two violinists automatically like each other? Clearly they have some common ground—but a little street sense quickly suggests ways in which they might be threatening to each other too. The key here is their *potential* to enhance and support each other.

The same harmony exists among the three Earth signs, and so on. The elements form families, and they can benefit from each other's company.

Going further, Fire (will; intention) mixes readily with Air (ideation; senses), while Earth (logic; patience) mixes readily with Water (the inner life). Fire and Air were called the "positive" or "masculine" elements, while Water and Earth were seen as "negative" and "feminine." While the greatest harmony exists strictly within each of the four elemental families, the Fire-Air community is a peaceful one and so is the Earth-Water community. Each Fire sign, for example, makes aspects to all three Air signs: two exciting, harmonious sextiles and one tense (or complementary) opposition. Always, the opposition aspect can be problematic, but of all the aspects it is certainly the most "romantic." When two people experience a feeling of being each other's lost half, we'll see lots of oppositions between their birthcharts.

So each Fire sign mixes with Air, either in a spirit of mutual excitation (sextile) or through the tense fascination of the opposition.

Similar logic links each Air sign to all three Fire signs, either through sextiles or oppositions. It also ties Earth to Water or Water to Earth in the same way.

But Fire doesn't know what to make of Water or Earth! They speak different languages. The misunderstanding goes both ways: water doesn't know what to make of Air. Earth can't easily find any common ground with Fire. Unsurprisingly, these are the elemental combinations we find in square aspects (friction) or in most of the various minor aspects, where the interactive pattern so often boils down to missing each other's meaning or failing to connect easily.

Aspects, then, are intimately linked to an understanding of the four elements. A Moon in the last degree of Capricorn trines a Venus in the first degree of Taurus, despite the fact that they are twenty-eight degrees out of orb. Both planets lie in Earth signs, and so they speak similar languages. That Moon seeks the natural evolutionary goals of the Earth signs: solidness, reality, steady growth, commitment. Exactly the same goals motivate the Venusian romantic instincts of the other person. The link would be more

152

vigorous if the interaspect existed more precisely, but there is a connection here.

What about the Moon in the very last degree of Capricorn and Mars in the very first degree of Aquarius? Are they conjunct even though they are not in the same sign? Yes, they are conjunct by degrees. That's what is called an "out of quality" aspect: an aspect by degrees but not by signs. Out of quality aspects are weaker than those not out of quality, and we recommend the use of very narrow orbs for them.

If you've hung in there with us so far, congratulations! Most of the technical material is behind us and we are almost ready to begin the more emotionally rewarding work of interpretation. But first, a subject that has perhaps been nagging at you . . .

Keeping Track of Interaspects

Typically, a handful of supercharged interaspects dominate a couple's astrological interactions. Unsurprisingly, these interaspects generally involve the primal triad of Sun, Moon, and Ascendant. Such broad-stroke interaspects form the bedrock of intimacy, at least from an astrological perspective. Achieving skill in synastry depends upon keeping these quintessential Sun, Moon and Ascendant interaspects clear. That's not as hard as it might sound; there are not generally very many of them.

The interpretive fish grows more slippery when we include all interaspects rather than limiting ourselves to the ones involving the primal triad. We leap from a handful of interconnections to dozens, and unless you can balance your checkbook blindfolded, you'll need a strategy just to manage all the astrological data.

Look at Figure Six on page 154. It's a synastry worksheet, filled out for Zelda Fitzgerald and F. Scott Fitzgerald, using whole sign aspects. We know it looks about as comprehensible as something copied off the inner walls of Dhufu's pyramid, but don't be nervous. All of those hieroglyphics are already familiar to you. The worksheet simply shows all the interaspects linking Zelda and Scott, even some relatively inconsequential ones.

153

FIGURE SIX: SYNASTRY WORKSHEET (whole sign aspects)

Scott's Impact Upon Zelda's Birthchart:

His ☉ falls in her 3rd house ⚹ ☉ □ ☽ ⚹ ☿ □ ♀ △ ♂ ⚹ ♃ ⚹ ♄ ⚹ ♅ △ ♆ △ ♇ △ ☋ ⚹ ☊ ⚹ ASC
His ☽ falls in her 10th house □ ☉ ⚹ ☽ □ ☿ ⚹ ♀ □ ASC ☌ MH
His ☿ falls in her 3rd house ⚹ ☉ □ ☽ ⚹ ☿ □ ♀ △ ♂ ⚹ ♃ ⚹ ♄ ⚹ ♅ △ ♆ △ ♇ △ ☋ ⚹ ☊ ⚹ ASC
His ♀ falls in her 3rd house ⚹ ☉ □ ☽ ⚹ ☿ □ ♀ △ ♂ ⚹ ♃ ⚹ ♄ ⚹ ♅ △ ♆ △ ♇ △ ☋ ⚹ ☊ ⚹ ASC
His ♂ falls in her 11th house ⚹ ☉ ⚹ ☿ ☌ ♂ ☍ ♃ ☍ ♄ ☍ ♅ ☌ ♆ ☌ ♇ ☌ ☋ ☍ ☊ ⚹ ASC
His ♃ falls in her 1st house ☌ ☉ ☌ ☿ ⚹ ♂ △ ♃ △ ♄ △ ♅ ⚹ ♆ ⚹ ♇ ☌ ASC □ MH
His ♄ falls in her 4th house □ ☉ △ ☽ □ ☿ △ ♀ □ ASC ☍ MH
His ♅ falls in her 4th house □ ☉ △ ☽ □ ☿ △ ♀ □ ASC ☍ MH
His ♆ falls in her 11th house ⚹ ☉ ⚹ ☿ ☌ ♂ ☍ ♃ ☍ ♄ ☍ ♅ ☌ ♆ ☌ ♇ ☌ ☋ ☍ ☊ ⚹ ASC
His ♇ falls in her 11th house ⚹ ☉ ⚹ ☿ ☌ ♂ ☍ ♃ ☍ ♄ ☍ ♅ ☌ ♆ ☌ ♇ ☌ ☋ ☍ ☊ ⚹ ASC
His ☋ falls in her 1st house ☌ ☉ ☌ ☿ ⚹ ♂ △ ♃ △ ♄ △ ♅ ⚹ ♆ ⚹ ♇ ☌ ASC □ MH
His ☊ falls in her 7th house ☍ ☉ ☍ ☿ △ ♂ ⚹ ♃ ⚹ ♄ ⚹ ♅ △ ♆ △ ♇ △ ☋ ⚹ ☊ ☍ ASC □ MH
His ASC falls in her 6th house ☍ ☉ ☍ ☿ △ ♂ ⚹ ♃ ⚹ ♄ ⚹ ♅ △ ♆ △ ♇ △ ☋ ⚹ ☊ ☍ ASC □ MH
His MH falls in her 4th house □ ☉ △ ☽ □ ☿ △ ♀ □ ASC ☍ MH

Zelda's impact upon Scott's birthchart:

Her ☉ falls in his 6th house ⚹ ☉ □ ☽ ⚹ ☿ ⚹ ♀ ⚹ ♂ ☌ ♃ □ ♄ □ ♅ ⚹ ♆ ⚹ ♇ ☌ ☋ ☍ ☊ ☍ ASC □ MH
Her ☽ falls in his 5th house □ ☉ ⚹ ☽ □ ☿ □ ♀ △ ♄ △ ♅ △ MH
Her ☿ falls in his 7th house ⚹ ☉ □ ☽ ⚹ ☿ ⚹ ♀ ⚹ ♂ ☌ ♃ □ ♄ □ ♅ ⚹ ♆ ⚹ ♇ ☌ ☋ ☍ ☊ ☍ ASC □ MH
Her ♀ falls in his 6th house □ ☉ ⚹ ☽ □ ☿ △ ♀ △ ♄ △ ♅ △ MH
Her ♂ falls in his 5th house △ ☉ △ ☿ △ ♀ ☌ ♂ ⚹ ♃ ☌ ♆ ☌ ♇ ⚹ ☋ △ ☊ △ ASC
Her ♃ falls in his 10th house ⚹ ☉ ⚹ ☿ ⚹ ♀ ☍ ♂ △ ♃ ☍ ♆ ☍ ♇ △ ☋ ⚹ ☊ ⚹ ASC
Her ♄ falls in his 11th house ⚹ ☉ ⚹ ☿ ⚹ ♀ ☍ ♂ △ ♃ ☍ ♆ ☍ ♇ △ ☋ ⚹ ☊ ⚹ ASC
Her ♅ falls in his 10th house ⚹ ☉ ⚹ ☿ ⚹ ♀ ☍ ♂ △ ♃ ☍ ♆ ☍ ♇ △ ☋ ⚹ ☊ ⚹ ASC
Her ♆ falls in his 5th house △ ☉ △ ☿ △ ♀ ☌ ♂ ⚹ ♃ ☌ ♆ ☌ ♇ ⚹ ☋ △ ☊ △ ASC
Her ♇ falls in his 4th house △ ☉ △ ☿ △ ♀ ☌ ♂ ⚹ ♃ ☌ ♆ ☌ ♇ ⚹ ☋ △ ☊ △ ASC
Her ☋ falls in his 4th house △ ☉ △ ☿ △ ♀ ☌ ♂ ⚹ ♃ ☌ ♆ ☌ ♇ ⚹ ☋ △ ☊ △ ASC
Her ☊ falls in his 10th house ⚹ ☉ ⚹ ☿ ⚹ ♀ ☍ ♂ △ ♃ ☍ ♆ ☍ ♇ △ ☋ ⚹ ☊ ⚹ ASC
Her ASC falls in his 7th house ⚹ ☉ □ ☽ ⚹ ☿ ⚹ ♀ ⚹ ♂ ☌ ♃ □ ♄ □ ♅ ⚹ ♆ ⚹ ♇ ☌ ☋ ☍ ☊ ☍ ASC □ MH
Her MH falls in his 2nd house ☌ ☽ □ ♃ ☍ ♄ ☍ ♅ □ ☊ □ ☋ □ ASC ☍ MH

As we've seen, Zelda's Sun squares Scott's Moon. Look on Zelda's half of the synastry worksheet. Find the glyph for the Sun. (☉) Read the list of aspects that follows it. That list shows every major aspect that Zelda's Sun makes to Scott's planets and sensitive points, as if her Sun had been placed in his birthchart. A square to his Moon, Saturn, Uranus and Midheaven (MH). Sextiles to his Sun, Mercury, Venus, Mars, Neptune and Pluto. Conjunctions to his Jupiter and south node. An opposition to his north node and Ascendant (ASC). At a glance you see how *her* Sun is wired into *his* birthchart.

Why are there so many interaspects? The answer is easy. Look to the other half of the Worksheet. Find the symbol for Scott's Moon (☽). There you see what aspects his Moon would make if it were placed in her birthchart. Sextiles to her Moon and Venus. A conjunction to her Midheaven. A square to her Ascendant, Mercury and Sun. There's the familiar square to her Sun—and that's our answer. Each interaspect is entered twice on the worksheet, once from the point of view of Zelda's chart, and then again from the point of view of Scott's chart. Her Sun squares his Moon. His Moon squares her Sun. As we'll see in the next chapter, both ways of phrasing the statement are instructive. Although this double entry procedure involves some extra clerical work, it's worth the trouble. One of the secrets of successful synastry is the ability to move fluidly from one person's frame of reference into that of the other person, without getting stuck in either viewpoint. A double entry technique on the worksheet will help you do just that.

In Chapter Thirteen, we'll offer specific procedures for interpreting these interaspects. Right now, our task is simply to provide ourselves with the raw information. How do we proceed? First, supply yourself with a synastry worksheet. Most astrologers use computers nowadays, and they can crank out one of these interaspect grids, also called synastry grids, in a few moments. You can also order an inexpensive one already filled out with a couple's data directly from us. (See the Appendix.) If you prefer, you can easily make your own based on what you see in Figure Six and fill it out yourself.

One more note: if you are filling out a worksheet by hand, jot down where one person's planets would fall in the other person's houses. As you can see from Figure Six, there is a space for that information. F. Scott Fitzgerald's Moon, for example, lies in four degrees of Taurus in his third house. Where would his Moon lie if it were placed in Zelda Fitzgerald's birthchart? Four degrees of Taurus lies in her tenth house, in other words. Therefore, we say that Scott's Moon falls in that zone of *her* birthchart. If you have an astrological computer program or you order the calculations, you'll always find this information listed.

What does it mean to have Scott's Moon fall in Zelda's tenth house? That's a big subject. We'll deal with it in Chapter Fourteen. We introduce it now only for the practical reason that it's a part of the synastry worksheet, and the information can be conveniently recorded while you are busy plotting the all-important interaspects.

One piece of fine tuning: although we define house cusps precisely, it's more practical to think of them as blurred areas a couple of degrees wide. Once a planet enters that territory, it is in effect thrown forward into the next house. For example, if a woman's Sun lies in 14 Scorpio and her partner's Seventh House starts at 15 Scorpio, it might seem that her Sun falls in his sixth house. Technically it does, but for practical purposes, we would say that her Sun conjuncts the cusp of his seventh house. Why? Because it is so near the cusp that its effects are thrown forward.

Here's our practical rule of thumb, used in our synastry worksheet for the Fitzgeralds: *Whenever a planet is within a degree and a half of a house cusp, its major impact is upon the following house.*

With your synastry grid or worksheet in hand—and with a grasp on the basic meaning of each of the two birthcharts individually—you are ready to dive into the crossfire of astrological intimacy. You've seen how to recognize an interaspect. Now let's figure out how to understand one.

CHAPTER THIRTEEN: INTERASPECTS

Fans of rock music will never forget the band called The Who. From their humble London beginnings in the early 1960s, through their semi-breakup in the early 1980s and beyond, they stretched the boundaries of a new kind of music. Fronted by lead singer Roger Daltrey and driven by the damn-the-torpedoes guitar style of composer Pete Townshend, The Who lifted the spirits of a generation.

The general crashing and banging that is such an elemental part of the music of The Who was not limited to their musical performances. Pete Townshend and Roger Daltrey were notorious for crashing and banging against each other, especially in print. Their infamous feuding nearly broke up the band on many occasions. In many ways they simply seemed not to like each other very much. And yet some force held them together, kept drawing them back into collaboration.

The men were opposites. Townshend: mystical, intellectual, angry, Steppenwolfish. Daltrey: playful, worldly, a classic "teen idol," even well into mid-life. Yet they were bound together. Rage—and fascination. Rebelliousness—and yet dependency. Escapism—but no exit. Immediately upon discovering such paradoxes in a relationship, we begin to think in terms of the *opposition* aspect.

Sure enough, when we look at their birthcharts on pages 158 and 159, that's exactly what we find. Pete Townshend's Moon lies in the fifth degree of Virgo (in his twelfth house.) It opposes Roger Daltrey's Piscean Sun (in Daltrey's third house). A Sun-Moon link—in working with interaspects, that's like striking a vein of gold. No matter what else is going on between the charts, we know those people pluck sensitive chords in each other.

How do we go about unraveling the meaning of such an interaspect?

Our first step is to understand each configuration on its own. Only then are we in a position to begin to unlock their interactions. Translation: you have to understand two people as *individuals* before you can say much that's meaningful about their *relationship.*

Townshend's *soul* (his Moon) is driven by an endless, insatiable hunger for perfection (Virgo). He *feels* profoundly the gap between the real and the ideal, between what he's actually accomplished and what he could have accomplished. He likely experiences that gap quite painfully at times. At best, this lunar configuration drives him toward excellence; at worst, it leads to self-destructiveness, shame and picky annoyances. *Where* is this energy

FIGURE SEVEN

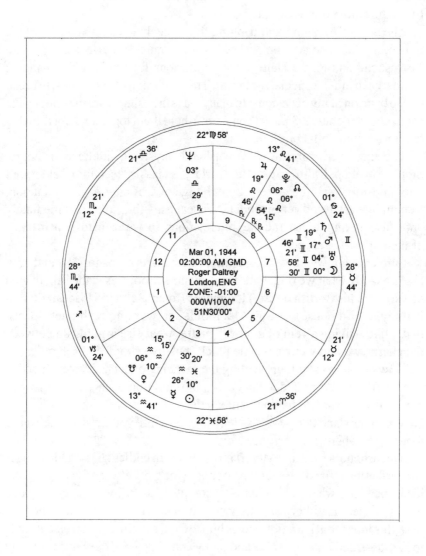

FIGURE EIGHT

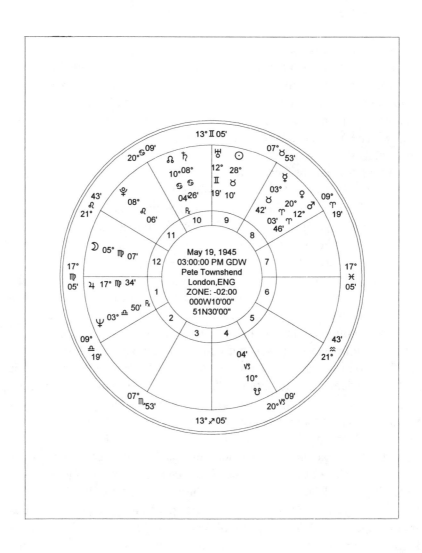

being released? In other words, what house does his Moon occupy? The twelfth—so his lunar soul is hungry for the twelfth house experience of mystical transcendence. He can sense *instinctively* (Moon again) what we might call the presence of God, and he feels a transrational drive to remain in that elevated state. Trouble is, if he falls prey to the self-doubts of Virgo, he can settle for surrogates, such as simply staying drunk or high. To the old astrologers, the twelfth was the "house of troubles." That's an unduly narrow and pessimistic assessment, but it's true that planets there have a tendency to run amok unless they are solidly anchored in what we might broadly think of as spiritual disciplines.

Pete Townshend, in other words, drives himself hard both materially and psychically. If he stays in balance, his accomplishments in both realms can be enormous. But if he fails to keep the shadowy side of the configuration under control, then he falls into moodiness, escapism, and self-punishment, along with a tendency to take out his inner tensions in picky attacks on the people closest to him.

Now put Pete Townshend on the back burner and consider Roger Daltrey.

Daltrey's basic *identity* (his Sun) is shaped by Pisces and expresses itself in the third house, the traditional "house of communication"—and Daltrey sings the lyrics, transmitting The Who's words. Communication is definitely a big part of this house, but *perception* is a better term for it. The goals of the third house are a radical open-mindedness to all types and levels of perception, without any preconceived notions. To a third house Sun, the world is not something to be classified or analyzed or understood or even judged: it is something to be experienced as a vast and endlessly fascinating mystery. Accomplishment and self-evaluation are not so important as a steady diet of interesting new experiences. There are no firm answers, only a plethora of ever-unfolding questions. For a Piscean Sun, the goal is self-transcendence. A recognition of the totality of one's being as something larger than the ego, body and personality. A merging with something greater than the self. That "something greater" might be consciousness, soul, Spirit, the inner self, art, music, the creative process—the list is long, and it's hard to avoid mystical language when discussing Pisces. For Roger Daltrey, even the exploration of consciousness needs to occur in a variety of third house ways, with no final judgments about what he perceives. Both the Piscean Sun (self-transcendence) and the third house (suspension of judgment and need for new experiences) denote a kind of scattering of focus in Daltrey's solar identity. The reason that he is so proficient at playing the role of a public

160

symbol is *not* that his ego is so strong and well-defined, but rather the opposite. Far more than most of us, Roger Daltrey is curious about and sensitive to the undercurrents that shape the mass mind. Ego, as we customarily understand it, never fully formed in him. He can tune into, communicate and mirror those social undercurrents. All in all, we find a sensitive, warmhearted man, devastatingly naked without a well-defined role to play.

What happens when these two men interact—one so hard-edged, driven and critical, one so impressionable, non-linear and inquisitive? Townshend's Moon and Daltrey's Sun are linked by an opposition aspect. Right away, we sense the dual qualities of *tension* and *complementarity* characteristic of this astrological configuration.

On the tension side, Townshend's sharply critical perfectionism can be rough on Daltrey's sensitivity. Meanwhile, Daltrey's "vagueness" and "irrationality" can infuriate Townshend's taste for precision and rigor.

On the complementary side, Daltrey's relative gentleness can perhaps soften Townshend's harshness—on himself as well as others. Daltrey is responsive to collective undercurrents; far more than Townshend, he has an instinct for what people want to see and hear. Townshend, on the other hand, is the consummate craftsman, driven by Virgoan visions of excellence. Had they not met and collaborated, it is difficult to escape the notion that Townshend would have made creative decisions that alienated his audience, perhaps long before he even had one. Balancing that, we must add that Daltrey might have become simply a hack, parodying whatever styles were current. But together they were able to accomplish much more, and not in spite of their differences, but rather because of them.

Shades of gray are the way of the world. Theoretically, the opposition interaspect between these two driving forces of The Who could have worked in blissful, conscious complementarity or in homicidal tension. But in the realities of the human world, we typically find a mix of the best and the worst, and much that lies in between. The astrologer's task, of course, is only to describe all the possibilities, make some recommendations about the higher ground, issue a few warnings about the garbage can, and leave the behavioral choices up to the individuals.

Let's dig a little deeper into the birthcharts of these two musicians, then try to deduce some elementary principles that apply across the board to all interaspects, even those belonging to people who spend less time in the fast lane.

161

The cusp of Roger Daltrey's seventh house is twenty-eight degrees and forty-four minutes of Taurus, and his Moon lies in the first degree of Gemini in his seventh house (the traditional house of marriage). A fortune-teller would say that he was destined to "marry a Taurus or a Gemini," probably an emotional one—the latter is the Moon's contribution. Here's a more modern and certainly more accurate way of phrasing it: Roger Daltrey's soul-intentions for this lifetime involve *healing* (Moon) some very basic issues around *trust* (the seventh house). If he succeeds in that, he has a lot of soulmate business to face, much of it with people who are lunar and Geminian or Taurean (because Taurus is on the cusp of the seventh house). What sort of people would that be? Men and women of imaginative, moody and subjective natures (Moon) who are concerned with Taurean issues (nature, music, security, concrete accomplishment, the body) or Geminian issues (communication, new ideas and information, a fast-paced, interesting lifestyle, a distaste for boredom). If those Gemini issues sound familiar, they should, because we touched upon them when we discussed Daltrey's third house Sun. Gemini, the third sign, has a natural affinity for the third house and for Mercury, the planetary ruler of Gemini, the third house *and Virgo.* (An interesting aside: a youthful quality frequently accompanies strong Geminian, Mercurial or third house placements. We saw The Who in concert a few years ago and were struck by Roger Daltrey's appearance. In his fifties at the time, he had the bearing, the energy and the voice of a much younger man.)

These lunar, Taurean, Geminian soulmates are guaranteed to appear in Daltrey's life at critical junctures, often sending him careening off in directions he could not have anticipated before their arrival—that's basic to a strong seventh house focus too. He must learn to *cooperate* with these soulmates without being *eclipsed* by them. That's the heart of the seventh house terrain: learning to establish equality and healthy, mutual *interdependency* in a long-haul partnership.

Into Roger Daltrey's life, at the tender age of nineteen, storms an emotional, creative Taurean *with a Mercury-ruled Moon and Ascendant*—Pete Townshend—who catalyzed a set of events that would leave an indelible mark upon Daltrey. Where exactly is Townshend's Sun? Near the end of Taurus, less than a degree from Daltrey's seventh house cusp, opposing his Ascendant, and less than three degrees from Daltrey's seventh house, Mercury-ruled Moon. A Sun-Moon conjunction by interaspect! The conjunction is weakened by the fact that it is what's called

162

"out of quality," because Taurus and Gemini are not the same sign. But it is a conjunction nonetheless. We can speculate that the out-of-quality character of the interaspect might have added to the tension between the two men. Conjunctions feel like fusion, and the closeness of the orb here can start to create that feeling—but Earth doesn't fuse with Air (see the discussion of the elements in Chapter Twelve). The more powerful aspect is the opposition of Townshend's Sun to Daltrey's Ascendant, and the simultaneous conjunction of Townshend's Sun and Daltrey's Descendant, the cusp of his house of marriage. The long, creative, albeit "oil and water" partnership between the two men has proven to be the "marriage" the fortune-teller would have prophesied. Its existence is suggested by the nature of Daltrey's birthchart. But its results—those are as uncertain as next year's teenage fad, and linked inextricably to the choices the two men make.

Perspective: an opposition links Townshend's Moon to Daltrey's Sun. Now we add that Daltrey's Moon conjuncts Townshend's Sun, and Townshend's Sun opposes Daltrey's Ascendant and simultaneously conjuncts his Descendant. Astrology predicts what history confirms: their destinies are interwoven. One Sun-Moon linkage is enough to imply the connection. Two, and the Sun-Descendant linkage, make the observation irrefutable.

Let's take this a giant step further.

Although a Sun-Moon opposition is a single configuration, it can be phrased in two ways. Each emphasizes a different interpretive perspective.

   * *Daltrey's Sun opposes Townshend's Moon.*
   * *Townshend's Moon opposes Daltrey's Sun.*

This inversion is far more than a word game. The statements are identical in meaning, but differ tremendously in terms of where they carry our thinking. The first phrasing emphasizes Daltrey's impact upon Townshend; the second, that Townshend impacts Daltrey. Understanding this bipolar flow of interaspectual interaction is the key to unlocking our general formula for all interaspects. Each one of them is a two way street, and a complete understanding only arises when we see them from both angles.

Townshend's Moon opposes Daltrey's Sun. What significance does this have? How does this interaspect feel? Something about Townshend's instincts and emotions (his Moon) flows into the core of Daltrey's personality (his Sun). Townshend floods Daltrey's solar ego with lunar feeling. Daltrey, in other words, always has an amplified emotional response to Pete Townshend, for better or worse. So long as they are together, his solar ego is filled with uncharacteristically lunar qualities, which he receives from Townshend. Put simply, Townshend makes Daltrey moody, even more so than he would be otherwise. He also affects him in such a way that Daltrey's creative imagination is stimulated—that's a Moon-gift too.

We would say that Pete Townshend's effect upon Roger Daltrey is to *lunarize* his Sun.

Townshend's Moon opposes Daltrey's Sun. Roger Daltrey's personality goes straight to Townshend's most vulnerable places, stimulating him to operate in a more active, solar way. Simply said, Daltrey's ego pushes Townshend's Moon into active manifestation. Potentials locked away in Townshend's psychic depths are triggered into active, extroverted development.

Daltrey, thus, has the effect of *solarizing* Townshend's Moon.

Here's our general principle:

When the Sun in one chart touches a planet in another chart, its effect is to solarize the action of that planet—that is, to charge it with solar vitality and inspire it to action. The Sun, in turn, is suffused with the qualities of the planet upon which it is acting. In our present example, the Moon lunarizes the Sun. But Mercury would *mercurialize* it, Jupiter *jovialize* it, and so on. Much of the rest of this chapter is devoted to a close analysis of each planetary transaction from this perspective.

Be careful never to assume that any such process is guaranteed to be dreadful or joyful. Ultimately everything depends upon the attitudes, determination, and level of commitment of the partners. In love, each planet can be a *Gift-Giver*—or a *Thief*. Which will it be? No way to answer that question astrologically. Everything depends upon the generosity, self-awareness, and motivation of the partners.

What if Townshend's Moon had *squared* Daltrey's Sun instead of opposing it? The process would still be accurately described as solarization, but the interaction would now have a different tone. Instead of the *fusion* associated with the conjunction, we would observe the *friction* that's connected with square aspects. In other words, solarization can happen in many ways, some of them harmonious, some of them explosive.

To put it all in subjective terms, we may like it when someone solarizes us—that's typically the case when the process occurs through trines and sextiles. Or we may not like it a bit—more likely the case with squares and oppositions. Those statements are fairly accurate subjectively. But don't forget that being pushed and stretched in love is one of the qualities that keeps a partnership alive, and that too much easiness and comfort often lead to somnambulism.

The general principle: *The planets forming the interaspect determine the developmental issues at stake—solarization, lunarization, and so on—while the specific aspect linking them determines the emotional tone of the process (tension, complementarity, friction, etc.).*

How intense will these processes of "jovialization" or "neptunification" be? Three factors figure in our understanding here.

* First, consider the *degree of precision* of the interaspect. Planets one degree apart from a perfect sextile interact far more vigorously than planets seven or ten degrees away from the perfect sextile.

* Second, consider how centrally each planet figures in the individual birthchart. In other words, if Neptune in one person's birthchart is the ruler of the Ascendant and in a tight conjunction with the Sun, then it's a powerhouse. Any interaspect it forms might prove to be the key to the whole synastry interpretation. On the other hand, maybe Neptune's role in the birthchart is relatively inconsequential. Then its interaspects are correspondingly less significant.

* Third, the intensity of an interaspect has to do with *the intensity of the relationship* itself. If you sit down next to a stranger who mercurializes your Sun, you're fairly likely to start talking about yourself. The stranger's Mercury pumps verbal energy into your solar ego. Should you marry such a person, you might very well write a semi-autobiographical novel. As the relationship becomes more charged, so does the response to the interaspect.

Interaspects are the cornerstones of practical synastry. Here are a few suggestions before we delve into them, one by one:

* Some of the planet-by-planet, "cookbook" interpretations below make reference to the higher or lower archetypes of the signs, so to refresh your memory about them, you might want to consult the Table of Archetypes in Chapter Two, on pages 26 and 27.

* For the following cookbook interpretations, a *flowing* aspect is typically a sextile (stimulation) or a trine (harmony), and a *challenging* aspect is typically a square (friction) or an opposition (tension). Remember, however, that in synastry, oppositions can also mean a romantic feeling of complementarity between two people.

* Conjunctions (fusion) are the most powerful of aspects. To do good work with your clients, it is best to pitch your synastric interpretations at the more flowing expression of a conjunction. However, we strongly suggest that

you think about the more challenging possibilities of that conjunction, too.

* Finally, because we wanted to devote more space in this book to the theories and techniques of evolutionary synastry than to the cookbook interpretations, they are necessarily limited in both length and scope. Please try not to take them out of the context of the chart as a whole, and consider them as guidelines to stimulate your own interpretive processes. We *guarantee* that some of what you read below about your own relationships will be completely wrong—ten interaspects pushing in one direction will overwhelm one pushing in the other direction. Also, for deeper understanding, read the longer description of each interaspectual process before going straight to the particular planetary combination.

An Important Note: *Some planetary combinations appear to be missing below—you won't, for example, find "Venus Mercurializes Mercury." That's because we already covered it under the heading of "Mercury Mercurializes Venus." All the processes are here. If you don't find the interaspect going one way, turn back a few pages and look for it going the other way.*

SOLARIZATION

PLANET: The Sun.
AS GIFT-GIVER: To charge and revitalize.
   To push into active manifestation.
   To encourage.
   To support.
AS THIEF: To eclipse.
   To overwhelm.
   To dominate.
   To burn out.

You are the first astrologer who ever lived. There is no astrological tradition on which to fall back, no preconceived notions about any of the planets, nothing but raw, direct experience. The King appoints you to invent astrology—and offers to cut off your head if you're not suited to the job. With that kind of encouragement you quickly get very creative. The King's first question is, "What is the Sun's significance?" You have three days to answer. You reason: summer is green and full of life; winter is dead and dreary. Cloudy days are sad days. Sunny ones are happy. Plants turn toward the Sun and wither in the shadows . . . you have your answer: the Sun signifies *the life-force itself.*

Now, ten thousand years later, no astrologer would disagree with you. The Sun still means life. It is the purest, simplest symbol of vitality. Energy. The gasoline in your existential tanks.

In synastry, the Sun floods the contacted planet with a tidal wave of energy. Spotlights it. Pushes it into dramatic development.

Is this always an unalloyed good? Not necessarily. Sometimes the Sun's force is overwhelming. Think of it this way: the electricity fails in an unfamiliar room. You need a bit of light to help you find the candles. You fumble in your pocket for a match. All you find is a small nuclear warhead. Now, that'll make a flash, but maybe a bit brighter than what you had in mind. That's exactly the danger with solar interaspects. The impact can be powerful—too powerful.

At its best, solarization can boost the contacted planet to a new level of energy. One who solarizes your Uranus, for example, brings out your natural Uranus qualities—your independence, your capacity for creative, divergent thinking, your free-spirited ability to lead your own life. You'll likely share some distinctly Uranian experiences—like winding up in Paris at two in the morning drinking Pernod with Madonna, when you thought you were only stepping out to buy a birthday card for Mom.

All that Uranian excitement can be wonderful, if you can handle it. The dark side is that maybe the framework of your psychic structure is simply not sturdy enough to cope with this onslaught of boosted (solarized) Uranian rebelliousness. What happens then? The dark side of the planet begins to dominate your behavior. You become eccentric, cranky, unrealistic, stubborn: Uranian disorders.

The rule of thumb across the board with all solar interaspects is that the healthier a response you are making to a planet in your own birthchart, the happier will be your experiences with someone who solarizes it. Why? Because the Sun's action is to vivify, to emphasize, to bring out—and it makes no distinction between your virtues and your blind spots. The Sun simply forces your hand. Maybe that's a gift; maybe it's the work of the Thief, stealing your balance and good judgment.

Sun is identity. Ego. When solarization occurs between two people, one person's ego is imprinted upon some aspect of the other person's individuality. Something of the solarizing person *enters* the other one. Thus, there are two critical dimensions to the process of solarization. The first,

167

which we have just explored, is that the solarized planet is simply pushed to the forefront of an individual's behavior, for better or worse. The second dimension is that the natural qualities of the solarized planet are not merely emphasized; they are also somewhat distorted, taking the qualities of the solarizing person. Something new, something alien, even unnatural, is added to the normal operation of that planet. A new voice, new values, new motivations appear. Thus, to allow one's self to be solarized is to allow another person into one's life in the most central and intimate of ways. That individual's impact, especially in an intense, committed relationship, will prove be huge. Life-shaping. Something of his or her individuality enters you and stays there.

What if you don't like it? Then minimize contact with that person. Other than your making a more conscious response to your own solarized planet, there is no other defense. Mere contact guarantees impact.

In our society we are taught to value independence and personal freedom. And yet love inevitably implies a lowering of defenses, a merging, a willingness to touch and be touched. Solarization—this loving acceptance of another's identity into the fabric of our own being—is an act of ultimate trust. We are changed. The path of our life is turned. Positively, as we internalize our partner's solar identity, our own life-process is fertilized, saved from the kind of psychic inbreeding that occurs if we never learn from anyone, never allow anyone to inspire or surprise us. Negatively, our partner can so dominate us that we lose track of our own course. We can be eclipsed. Humiliatingly, we can be reduced to a mere clone of the other's personality. A puppet.

If you are solarized by someone you love, learn from him, trust her. Let that individual into your heart and mind. Don't worry if you find yourself picking up certain of that person's characteristic gestures or turns of phrase. That's a normal part of solarization. But guard your freedom too. Find a middle course. Listen to yourself as well as to your lover. Let yourself learn. Let yourself be changed. Then make that learning and those changes your own.

If you find yourself in a relationship in which you solarize the other person, be gentle. You probably don't fully comprehend the power you wield, and that makes you extremely dangerous! Recognize that however egalitarian your ideals might be, you still have a vast influence upon your partner's destiny. The planet you touch in that individual is almost like clay in your hands, ready to receive your imprint. Take that responsibility

168

seriously. Imagine yourself to be quietly guiding the development of that dimension of your partner's life. Be a good guide. Not too dominant. Not too stultifying. Not too convinced of your own infallibility. And if your partner seems to be defensive, putting up mile-high walls, consider the possibility that he or she senses the overwhelming solarizing danger in you and is instinctively undertaking a process of self-preservation. Honor that instinct, and back off.

Antonio Banderas solarizes his wife Melanie Griffith's Sun, Uranus, Ascendant, Moon and Saturn. She solarizes his Sun, Uranus, Moon and Jupiter. Their Suns are conjunct in Leo. Here's a grand solar gesture: when she was shooting one of her movies, he sent a white rose to her on the set every forty-five minutes.

SUN SOLARIZES SUN:

Flowing aspects: Sun-energy is ego energy, and that's not a bad thing. Without our egos, we would just sit and stare into space, and without a healthy ego-function, we would never trust ourselves enough to reach very far beyond the refrigerator or the remote control. With your Suns in a harmonious association, there is a natural tendency to energize and encourage each other. That linking force is always there between you. There is a distinct tone of friendship here, of being on each other's team, which is very good news indeed when it comes to longevity in a relationship. Always, however, when ego-energies support each other in this way, you and your partner must be on guard about being too quick to enhance each other's defenses: you might be blind to the same dangers at the same time, which would be less of a risk for people who saw the world more differently. Still, this harmonious connection between your Suns is a classic sign of astrological compatibility.

Challenging aspects: Traditionally, a challenging aspect between two people's Suns was the kiss of death for a relationship, but we're not going to take quite so dim a view. The essential point is that the two ego functions work in very different ways. If you were both computers, one would be a Mac and the other a PC. There can be a clash of values here, since you don't always share basic aims and desires with each other. The good news is that the differences between you two can breed a very wide perspective on life. It can supply you jointly with a formidable array of distinct skills, rendering you a team to be reckoned with—if only you recognize each other's unique "rightness," rather than spinning your wheels with each one trying to turn the other one into something he or she was never born to be. If those ego-wars start, it could get ugly. Each of you could trigger the more shadowy manifestations of each other's solar archetypes. With enough communication and respect, none of that is necessary—but fear of it is what made the old astrologers so nervous about this passionate, tricky combination.

SUN SOLARIZES MOON
Flowing aspects: Here is a peaceful, supportive flow between the stimulating, vitalizing energy of the Sun and the softer, caregiving energies of the Moon. The Sun person has an animating, supportive impact on the Moon partner's spirits, mood, and attitude. This gift of enlivenment flows the other way too, but in a distinct way. Deep in the Moon partner's chest, there are moon-instincts that create a mood or vibration which is extremely nourishing to the Sun person, leading him or her to live a little more gently, to feel the present more deeply, and in general to take better care of himself or herself.

Challenging aspects: There is something about the Sun person's ego that *bothers* the Moon partner, and simultaneously something about the Moon partner's attitude that can have an annoying, stifling effect on the Sun partner's spontaneity and ease about simply being himself or herself. These problems are addressable, but they require two very different kinds of efforts, one from the solar person and another from the lunar person. For the lunar person, the effort lies in getting past a set of reflexive instincts connected with the power that the inner archetype of his or her Moon sign holds over him or her. The Moon person of course has legitimate emotional needs in that regard, which must be honored—but the challenge here is to escape a narrowness of perspective which could blind him or her to the solar person, and to find a way to respect the solar person's basic individuality, which is so charged with the spirit of that particular solar archetype. For the solar person, on the other hand, the challenge lies in rising above a kind of self-centered interpretation of that same archetype, and to temper being true to himself or herself with a little gentleness, caring, and a broader imagination about the care of the lunar person's soul.

SUN SOLARIZES ASCENDANT
Flowing aspects: This harmonious blending of the Sun and the Ascendant is a particularly merry synastric contact. There is something about the Ascendant partner's style that brings out confidence in the Sun person, and

something about the Sun person's basic character that encourages and energizes the showmanship of the Ascendant person. Specifically, the Ascendant person wears the mask of the archetype of his or her Ascendant sign—his or her style automatically takes on that spin as it comes out into the world. The Sun person just eats that Ascendant energy for breakfast, since it inspires the deeper and more effective expression of that person's own core solar archetype. Thus, these two people bring out something close to theater in each other, each one rendering the other one more colorful, effective, and alive. The catch? Well, whenever egos start reinforcing each other, we need to be alert to lies and illusions upon which we unconsciously agree . . . but hopefully some of the more challenging aspects between the charts will flush out those illusions.

Challenging aspects: The inharmonious blending of Sun and Ascendant is a problematic interaspect in synastry. Both Sun and Ascendant are self-centered symbols in general, and there is the possibility of an unseemly ego-war here. There is something about the Ascendant partner's style that rubs the Sun person the wrong way, and something about the Sun person's more narrow, self-centered side that can trigger volatility and "shutting out" behavior in the Ascendant partner. When it gets bad, the Sun person winds up looking like a sorry archetype of that particular Sun sign, while the Ascendant partner resembles a lower archetype of his or her Ascendant— remember to look at our Table of Archetypes in Chapter Two if you need a refresher on the specifics. How can this messy scenario be avoided? Start with the recognition that *pride* is the basic problem here. If the couple feels loving and humble towards one another, they can make soft, open eye contact. If they are caught in the nets of this Sun-Ascendant tension, they can't—their ego-walls are up.

SUN SOLARIZES MERCURY
Flowing aspects: Here is an effortless, uncomplicated connection between the Sun and Mercury, which mightily stimulates the flow of communication. While this doesn't always indicate that two people have exactly the same interests, it often suggests a kind of complementarity between them in that regard. Also, as everyone knows, good communication is one of the basic building blocks of ongoing intimacy, and every indication is that these partners have what it takes simply to understand each other, even if that doesn't always mean agreement on every subject.

171

Challenging aspects: This rather vexing connection between the Sun and Mercury can unwittingly distort the flow of communication within the couple, as if their dictionaries had all the same words but different definitions. While this doesn't always breed catastrophe, it does indicate that particular effort must be made simply to understand each other's meaning, especially when discussing something with emotional charge. One specific point: the Sun person needs to guard against seeming autocratic or closed-minded, while the Mercury person needs to take particular care to choose his or her words efficiently and not overwhelm the Sun person with too much chatter.

SUN SOLARIZES VENUS

Flowing aspects: The Sun partner's basic identity makes a harmonious, enhancing contact with the other partner's Venus. The "love goddess" in the Venus partner is pushed and stimulated mightily in this relationship, filling that person with amorous emotions, an attitude of fondness, and a distinct desire to express all those energies erotically. Meanwhile, the flow back to the Sun partner softens and warms him or her, adding a simple grace to life that wouldn't be there as strongly otherwise.

Challenging aspects: The ego of the Sun partner is operating in a tense relationship with the Venus person's romantic, erotic sensibilities. In intimacy, this is obviously not a comfortable situation, although it does keep a certain quality of intensity alive between the partners. The Sun person needs to cultivate an attitude of receptivity toward the Venus person's natural style of interconnectedness, and also toward his or basic desires regarding how he or she wants to be courted, appreciated, desired—and treated in bed. Conversely, the Venus partner benefits the relationship enormously by emphasizing an appreciation of the Sun person's actual essence, and by not asking him or her to live up to some arbitrary ideal that may have little to do with an authentic expression of the Sun person's true nature.

SUN SOLARIZES MARS

Flowing aspects: There is a fiery tide of positive cross-stimulation between one person's Sun and the other one's Mars. Even with this harmonious interaspect, we need to remember that Mars is the god of war. That doesn't have to mean horrible fights—more like passion in general: there is an abundance of that here. The fights may be glorious, but they tend to be resolved in ultimately useful ways, even if the road to that resolution resembles World War Three. There is also an excellent chance that erotic fire will have a long life in this couple. These two may make each other's blood boil at times; and each person may press all the buttons that the other one has. But in the end there is a fierce loyalty between them—and a heat of the blood that won't go away.

Challenging aspects: There is a fiery flow of irritation between one partner's Sun and the other one's Mars. When the slightest whiff of disagreement is in the air, things can go ballistic. There is something about the way the Mars person breathes that can bring out a haughty, judgmental side of the Sun person's character—at least that the way it looks to the Mars person. Turning it around, from the Sun person's perspective, when faced with even minor discord, the Mars partner is unnecessarily abrasive, defensive, and prickly. Who's right? Both of them, of course. There is passion in this bond, and that's a precious thing. But living happily with it involves learning to tolerate each other's style, and to avoid patterns of pointless emotional *escalation* in the face of life's inevitable skirmishes.

SUN SOLARIZES JUPITER

Flowing aspects: The Jupiter partner is the Sun partner's biggest fan, most faithful coach and loudest cheerleader, while the Sun person inspires the Jupiter person to realize ever-higher dreams and aspirations. There is some danger of these two pushing each other into ego-inflation, but in any intimate relationship, that beats the opposite possibility by a country mile. This is another one of those "crown jewel" interaspects in synastry.

Challenging aspects: There is an expansive, positive, humorous energy between the Sun and Jupiter, even when linked in this tense manner. Where the potential for troubles comes in is that these partners may simply expect too much of each other—and then begin to perceive each other as demanding or overbearing as a result. Humility—an acceptance of each other's humanness—is the key to developing this interaspect in a way where its benefits outweigh its liabilities.

SUN SOLARIZES SATURN

Flowing aspects: The Sun person brings cheer and energy to some brooding and rather lonely parts of the Saturn person's character, while the Saturn person supports a more disciplined, mature side of the Sun person. This flow of energy within the couple, and the potential for a deep, responsible and heartfelt commitment, can grow more obvious and more precious with every passing year, and contribute mightily to the longevity of any human bond.

Challenging aspects: There are serious challenges inherent in the tough connection between the Sun and Saturn, and a kind of unspoken script that must at all costs be evaded by this couple. In that script, the partners polarize, with the Saturn partner becoming the controlling, sober "police officer," while the Sun person struggles childishly and egocentrically against those limits. The frustrations for both people could eventually charge the bond with so much anger and resentment that it would just run out of gas.

SUN SOLARIZES URANUS

Flowing aspects: There is a zany side to the Sun person's character which the Uranus person seems custom-designed to tickle. Meanwhile, the Sun person brings a loosening, unconstrained kind of energy to sharper focus in the Uranus person. There is a wild card element connected with this interaspect—unusual, unexpected events abound, and both partners are made somewhat stranger by the relationship, at least in the eyes of conventional folks.

Challenging aspects: There is a rebellious dimension to the Uranus partner's character which the Sun person seems tailored to exaggerate. Meanwhile, the Uranus person brings a more autocratic, self-centered kind of energy to sharper focus in the Sun person. The obvious problems that kind of interaction might create can be minimized by one simple remedy: each partner needs to guard the other one's right to have a life outside the relationship and independent of it. They would do well to have some separate projects, friendships, beliefs: in short, anything that alleviates the fear that one morning they will awaken as Siamese twins, or locked in the ancient drama of the autocratic king and the self-righteous rebel.

SUN SOLARIZES NEPTUNE

Flowing aspects: The easy interaspect between the Sun and Neptune is a sweet astrological building-block, and one that can contribute profoundly to the sense of depth, magic and sacredness in a relationship. Rather automatically, it gives a taste of soul-connection, but with a little conscious cultivation that connection can become profound. The Sun person needs to let the Neptune partner impact their shared spiritual life in a guiding way, while the Neptune partner benefits from the Sun person's practical instincts about anchoring dreams and visions in the concrete world of everyday reality. Once that flow starts, the bond can become a living experience of the presence of Spirit, growing more precious by far than any metaphysical dogma, religion or philosophy.

Challenging aspects: The tense connection between the Sun and Neptune is fraught with possibilities of misunderstanding. It is as if neither partner sees the other one very clearly. That can frustrate both of them in ways that are hard to trace or analyze, leading to ungrounded positive expectations of one another which are inevitably dashed—or to ungrounded fears and misgivings which breed hurt out of thin air. There is a spiritual core to this relationship, and it offers the higher road: the partners don't need to share a religion, but benefit deeply from sitting together in silence, attuning to each other without the veil of words between them.

SUN SOLARIZES PLUTO

Flowing aspects: Pluto is never an easy planet. It's the part of us that is equipped to deal with difficult psychological realities. With a Pluto-Sun interaspect, a relationship takes on a penetrating, exacting quality, even with the flowing aspect. There is something about the Sun person that brings out the psychoanalyst in the Pluto partner in particular, although that's really a two-way street. The partners can and probably will help each other grow wiser and saner, although naturally the process will have its exhausting, edgy moments. Still, there's an underlying sense of being on the same side, and nothing brings people closer than a tradition of successfully risking stark naked, terrifying honesty.

Challenging aspects: Again, Pluto is never an easy planet—it's the part of us that delves into regions that are touchy psychologically. With a difficult Pluto-Sun interaspect, relating takes on an intense, probing, exacting quality just as with the flowing aspect above. However, now there's a much more explosive, volatile note. There is something about the Sun person that brings out a shoot-from-the-hip psychoanalyst—accurate maybe, but not gentle—in the Pluto person in particular, although once the so-called insights start flying, it may be hard to determine who shot first. A real bottom line here is that the partners can be of inestimable value to each other in terms of the long process of growing wiser and saner. Succeeding gracefully in that process depends mightily on both parties knowing when enough is enough, when their own passions have distorted or sensationalized their insights into one another, and when a smile and a hug are more therapeutic than a thousand supposedly constructive criticisms.

LUNARIZATION

PLANET: The Moon.
AS GIFT-GIVER: To sensitize.
To deepen.
To comfort.
To inspire.
AS THIEF: To emotionalize.
To upset.
To smother.

What does moonlight mean? Let the poet in you answer, not the rationalist. The Moon is a creature of the night. To decipher its significance you must respond from the night-side of your own being, from your unconscious, from your dreams and fantasies. Your day-self is useless here. It speaks another language, a more rational one. With the Moon you must *feel* the answer.

The Moon's meaning? Magic. Intuition. Passion. True enough—even Hollywood's Moon-worshippers understand that much astrology.

Go further. There's more here than kisses in the moonlight. The ghostly sickle shining through the bare trees on a black, windy night. Tattered clouds. The old graveyard. A cat startles at—nothing. What do you feel? Something other-worldly. Something surreal, vaguely ominous. Something unsettling. That's the Moon too.

Once, in the minds of men and women, there was a Goddess. She was the Mother, and she was feminine. But she wasn't Betty Crocker. Long ago the feminine was a primal power, equal in every way to the masculine, but different. She ruled a distinct domain: the night. And she wasn't always gentle. The realms of dreams and nightmares. The realm of birth and death. A realm of tender nurturing—and of inexplicable, lightning-swift violence. The Goddess, in other words, had teeth. As humanity lost its sense of the primordial feminine, a madness of unchecked, unbalanced power corrupted the decisions of active, aggressive, solar people, and a corresponding madness of powerlessness overtook the lunar poets, dreamers, and visionaries.

In synastry, if we are to understand the process of lunarization, we must recover the old, half-forgotten Moon goddess. We must recover our ancient respect for the powers of the night.

176

When the Moon in one birthchart contacts a sensitive point in another person's birthchart, that zone of life is flooded with emotion. That planet is made to *feel itself* as never before. Awareness itself is boosted. You might never think of your teeth, until you have a toothache. You might never consider your back, until someone is kind enough to scratch it. That's the kind of impact lunarization generates. All the inner, subjective processes associated with the lunarized planet are heightened. Much that was unconscious or subliminal suddenly flashes into awareness. *The volume is turned up on all the emotions, pleasant or unpleasant, sane or certifiably bonkers, connected with that planetary function.*

Is lunarization a positive effect? Stirring up the unconscious is not terribly difficult, any more than opening Pandora's box was difficult. The problem lies in the next step. Now that all those demons and pestilences are stirred up, what are we going to do with them? One of the best psychotherapists we know warns his clients in the first session: Are you *sure* you want to undertake this process? Are you confident you know what you are getting into? The same can be said for lunarization. It's potentially healing—and potentially very spooky.

The Moon is the Mother. In lunarization the Moon wants to nurture the planet it touches, bringing it from weakness to strength, from infancy to maturity. It wants to comfort that planet, to fill it with vision and imagination, to make it happy. How does Luna go about realizing her aim? Crudely, sometimes. She's like a person who believes passionately and dogmatically that psychotherapy is the answer to any question. "What do you feel? Why do you think you feel that way? How do you feel about feeling that way?" It's easy to lampoon this process—but it works. It succeeds in opening up the unconscious: Pandora's box again. Trouble is, the Moon might find the box is harder to close than it was to open.

A trusted friend lunarizes your Venus, filling your bonding mechanisms (Venus) with emotion, helping you to feel your intimacy needs more deeply, nurturing your capacity to enter into ongoing, mutually supportive associations. So far, so good. Perhaps in so doing your friend helps you get in touch with some fundamental vacuums in your primary relationship. That too can be helpful, maybe. But let's not be naïve: everything depends on what steps you take as a result of gaining that knowledge. Perhaps you bring that wisdom home to your mate and begin to work actively on deepening your relationship. That's a practical example of the Moon's *Gift*. But maybe the *Thief* twists the healthy pattern, sewing only childish seeds of discontent—you leave your marriage or wreck it with an affair, only to realize that, in this case at least, you were better off without the Moon's "wisdom."

Our key principle is that the Moon goddess has teeth. The unconscious mind is a stormy, dangerous sea. We must sail those waters if we are to become wise. But we must sail them cautiously and know when to make for harbor rather than challenging hurricanes in our pea-green boat.

Positively, as we are sensitized to our own inner processes through lunarization, we do become wiser—that is, happier, less driven by neurotic, unconscious dimensions of our character, kinder toward ourselves. Our lunarizing partner might help lead us to new levels of self-understanding, new insights into our foibles and mad hungers. That's the good news.

The bad news is that, in lunarization, we can be driven *regressively* back into childishness and narcissistic emotionalism. Why? Because lunarization empowers the unconsciousness to a dangerous degree. Irrational fears, self-damaging "needs," and developmental glitches rooted in our early years—all these can be energized, lifted from the crypt like some ancient zombie we thought we had successfully laid to rest. Then we deal with them. Or they deal with us. In short, lunarization can *infantilize us*—turn us into whining, demanding children.

If you are lunarized by someone you love, prepare for a very emotional relationship. You'll know tenderness and caring as never before. You'll also likely embarrass the pants off yourself from time to time with moodiness, irrationality, and childish tantrums. Let yourself be mothered, but don't allow yourself to be smothered. The child's task is to grow up, and that's a delicate, ironic process. The child needs the mother and also needs *not* to need her. Your lunarizing partner creates an incubator for your growth. Use it, but know when to climb out into the world, dry your eyes, and take a grown-up stand.

If you find yourself in a relationship in which you lunarize your partner, prepare to be very vulnerable. Like any mother, you will be clobbered sometimes. Whether or not you put it into words, the aura of your being exhorts that person to feel, feel, feel. Perhaps he or she feels love and admiration for you. Wonderful. That's easy to get used to. But perhaps he or she also feels anger and frustration. Maybe decades ago mommy forbade that third bowl of ice cream, and those enraged, violent, childish emotions are now released—at you! You are the "psychotherapist," at least in this part of your relationship. No escaping that role. So be a good one. Know when to love actively. And know when to back off. Know when to encourage emotion, and when to balance emotion with adult rationality and responsibility. Above all, don't fall into the trap of encouraging your partner to feel and grow and explore—and then leap down his or her throat the instant that unsettling process jostles you.

The late Linda McCartney's Moon lunarized Paul McCartney's Venus, Ascendant, Moon and Mercury. In turn, he lunarized her Moon, Venus, Ascendant, Jupiter and Mars. By all accounts their union was a happy one; they not only worked together but "nested" well, raising a family, and she persuaded him to become a vegetarian.

MOON LUNARIZES MOON
Flowing aspects: This interaspect suggests that the couple's hearts and souls share a fundamental understanding or sympathy with each other. Their moods are harmonious. By instinct and reflex, they comfort and nourish each other. The Moon is a domestic symbol, and generally when this interaspect exists, two people tend to live together pretty easily, sharing a kind of attitude that resolves a lot of lifestyle questions before they even pop up. Attitude is really the key concept here—and, happily, these partners' attitudes are similar enough to allow an enviable kind of ease and familiarity around each other. This is another one of those "crown jewel" aspects in synastry.
Challenging aspects: The Moon is the heart, and so having two partners' Moons in tense interaspect is not a very reassuring sign. It suggests that the couple's hearts and souls may at times lack a fundamental kind of understanding or sympathy with each other. There's a clash of mood and attitude, and the conflicts which arise are knotty and hard to address because they're really *symptomatic* of these underlying differences. If the couple lives together, separate spheres of influence in the domestic environment can avoid a lot of unnecessary friction. The Moon is moody by nature, and not very rational regardless of its pretenses in that department. When this harsh Moon contact is starting to go sour, there are warning signs. Each person will start to display his or her dark Moon archetypes. If that happens, first the couple should take time away from each other. Then they should sit and listen to each other without interrupting, knowing that emotional heat might run high enough in these matters to cancel out what's best about each person, if they let it.

MOON LUNARIZES ASCENDANT

Flowing aspects: Here we have a glorious, happy-go-lucky spirit of accord between two critically important astrological features. The Ascendant partner's outward style is perfectly suited to encouraging the deepest, shyest innermost heart of the Moon person to come forth and express itself. And that feels good to both parties, even if they don't think about it. Turning it around, the Moon person seems to have a behind-the-scenes nourishing, supporting impact on the Ascendant partner's poise and self-assurance, helping him or her fully inhabit his or her body and natural style. This is a bedrock, positive interaspect in synastry.

Challenging aspects: When this interaspect goes sour, the Moon person can seem like a moody wet blanket to the Ascendant person, while the Ascendant person can seem like a shallow, posturing phony to the Moon person. The solution? First, realize that no one is being difficult on purpose. The Moon is often quite unconscious of its own reactions, and of how its attitude can cast an off-putting pall over a relationship. The Ascendant is someone's natural style, not a fake one, and the Ascendant person needs to adopt that style or feel naked in the world. Second, the Ascendant person needs to cultivate tolerance and humor, especially an ability to laugh at oneself—and express that perspective to the Moon person. Third, they both need some places, either in the relationship or with friends, where both that Moon and that Ascendant can be expressed without restraint.

MOON LUNARIZES MERCURY

Flowing aspects: When it comes to the gentle art of simply talking to each other, there's an effortless, relaxed fit here. That may seem like a small thing, easily taken for granted, but there are many relationships that founder for the lack of what comes so naturally here. A certain amount of homely, forgettable chatter is one of the daily building blocks of this relationship, and given half a chance these partners will fascinate and comfort each other that way for hours.

Challenging aspects: There is an awkward mismatch between Moon and Mercury here. Translation: something doesn't work easily between the Moon person's heart and the Mercury partner's mouth. This doesn't imply any negative or destructive motivations on either part, only that the Moon person needs to strain to find the soul behind the Mercury partner's words, while the Mercury partner needs to make an effort to hear the words that the Moon person doesn't actually say out loud, but which are there in body language, attitude, and vibrations.

MOON LUNARIZES VENUS

Flowing aspects: The Venus person's cuteness charms the Moon person's soul, while the Moon person's natural warmth of heart nourishes, encourages, and supports the Venus person's capacity to relate. For the sheer sweetness of human love, it's hard to beat gentle links between the Moon and Venus. They help us forgive. They represent a spirit of trust and deep closeness. Their joy—and their curse—is the peace they bring to a relationship. Neither the Moon nor Venus are particularly rational, nor particularly versed in how to set boundaries—the spirit of generosity and forgiveness that reigns here overrides all that. This couple definitely benefits from a few challenging interaspects too, just to keep from sweetly falling asleep in each other's arms.

Challenging aspects: The Moon always represents a rather shy, inward part of the human psyche: it is our vulnerability, after all. Venus, on the other hand, reaches out and connects whenever it can—it is the human impulse toward intimacy. There is something about the way the Venus person approaches the Moon person romantically that brings out something closely akin to shyness in the Moon person. This can be frustrating for both people, and is only resolvable if the Venus partner is patient, while the Moon partner commits to the slow, scary process of opening up. The good news is that *any* contact between Venus and the Moon represents one of the deepest and most instinctive kinds of human bonds imaginable.

MOON LUNARIZES MARS

Flowing aspects: The easy connection of Moon-feelings and passionate Mars-energy is a torrid, ardent, and inherently unstable combination, even with the flowing aspect. The Moon person encourages and enhances the development of the Mars partner's sexual confidence and fire, which is of course good news. The Mars partner, meanwhile, possesses a kind of native eroticism which seem custom-designed to go right to the Moon person's mammal brain, filling the Moon person with passion and also the lunar urge to make a nest and protect it. The instability of the aspect arises from the fact that the Moon and Mars are both emotional and inclined toward irrationality, which is great when it comes to the expression of love, but explosive when conflicts arise. Even with the easy astrological aspect between them, this couple's blood is simply heated in every sense by this relationship.

Challenging aspects: The Moon person stimulates the development of the Mars person's sexual confidence and fire, which is good news for physical intimacy. But there's a paradox here: that intensification of the Mars partner's nature can backfire, leading that partner to seem overly aggressive either sexually or in negotiations with the Moon person. Meanwhile, the Moon person experiences a flow of Martial energy to his or her Moon, which can create a chronic mood of touchiness. This is not an easy aspect when it comes to the mellow elements of domestic life for which couples naturally hope. Balancing that, it is a strong vote for the long-term survival of this couple's desire for one another.

MOON LUNARIZES JUPITER

Flowing aspects: The easy connection between the Moon and Jupiter adds two welcome elements to the larger synastric tapestry: a good mood and a sense of comfort. Above all, Jupiter-Moon links are *happy* ones. Putting it under the microscope, inside the Jupiter partner there's a clown who equips that person extremely well for simply putting a smile on the Moon person's face. At the same time, the Moon person seems uniquely gifted when it comes to nurturing and encouraging the Jupiter person's expansiveness and self-confidence, as well as supporting his or her dreams and aspirations.

Challenging aspects: An uneasy interaspect between the Moon and Jupiter isn't terribly problematic—neither symbol has rough enough edges to create serious difficulty. It's mostly a question of good intentions gone awry. The Moon person may feel uncomfortable when the Jupiter partner misunderstands a passing mood and tries to cheer him or her up, while the shoe may be on the other foot when the Moon person encourages the Jupiter partner in areas where that person doesn't feel he or she really needs it or about which that person simply doesn't care.

MOON LUNARIZES SATURN

Flowing aspects: A wonderful partnership exists between the Moon and Saturn here, even though the two symbols are as different as night and day. Basically, Saturn is practical while the Moon is emotional. These two qualities complement each other nicely, allowing the development of a pattern of practical support, unquestioned loyalty, reliability and trust between the partners. Like some fine wines, such astrological contacts grow more delicious given a few years in the bottle. Everything else being equal, this interaspect correlates with a long-lasting capacity simply to live together, interwoven, accepting and content.

182

Challenging aspects: This tense connection can easily create a very particular kind of misunderstanding: Saturn is practical while the Moon is emotional, and those parts of the human mind speak very different languages. The risk is that when the Moon person needs nurture and kindness, the Saturn partner might be inclined to offer stern, clear counsel—well-intended, on target, but poorly timed. And of course we can turn it around: the Saturn partner might need concrete commitments, clarity and reason, and feel that the Moon person is offering fuzzy reassurances more suitable to the needs of a child. Patience, translation, and careful listening will help.

MOON LUNARIZES URANUS

Flowing aspects: There is a wild, merry, unpredictable element connected to the easy aspect linking the Moon and Uranus. Regardless of how steady either person is as an individual, when they are together, spontaneity and mischief are in the air. Often, on the surface, it may seem as if the Uranus partner is the instigator, but one needn't be Sherlock Holmes to detect the encouraging smile on the Moon person's face. Some of the unconventionality promised by this interaspect may be evident in the decoration of any home they might share.

Challenging aspects: From the Moon person's point of view, the Uranus partner is a chaos-monster, bringing unwelcome elements of disorder, upset, and perhaps plain messiness into an otherwise happy home. From the Uranus mate's point of view, the Moon person has a closed, conservative streak that could use a little shaking up—and which is hard to resist baiting. A sense of humor on both sides goes a long way to helping this tense interaspect along.

MOON LUNARIZES NEPTUNE

Flowing aspects: The Moon and Neptune represent two of the least boundaried parts of human consciousness, and their easy interaction is extremely conducive to feelings of deep, undefended intimacy and empathy, as well as a demonstrably uncanny psychic connection—examples of extra-sensory perception very likely abound in this couple. This splendid state of affairs seems uniquely gifted when it comes to the Moon person's nurturing and encouraging the Neptune mate's dreams, aspirations and creative imagination.

Challenging aspects: Neither the Moon nor Neptune guard themselves very easily, at least not in the context of a trusting relationship. On top of that, their interaction is often associated with uncanny psychic connections.

183

Examples of knowing what the partner is thinking before that person speaks can be abundant. Where the difficulty of the interaspect comes into the picture is when we realize that humans need boundaries, a sense of personal space, even perhaps secrets. The level of primordial soul-intimacy here can be so intense as to create resistance and fear. There is almost no way to avoid some degree of mutual soul-invasion. A few judicious hours or days apart can work wonders, especially during periods characterized by "growth experiences" in the relationship.

MOON LUNARIZES PLUTO

Flowing aspects: A hug or a kiss can help people feel intimate and connected, but there's little that will carry a couple further in that direction than honest talk about painful, difficult, or embarrassing subjects—and that's the domain of Pluto. There is something about the way the Moon person is wired that seems to disarm the Pluto person's defenses, opening him or her up. So long as they both see to it that it doesn't become a one-way street, this supportive, intense interaction between the Moon and Pluto helps create an unparalleled sense of psychological intimacy.

Challenging aspects: Psychological truthfulness is strong medicine and needs to be tempered with kindness on the part of the Pluto person here. The Moon person should try to remember that ultimately one of the kindest, most loving actions anyone can take is to risk triggering the partner's natural defenses by telling the truth as he or she sees it. Our point is not that the Moon person is so defensive or that the Pluto mate is so nasty . . . only that they can look that way to each other when the darker side of this difficult interaspect is showing its face.

ASCENDANTALIZATION
(accent the third syllable)

AS GIFT-GIVER: To socialize.
   To stimulate.
   To stylize.
   To "egg on."
AS THIEF: To trivialize.
   To caricaturize.
   To make a fool out of someone.

There is a French expression for feeling good—*"Je suis bien dans ma peau"*—that can be translated as "I am at ease in my skin." Those words spring directly from the part of human awareness that astrologers call the Ascendant. What does it mean to be at ease in our skins? It implies well-being, certainly. But more: poise. Feeling centered. Self-acceptance.

To learn about the Ascendant there is no need for lofty meditations or for long hours spent peering into astrology texts. Instead, just go to a party—and the more brash and phony the party, the better. Watch how people act—and the word "act" is of course appropriate under such circumstances. Who can be "real" with the music blasting and the drinks strong, while circulating through a horde of posturing strangers? Acting is the only option.

Some of us like parties. Some of us don't. There's room in the world for all of us. But in the everyday course of living, all of us are compelled to streamline our psyches in a way that allows us to relate as actors in the immediate social environment. If we do that well, we feel "at ease in our skins"—and we make a strong response to our Ascendant.

Someone might have Leo or Libra rising. Everything else being equal, such a person will likely appear to be right at home in social situations. Those are friendly, expansive signs—good at parties unless the rest of the birthchart pushes strongly in the opposite direction. But what if a person has a more introspective sign on the Ascendant, such as Scorpio or Cancer? He or she can still be "at ease in his skin," just more quietly. Not everyone in the room needs to be the life of the party. The trick with the Ascendant is not to be the smooth-talking fashion model surrounded by a gaggle of admirers. Rather, it has to do with a self-accepting knowledge of one's own natural style, a capacity to use that style effectively in social circumstances—and a sure fix on the difference between an honest adaptation to social reality and mere posturing and phoniness.

In synastric interaspects the Ascendant plays a significant role. In keeping with our general formula, the significance of the Ascendant is to *ascendantalize* whatever planet it touches in a partner's birthchart. In other words, qualities associated with the Ascendant—poise, style, social confidence—are grafted onto the ascendantalized planet.

A woman is an eighth-house Pisces with Cancer rising and Saturn in the first house: not exactly a social butterfly. Yet she has Mercury in Virgo in the third house, which is a highly verbal, communicative feature. Clearly there is tension here. How does an introvert with strong language skills resolve that paradox? Perhaps she doesn't! Perhaps she simply feels bottled

185

up inside herself. Perhaps she's silent for long periods then bursts out with spells of pointless nervous chatter. But maybe her response is stronger. She makes peace with the inwardness, capitalizes on her vivid imagination—and becomes a talented fantasy novelist. And she's still quiet at parties.

She befriends a woman who ascendantalizes her Mercury. Initially, as their friendship is forming, the impact of this interaspect is simply to encourage the novelist to speak. She talks with uncharacteristic spontaneity about book plans, her feelings, the weather, politics. Quite unintentionally, through practice with this ascendantalizing friend, she improves her spoken verbal skills. Before long, she notices that when the two women are together in a group situation, she feels better about herself. More at ease. Words come to her more quickly. She knows what to say. She's urbane, entertaining, informative, interesting . . . and she's received a Gift.

In common with all astrological processes, ascendantalization has few guarantees. The Thief can strike just as easily as the Gift-Giver. The ascendantalized planet is pushed into more active, social operation. That's all we know for sure. At best this encourages its poise and maturation. At worst the Thief can take over, simply trivializing the contacted planet, pushing it into premature, unconsidered self-expression. Our novelist can find that whenever she's with her friend in a social situation she tends to open her mouth before her brain is engaged, with embarrassing results.

What determines whether we'll see the Thief or the Gift-Giver? It boils down to how solid a response the ascendantalized individual has made to the planet being contacted. If our introverted novelist has been taking her writing seriously, polishing her craft, feeding her intelligence with curiosity and openness, then she'll likely have reason to welcome ascendantalization. Her Mercury is healthy; one push from her friend and it shines. On the other hand, perhaps the novelist has been lazy. Perhaps she's settled for clichés. Perhaps she's not a novelist at all—there were less self-actualized possibilities in her birthchart. Then, when that starved Mercury is pushed, its illness is made apparent to anyone who's listening.

Italian director Roberto Rossellini ascendantalized Swedish actress Ingrid Bergman's Sun, Venus, Pluto, Mars and Saturn. She ascendantalized his Mercury, Moon, Pluto and Sun. She scandalized the world of 1949 by leaving her husband for Rossellini, and by having a child out of wedlock with him in 1950. At least at first, he gave her an opportunity for more challenging film roles than her previous ones. Their marriage lasted from 1952 to approximately 1957.

186

ASCENDANT ASCENDANTALIZES ASCENDANT

Flowing aspects: The Ascendant is the mask we wear in the world. There's nothing necessarily phony, shallow, or hypocritical about it—it's just our style. This symbol doesn't provide the deepest *psychological* information, but it's still quite significant: skin isn't very deep either, but we'd be hard to recognize without it! With these partners' Ascendants in an easy interaspect, their styles get along swimmingly. Their outward expressions are harmonious and allow for an easy flow of body language, daily rhythms, and stylistic meshing between the partners. They probably even look good together. This is a great assistance when it comes to sharing intimate physical and emotional space with another human being, but paradoxically, it's often so reflexive that we are unconscious of it, and perhaps don't celebrate or appreciate this almost primeval familiarity deeply enough.

Challenging aspects: There's nothing necessarily phony, shallow, or hypocritical about the Ascendant—it's just our style, our mask. The tension here can work almost unconsciously, through body-language and subliminal cues, producing frustrating feelings that have no clearly understood source. It's a lot like how tiring it can be to hang out with people from a foreign culture and not much command of English, even with good attitude all around. If that annoyance isn't traced to its source and discussed in a non-judgmental way, then pretty soon each person may start wearing the lower archetypal version of his or her mask, rather like a dog growling to say, "Back off!"

ASCENDANT ASCENDANTALIZES MERCURY

Flowing aspects: Both the Ascendant and Mercury operate pretty close to surface of the psyche, the Ascendant being our outward style and Mercury the way we communicate. The potential of a ready flow of communication and a shared language exists in this couple. This interaspect works like being presented with a terrific set of tools when building a house. The task still lies ahead, but the essential communicative equipment is there.

Challenging aspects: With one person's Ascendant in tension with the other partner's Mercury, both people need to be wary of a quick, slippery slope that leads to serious misunderstandings. Sometimes the Ascendant person will make a gesture or express an apparent attitude that throws the Mercury partner into interpretations that are misleading. Or the Mercury partner's word choice or tone of voice will do the same thing to the Ascendant person.

The point is, this kind of thing can happen at the speed of light and create the experience of problems where none really exist. Each person should slow down and make sure he or she heard what other one really meant to say. Ask, don't assume!

ASCENDANT ASCENDANTALIZES VENUS

Flowing aspects: The effortless flow of support and reassurance that courses between the Ascendant and Venus is one of the most precious links in synastry. Venus is deeply connected to the human ability to feel fond, loving emotions. The Ascendant is all about self-expression. With this easy, enhancing interaspect, each person simply makes it easy for the other one to express tenderness, verbally, in acts of simple kindness, and erotically as well. That latter gift is particularly delightful, in that it helps maintain the sexual spontaneity and inventiveness that is of course one of the greatest challenges facing lovers who are committed to each other for the long haul.

Challenging aspects: This interaspect is no disaster, but it does require some effort at communication, lest little stylistic differences lead to big misunderstandings. The Venus person's ways of signaling affection and erotic openness don't always get through to the Ascendant person. It's not the Ascendant person's fault, or even that he or she is being thick-skulled, although it will certainly look that way to the Venus partner from time to time. The Ascendant person, on the other hand, may sense that his or her right to behave in a spontaneous way and without self-consciousness is being challenged. That's especially sensitive in sexual areas. The answer lies in directness. The pitfalls boil down to minor resentments, misinterpretations, and frustrations held inward, festering.

ASCENDANT ASCENDANTALIZES MARS

Flowing aspects: Exhilaration, aliveness, and vivacity abound when ardent Mars energies are pushed into outward manifestation through contact with another person's Ascendant. The cross-fire of these two forces adds speed and candor to the relationship, and spices it with the hint of sexuality, even in mundane interactions. Astrology always involves balancing a lot of forces, but this aspect contributes strongly to the necessary expression of routine annoyances. That may make for more frequent spats than a more tranquil couple might have, but the bottom line is that this way is healthier than saving up mutual vexation, then letting it all blow up months later in a great

188

Apocalypse. A sense of rough camaraderie, and humor mixed with deep loyalty, is the soul of this planetary contact.

Challenging aspects: There is often a prickly, stormy quality to this relationship. Something about the Ascendant person's natural style of self-presentation just seems to get the Mars partner's goat. The key to living peacefully with this astrological aspect lies in remembering that the tension is stylistic, and doesn't have much to do with either mate's real essence. Compromising one's essence is always a catastrophe in a relationship, but failing to compromise on trivial questions of style is just egoism and self-righteousness. The Mars partner needs to lighten up, and the Ascendant partner to show some diplomacy and empathy.

ASCENDANT ASCENDANTALIZES JUPITER

Flowing aspects: Here's a blessing for simple joy—a happy interaspect between the Ascendant and Jupiter. There's a delightful tendency toward mutual support and expressions of encouragement. These two have a touching kind of faith in each other, and they show it. Each is the other one's coach. Psychologically, that pushes both partners toward higher levels of self-actualization. But it's not just psychological: synchronistically, it can also trigger the welcome phenomenon we call luck.

Challenging aspects: The Jupiter partner sincerely wishes the Ascendant partner joy and success in life and tries to be supportive of that. But sometimes the Jupiter mate's sense of what the Ascendant person actually needs or wants is skewed. That means the intentions are laudable, but the effect may feel distorting or even overbearing to the Ascendant person, who may then respond with touchy body language. That of course will seem ungracious to the Jupiter partner, who meant well. For both partners, the key here lies in recognizing the pattern and putting the cards on the table.

ASCENDANT ASCENDANTALIZES SATURN

Flowing aspects: Interaspects involving the planet Saturn aren't usually full of fireworks, but they are absolutely precious in the context of long-term relationships. In fact, their full glory generally takes time even to appear. Here, the Ascendant person slowly, steadily helps sustain the development of the Great Works in the Saturn partner's life, while the Saturn partner brings a persistent, firm pressure to bear upon the maturation of the Ascendant person's outer character, so that the Ascendant person's natural qualities of authority, quiet self-confidence, and dignity increase year by year under the subtle impact of the Saturn mate's expectations and vision.

Challenging aspects: When the Ascendant person is simply expressing himself or herself spontaneously, there is something in that person's outer mask which presses the Saturn partner's buttons, leading the Saturn person to respond with a repressing, judging, or controlling attitude. Naturally, that response annoys the Ascendant person, who may persist rather self-righteously in the behavior, which was in fact innocent—but we can't say the same for the self-righteousness. If this relationship isn't going to be plagued with childish conflicts, the Saturn partner needs to loosen up and be more tolerant of the Ascendant person's style, while the Ascendant person needs to be willing to make some superficial behavioral adjustments out of love, generosity and respect toward the Saturn person.

ASCENDANT ASCENDANTALIZES URANUS

Flowing aspects: There's a gleeful, playful zaniness to the mutually-reinforcing connection between one person's Ascendant and the partner's Uranus. They seem to egg each other on in unconventional directions, supporting a "who cares what anyone thinks" attitude. They can have more existential liberty as a team than they might on their own. The trick, if one is necessary, lies in remembering that reality contains some hard limits: keep the ratio of mischief in reasonable proportion to the possible proximity of police officers!

Challenging aspects: The Ascendant person triggers rebellious, defiant qualities in the Uranus person, that in the worst case scenario may incline the Uranus person toward petulant, childish tantrums. In so doing, the Uranus person may put the Ascendant person on the defensive—which in this case would manifest as semi-intentionally "dummying up" and failure to make truly open, respectful, intimate contact. Treating the Uranus partner as a child, in other words. And then the whole sorry system can go into loop-mode, reinforcing itself. In that scenario, conflicts arise that might lead an outside observer to imagine that the couple is more asinine than it is actually is. A healthy dose of common sense, mutual respect, and cooling off goes a long way here.

ASCENDANT ASCENDANTALIZES NEPTUNE

Flowing aspects: The partners are blessed with the magical ability to look into each other's eyes rather than merely at them. That may sound subtle, but to the human soul it is a huge distinction. The trick here lies in remembering to make time for this kind of communion, because it is one of the basic nutrients of the relationship. And, while this may seem unfair, in practice it will be mostly up to the Ascendant partner to initiate those quiet moments of spirit-connection.

Challenging aspects: The manifestations of strain between the Ascendant and Neptune are subtle, but we need to be alert to them. In a nutshell, the Ascendant person can seem to make the Neptune person spacier or perhaps even more passive than that person would be otherwise. This can lead the Neptune person toward acquiescence initially, then toward an overreaction to that problem. The Neptune partner may accuse the Ascendant person of steamrollering behaviors of which the Ascendant person is probably innocent, at least in terms of intentions.

ASCENDANT ASCENDANTALIZES PLUTO

Flowing aspects: Revealing talk about serious psychological material is an essential part of any truly intimate relationship, but it is never a totally comfortable process. Still, these partners have the potential of doing very well in that department. Their styles blend well in that regard, but like most flowing aspects, the secret lies in remembering to take advantage of the strength—and in that, the Ascendant partner will often be the one to take the initiative. Whatever issues the Pluto partner has are going to be pressed into expression by the relationship.

Challenging aspects: Working through serious psychological material—childhood wounds, sexual issues, karmic ghosts, and so forth—is a critical part of any truly intimate relationship, but it is also a scary process. These partners have a big Plutonian element operating between them, which suggests they have work to do in that department. Their styles don't blend very well there. Each person needs to make adjustments. Specifically, the Ascendant person needs to commit to the highest degree of genuine openness and honesty which he or she is capable of attaining. Meanwhile, the Pluto partner must drop a certain "psychoanalyst" persona that he or she might adopt when frightened, and temper wisdom about the Ascendant person with humility, gentleness, and simplicity. They'll bring out the very worst in each other sometimes. The good news is that, with enough forgiveness, the worst—which was there anyway—can be healed.

MERCURIALIZATION

PLANET: Mercury.
AS GIFT-GIVER: To inform.
    To excite intellectually.
    To enliven.
    To encourage speech.
AS THIEF: To confound.
    To fluster.

In her wonderful book, *The Faces of Science Fiction*, photographer Patti Perret quotes one of the genre's grand old masters, Fritz Lieber: "I occupy one of the half billion or so stations in the speech web of story-telling, gossip-trading, observation-sharing, English-speaking minds . . . It's my job to keep my station in good working order, busily receiving and sending . . . and with my antennae burnished and honed to catch, embellish, reweave, and retransmit hints of the strange, the mysterious, the wondrous."

We don't know Fritz Lieber's birthchart, but it's clear that he is a master of Mercury. This is the planet of data-transfer. Pure information, coming and going. "Intelligence" is a key word here. So are "speaking" and "listening." But most central is that miracle-seeking, wonder-loving inner state we call *curiosity*.

In *mercurialization,* the contacted planet is asked to *think.* That's the heart of the process. How is such cogitation encouraged? By giving the planet something to think about! Information is everything. When we're bored, we're dull. Kids growing up in environments lacking stimulation have been proven to grow up less bright and alert than kids who are given access to varied experiences, interesting objects, changing viewpoints. Mercury floods the planet it touches with ideas and experiences. Sometimes it argues. Sometimes it recommends books. Often it simply plays mind games. Not infrequently it shows up with tickets to a movie—or tickets to Lisbon.

Mercury encourages the planet it touches, once stimulated, to speak its mind. First it enriches the information environment. Then it presses for speech, usually through dialog and questions.

A man has Saturn in the tenth house (career; community). A tennis buddy mercurializes it. Here's what that buddy says: "You mentioned the other day that you were interested in incorporating your business. I happened to have some literature about that; here it is. By the way, I had a friend who incorporated. They had to pump his lungs—he nearly drowned in a sea of paper. But I know this other guy who really should have incorporated. He's a house painter. Or was. He spilled a can of paint on this old lady's marble-top antique chessboard. Belonged to Napoleon. Or so she said. Anyway she sued him for everything but his toenails . . . so, what do you think you're gonna do?"

Mercury the Thief operates by never shutting up—or by attempting to put prefabricated thoughts into the other person's head. With its verbal agility it can *fluster* the planet it contacts, tie it up in knots. *It can win arguments, even when it's wrong.* The Gift-Giver shares what it knows, then listens. The Thief insists upon agreement.

If you mercurialize someone you care about, first consider what planet your Mercury contacts in that person. What issues does it represent in that individual's life? The answer, of course, depends not only upon the name of the planet, but also upon its sign and house and its role in the larger patterns of the birthchart. Once you've understood the big picture, then realize that you have access to certain information or certain ways of thinking that can be extraordinarily useful in that department of your partner's life. Share them. Engage the partner in dialogue. You're not a teacher, exactly—you're more like a library. Stimulate, inform, ask hard questions, facilitate clear thinking as best you can. But don't try to enforce any decisions.

If you find yourself in a relationship in which you are mercurialized, start by accepting that unless you're an Enlightened Being, the contacted planet in your birthchart is not all-knowing. It has a blind spot or two. There are important realities it's not seeing clearly, and your partner can help. He or she has the information, or at least the method for finding it. The difficulty and the delight are that you must discover the missing pieces of the puzzle together. Think of that partner as a library—but a library in total chaos. The books are scattered. There is no card catalog. Half the volumes are written in extinct languages. To find what you need you'll have to search together, comparing notes, talking, exploring, questioning.

The poet Percy Bysshe Shelley mercurialized the chart of his wife, Mary Shelley. His Mercury stimulated her imaginative Neptune through a sextile interaspect and simultaneously complemented her shadowy Pluto through an out of quality opposition. Would she have written *Frankenstein* without him? Or did he help give voice to that creature from her Neptunian-Plutonian depths—just as her Neptune and her Pluto fed gutsy, transcendental vision into his glib Mercury?

MERCURY MERCURIALIZES MERCURY

Flowing aspects: With their Mercuries in such a stimulating interaspect, a gush of language and ideas courses naturally between these partners. As always with flowing aspects, the key lies in really using the tool. Chit chat is fine, but the real soul of this treasure lies in what happens when this couple takes the time to turn off the television and really gets into sharing ideas—talking about books they've read, provocative films they've seen, ideas they've been entertaining. It's a delight, and one that can cement their connection.

Challenging aspects: A torrent of stimulating language and ideas is trying to break through between these partners. But as always with challenging aspects, obstacles must be surmounted before the higher ground can be attained. The bottom line is that these people have very different mental and communicative styles. If they really listen to each other, each will see things that otherwise would remain invisible. They need to shun cheap ways of avoiding each other—turn off the television, in other words—and really start talking to one another. Build the skills, and the Mercury-link turns from a problem to a source of enlightenment.

MERCURY MERCURIALIZES VENUS

Flowing aspects: The Mercury person's style of communication supports the Venus person's ability to verbalize emotions, creative visions and relationship needs. Each person benefits a lot from this encouragement, finding new levels of intimacy that way. Meanwhile, there is a softening, graceful flow of tenderness from the Venus partner which helps the Mercury person feel interesting and sexy. And of course anything that enhances the quality of communication in a relationship is priceless.

Challenging aspects: The Mercury partner's style of communication may interfere with the Venus person's ability to feel romantic or erotic openness. Whether it's a question of the Mercury partner talking too much or too little is hard to say, but as with most problems in a relationship, it's misleading to lay the whole thing on the Mercury mate's doorstep. The Venus person may be behaving in too nice or tolerant a way, rather than simply expressing what is or isn't working for him or her. If the Venus person changes that, he or she may be quite surprised at how receptive the Mercury partner turns out to be.

MERCURY MERCURIALIZES MARS

Flowing aspects: This easy connection suggests a kind of playful, sassy vibration expressing itself verbally between the partners. It may occasionally

194

go a bit over the top in terms of the Mars person's teasing and the Mercury partner's kind of setting himself or herself up for teasing, but basically this is a lively, mentally stimulating planetary combination and one of the treasures of this relationship.

Challenging aspects: This edgy connection between Mars and Mercury may lead to suddenly, unintentionally escalating tiffs. When that happens, each may blame the other, but an outside observer would hard pressed to say exactly who had started the war—it all happened so fast. Both partners need to be aware of this volatile dimension of the relationship, and choose *moderate language* instead of spectacular, over-the-top one-liners that work better in movies than they do in real life, between real people, with feelings that can get hurt—and claws that can scratch back.

MERCURY MERCURIALIZES JUPITER

Flowing aspects: Humor is precious and abundant between these partners. Life contains situations where we either laugh or we cry. These two excel at taking the merrier road. More seriously, the Mercury person's ideas support and inform the Jupiter mate's dreams, while the Jupiter mate's faith deepens the Mercury person's mental, intellectual self-confidence.

Challenging aspects: The Mercury person may perceive the Jupiter partner as overly fixed in his or her opinions, as if that person tends to pontificate. Meanwhile, the Jupiter mate may view the Mercury person as overly critical or nitpicky when it comes to his or her ideas, dreams, and speculations.

MERCURY MERCURIALIZES SATURN

Flowing aspects: The Mercury person feeds the Saturn partner stimulating ideas and useful information that often open him or her up to liberating possibilities, helping the Saturn mate get out of stuck places. Simultaneously, the Saturn partner has a steadying, grounded, realistic impact on the Mercury person's mental creativity, helping to keep him or her on task.

Challenging aspects: Communication faces some blockages here. To get past them, the Mercury person needs to focus on staying grounded, undistracted, and realistic, and on using language efficiently. Meanwhile, the Saturn partner helps things along by allowing the Mercury person space to speculate, and not being quite so quick to point out minor inconsistencies, difficulties, or irrelevancies.

MERCURY MERCURIALIZES URANUS

Flowing aspects: The intellectual and mental cross-fertilization between these partners is one of the Wonders of the World. They bring out each other's innate genius, sprinkle it with wit, and encourage its expression and development. At the simplest level, this is plain fun. At higher levels, they can generate tremendous creativity together.

Challenging aspects: There's a communicative hair-trigger between these partners in which a simple conversation can flare into disagreement in three seconds. One of the best ways to get beyond the problem may sound like a chapter from Miss Manners: each person needs to resolve never to interrupt the other one! That simple courtesy will take half the teeth out of the tension.

MERCURY MERCURIALIZES NEPTUNE

Flowing aspects: Some of the conversations that these partners have with each other would be pretty hard for an outsider to follow. They have a kind of psychic link that seems to transmit unspoken paragraphs of information, when all that's actually said out loud is a word or two. This makes for a feeling of closeness that's really quite enviable; to take it over the top, the couple needs lots of quiet, meditative time together. They bring a lot of joy into the bond through sharing creative projects.

Challenging aspects: Communication between these two can be muddied. There is something about the Neptune partner which nonplusses the Mercury partner, leading the Mercury partner to lose track of his or her train of thought. What really triggers the problem is when the Neptune partner is actually woolgathering, even when his or her appearance suggests rapt attention. The Mercury partner seems to pick up that vagueness subliminally, and get derailed by it.

MERCURY MERCURIALIZES PLUTO

Flowing aspects: Verbalizing our most vulnerable, psychologically-charged places is never an easy thing to do, but there is an admirable Mercury-Pluto chemistry between these partners which facilitates it. The usual caveat about flowing aspects applies: they often lack dynamism and must therefore be developed consciously—otherwise, the energy will just sort of sit there, manifesting as idle gossip, or merely as something like a shared interest in murder mysteries. What conscious development means here, in practice, is that the Mercury partner will need to initiate such conversations intentionally, and the Pluto partner will benefit both of them by going along with the process, adding his or her uncannily penetrating insights.

Challenging aspects: Verbalizing our vulnerability and our issues honestly is never an easy thing to do. While these partners have a desire to do that, they also have a Mercury-Pluto tension that makes it harder. First, a psychological fact: an impulse toward defensiveness is absolutely natural when defended places inside us are scrutinized. With that said, here's the key: the Mercury person's defenses revolve around talking too much and too cerebrally, while the Pluto partner's defenses revolve around hiding behind the role of self-appointed psychologist, or simply clamming up. Now add one more ingredient: getting to the heart of real Mercury-Pluto truthfulness always involves surrendering one's defenses.

VENUSIFICATION
(Ve-NOOSE-ification)

PLANET: Venus.
AS GIFT-GIVER: To attract.
    To refine.
    To warm.
    To soothe.
AS THIEF: To seduce.
    To manipulate.
    To lull.

Males have played a disproportionate role in establishing the myths and symbols upon which Western (not to mention Eastern) culture is founded. One effect of that historical twist is that the planet Venus is almost universally viewed as a pretty woman. Ask ten men—five thousand years ago or today—to invent an image that conveys attractiveness, juicy irresistibility, and seductive warmth. What do you get? Nine of them come up with something not far from the goddess Venus: feminine, curvaceous, misty-eyed, draped in a sexy marble Greco-Roman negligee. (The other fellow is gay, and may God bless him too.)

You can hardly blame the boys. But if the balance ever shifts and women become the dominant symbol-weavers, you can safely predict that Venus will be packed off to Sweden for that famous operation . . .

Attraction: with Venus, that's the key. When someone venusifies you, there's an excellent chance that you're going to like the sensation. How does it feel? That depends upon which planet in your own chart the other person's Venus is contacting. If Venus contacts your Mercury, your mind is attracted. You find that person fascinating. If he or she venusifies your Neptune, then your sense of magic and wonder is alerted. Should Venus contact your Saturn, you will likely be drawn in by Saturnine feelings—that person might fill you with a combination of longing and respect, as if he or she represented some unattainable ideal.

The sexual world is treacherous in many ways, full of two-legged predators. Most of us, as a result of an accumulation of disappointments, hurts, and fears, gradually accrete a protective shell. Naïvely, some of us imagine the shell to be bad. Cynically, others imagine it to be good. A better, more neutral word might be "inevitable." However necessary that shell might be and however inevitable its acquisition, one observation is certain: finding someone with whom we can drop the shell is one of life's most blissful experiences.

Venus melts the shell. When we are venusified, we immediately sense warmth in our hearts, trust, understanding, interest, attraction, as if some great magnetic void has opened up between us, pulling us in, drawing us together.

At best our being is engaged in that most healing of human activities: *loving.* In fact, apart from basic Sun, Moon, Ascendant linkages, strong Venus contacts are perhaps the single most common astrological features in happy sexual unions and lasting friendships. Simply liking each other is essential if any two people are going to survive the bumps and wrinkles of intimate human interaction. Strong Venus links come nearer to guaranteeing that kind of affection than any other kind of planetary configuration.

So where's the catch? Have you ever really liked someone, really trusted, really opened yourself—and gotten nailed to the wall? We thought so. Looking back, would you say that the catastrophe stemmed from misunderstanding and wishful thinking on your part, exaggerated by some form of misrepresentation on the part of your partner? If you can identify with this scenario, you need no introduction to Venus the Thief.

The old saw "love is blind" offers helpful insights into Venusian interaspects. If someone venusifies you, it is as if that mere man or woman were suddenly surrounded by a sparkling aura of wonderfulness. Violins swell in the distance. Intoxicating mists rise up from somewhere down around your socks. Before you know it, you get attached. Your thinking is not as clear as it might normally be. You want to see that person as the embodiment of all that is decent in the universe. This is a mixed blessing, or mixed curse, if you prefer. The up side is that you get a flash of something approaching unconditional love: a spirit of generosity, a quickness to forgive. And that's a fertile growth medium for genuine commitment. The down side is blindness. If you are venusified and if that person's motives are predatory or simply whimsical, you've really let the cat in with the mouse.

If you venusify someone, strive to represent yourself honestly to that person. He or she expects a lot of you, probably more than you can deliver in the long run. Soften the blow in advance with the disciplines of truth.

The rock band The Rolling Stones have never been nominated as paragons of virtue, nor have they sought to appear that way. The undercurrents of violence and recurrent elements of sexism in their music have alienated a lot of people. Yet there is irony here. Due to various cultural toxins, lasting friendship between men is often rare, and yet Mick Jagger and Keith Richards have quietly carried the torch as pals for half a century, never publicly mythologizing their relationship or capitalizing on it, and yet successfully weathering together the storms and temptations of fame, divorces, corporate politics, mid-life crises, wealth, changing musical styles, and sundry legal difficulties, not to mention Keith's long destructive bout with narcotics. Unsurprisingly, when we compare the two men's birthcharts, we find rampant venusification. For starters, the Venuses themselves share a sextile interaspect. Beyond that, Jagger's Venus conjuncts Richards's Moon and trines his Mercury, while Richards's Venus opposes Jagger's Mars and squares his Jupiter, Mercury, and his Pluto. Those Venusian interaspects are of course relevant to the fact that their partnership is artistic as well.

VENUS VENUSIFIES VENUS

Flowing aspects: You could hardly ask for a more elemental astrological aspect of affection, fondness, and warmth between two people. Typically, this harmony extends into other Venusian areas: complementary tastes in music and art, and similar senses of courtesy and social behavior.

Challenging aspects: A tense, uncomfortable association—and yet with a strong element of attraction inherent to it. There are frustrations in to this aspect: the partners have different romantic styles. Sexually and romantically, they often make radically different assumptions. The heart of

199

the difficulty can be understood more precisely if we think about the clashes between the archetypes for each person's Venus sign. They have agendas and values that aren't naturally complementary. Still, it's important to keep perspective here. The deep, core erotic energies in both people are linked—that's what Venus is all about, after all. There is passion, both creative and sexual, inherent to the tensions we describe.

VENUS VENUSIFIES MARS

Flowing aspects: Classically, Venus and Mars represent feminine and masculine sexuality. While nowadays we're not so quick neatly to package people according to their genders, it's still quite relevant to observe that when the archetypal male meets his female counterpart, the pheromones get pretty thick! This harmonious aspect between Venus and Mars is as erotic as they come, and suggests a high level of comfort and spontaneity, not to mention enthusiasm, in the sexual department regardless of whatever else might be going on between the people. An interesting twist is that the Venus person will be pulled toward more traditionally feminine roles of receptivity in this relationship, while the Mars person will be pulled in the opposite direction—independently of their physical genders.

Challenging aspects: Venus and Mars, in the classical traditions, represent feminine and masculine sexuality, although we're not eager to define a person's nature too strictly according to his or her gender. The inharmonious aspect between Venus and Mars still represents a strong link between these sexual forces, and promises a strong initial erotic reaction between these partners. Whether it lasts depends on the rest of the charts, as well as how they handle the tensions inherent to this aspect. The Venus person will be pulled toward more traditionally feminine roles of receptivity in this relationship, while the Mars partner will find himself or herself pulled in the opposite direction, into more masculine assertiveness and heat. The Venusian person may feel bumped by the "animal" sexuality of the Mars person, while the Mars person may feel disrespected by the "prim" Venusian.

VENUS VENUSIFIES JUPITER

Flowing aspects: In traditional astrology, these are the lucky planets, so having Venus get along well with Jupiter definitely strikes a cheery note. The basic drive of Jupiter lies in its capacity to *encourage,* so we find that there is something about the Jupiter mate's energy that encourages the Venus person's basic romantic drives and sensibilities, sexual confidence, and the capacity to express them. As always, the aspect works both ways, so we also find that the Venus person's kindness and love tend to have a very supportive impact on the other person's Jupiter, which is to say his or her self-confidence and sense of being in a position to be generous.

Challenging aspects: These are the benefic planets of traditional astrology, so having any kind of connection between them strikes a hopeful note, even when the aspect linking them is a difficult one. There is a feeling of tremendous *promise* in this relationship. That promise has a valid basis, but both people need to work with care toward realizing it. The bugaboo here is *expectations.* They may be too high, and lead to a tiring cycle of inflation and deflation in terms of whether the relationship is working at any given moment. Both partners benefit from accepting—and expecting—each other's human faults, and maintaining awareness of the limits on how much fulfillment one person alone can bring into another's life.

VENUS VENUSIFIES SATURN

Flowing aspects: Saturn is serious. It's not a planet of wide-eyed romance. But it is the planet of commitment and of deep-sworn vows. A harmonious link between Venus and Saturn suggests a sober, reflective quality in this bond. In an easy, generally unobtrusive way, the Saturn partner has a maturing, stabilizing impact on the Venus person's sexuality and relationship skills. Meanwhile, the Venus person can charm his or her way into some very guarded, cautious parts of the Saturn person's character. This combination breeds longevity and promises that are kept.

Challenging aspects: A tense interaspect between Venus and Saturn calls for considerable, skillful effort from both people. The good news is that Saturn aspects correlate with commitment and longevity in relationships, and any contact with Venus can be a big help in that department. The bad news is that Saturn is also about emotional blockages and control-issues. On the simplest level, there is something about the Saturn partner that seems to inhibit the Venus partner's romantic and sexual responses. The Saturn partner may need to loosen up and just let the Venus person be himself or herself a little bit more. On a more complicated level, the Venus person needs to recognize that his or her own issues around trust might blind him or her to the Saturn person's many gifts. The Saturn person's behaviors could then be misinterpreted as more inhibiting or controlling than they really are. Untangle that one, and the deeper, bonding elements of this aspect are free to express themselves.

VENUS VENUSIFIES URANUS

Flowing aspects: The planet Uranus is astrology's wild card, full of unpredictable elements and long-shot mayhem of both the enlivening and frightening sort. Here, the accent is on the merrier side of the equation, as Uranus throws a supportive aspect to Venus. As long as the couple remains in this relationship, the Venus person's sexuality and romantic propensities are going to be stretched and made more novel, as the Uranus partner simply pushes the Venus partner in that direction. In return, the Venus person has a gentle, civilizing impact on the "wild child" inside the Uranus person, calming and reassuring a part of that person's inner being which might otherwise tend to bolt.

Challenging aspects: Uranus is the wild card, bringing lightning bolt strokes, unexpected developments, and sudden changes. Here, the accent is on the jagged side of the equation, as Uranus throws a challenging aspect to Venus. Each person faces some hard learning from the other. For the Venus person, there are lessons having to do with allowing the Uranus partner freedom and autonomy—and not being too quick to interpret the Uranus person's desires in that department as personal rejections or betrayals. For the Uranus partner, the lessons have to do with realizing that there is a part of his or her being that is spooked by the compromises that real commitment entails, and that he or she needs to stop rationalizing and either accept some of those compromises, or elect a solitary path.

VENUS VENUSIFIES NEPTUNE

Flowing aspects: Neptune is the planet of higher love, the mystical, soul-gazing sort. With an easy interaspect between Venus and Neptune, there's a wonderful potential for a kind of soul communion here that goes deeper than the flesh, deeper than psychology and emotions—and yet manages to include those layers most wonderfully too. The rub? Well, there is one, and it can be serious. Even a taste of that garden is intoxicating. Afterwards, anything less feels like robbery. For these partners, there are two challenges: one is learning to create the time and space that are conducive to magic. The second challenge lies in learning to see those high moments as Gifts of Grace to be appreciated, not some kind of cosmic entitlement program, to be resented when it fails to appear on schedule.

Challenging aspects: There is a lovely delicacy to any contact between Neptune and Venus, even a difficult one, as we observe here. Together, these two planets represent a fusion of forces that lucky lovers understand far better than any moralizing bishop: spirit and flesh, sex and higher consciousness—*the genital magic of the soul.* That kind of wonder is quite available to this couple, but their access to it is unstable and requires a lot of attention. The bottom line is that to maintain that depth between them, each person needs to be very wary of toxic *illusions* poisoning their trust of one another. Unfounded jealousies can abound here, as can gross misunderstandings and misinterpretations of each other's attitudes toward the relationship. As is so often the case, maintaining the essence of the higher path depends on clean, timely communication and grounded reasonableness.

VENUS VENUSIFIES PLUTO

Flowing aspects: There may be an easy interaspect here, but it's helpful to remember that these two planets aren't naturally very friendly toward each other. Pluto is about hard psychological truth. It is challenging and confrontive, while Venus is in all things more moderate. The Pluto partner brings a kind of confrontive intensity to bear on the Venus person's relationship patterns, instincts, and history—a quality which the Venus person may not appreciate every minute of the day. Still, this exchange works better than we might expect, and the end result is that the Venus person gradually becomes more savvy, psychologically naked, and honestly communicative, while the Pluto partner learns some necessary lessons about patience, courtesy, timing, forbearance, and humor.

Challenging aspects: Fireworks, due to this tense interaspect, exist here, and Venus and Pluto aren't naturally very friendly to each other in the first place! Pluto is always about hard psychological truth, delivered clear and cold. Venus is far gentler. The Pluto partner brings a confrontive, challenging intensity to bear on the Venus person's relationship patterns, instincts, and history. This intensity can push the Venus person harder than the Pluto person realizes, at least until the Venus person flares. If this interaspect isn't handled with patience and a sense of humor, there is danger that the partners will damage each other in psychologically and spiritually serious ways. Yet if this probing energy is handled with tolerance and forgiveness, one end result is that the Venus person can become increasingly wise and articulate about areas in which he or she is wounded. Another result, just as central, is that the Pluto partner can learn some necessary lessons about patience, forbearance, and humility.

MARTIALIZATION

PLANET: Mars.
AS GIFT-GIVER: To excite.
    To embolden.
    To arouse.
AS THIEF: To terrorize.
    To irritate.
    To enrage.

Passion. Adrenaline. Heat. Fire. Those are Mars words. Feel them in your body and you'll feel the ambiguous relationship the human spirit has with the red planet. We love it and hate it, fear it and seek it.

A passionless life. A passionless marriage. The phrases feel like indictments. Or maybe death sentences. Yet passion frightens us. We turn from it—and then look back longingly. We pay dearly for it—and then smother it as quickly as we can, just to control it.

The Martial thermostat has only two settings: freezing and boiling. That's the difficulty with the planet. Feast or famine. Too much intensity. Or too little.

Imagine that you and I are caricatures of suburban values in the 1950s. We share a back fence. We're both out there, weeding our tomatoes, gossiping about another couple in the neighborhood. "I've known them for fifteen years. I tell you, those two have the best marriage I've ever seen—fifteen years, and they've never once had a fight." You nod your head with a faraway look in your eyes. In this scenario, of course, we both privately compare our own relationships unfavorably to that of our allegedly blissful friends.

Nowadays, hopefully, we're a little smarter. We might say, "Fifteen years without a fight! *What are they saving up?*" And if we're a little smarter still, we might add, "And how well do they know each other?"

Intimate conflict is a thoroughly miserable experience. That much is certain. But if undertaken fairly and honestly, it can also be a form of communication. It can break up the icy veneer of lies and half-truths that begin automatically to build up in any bond that's more than a few months old.

Like most experiences that threaten us, Mars—and martialization—is a process fraught with taboos. There are certain observations we're not supposed to make, certain common human behaviors we've all agreed to ignore. Scratch an old tomcat behind the ears. Stroke his back. He stretches, luxuriates—and then bites you. Why? He's aroused sexually. And he responds violently. Fighter pilots have occasionally spoken of getting erections as they flew into battle. Go to the typical movie. What do you see? *Sex* and *violence.* Why are they so often linked? A sexy man or a sexy woman often exudes a certain undefinable aura of danger. Why?

Mars is the common denominator. All those energies are Martial. If astrology is the wiring diagram of the human mind, we learn that passion and rage—sex and violence—*run on the same circuit.*

As we write these words, we feel tremendous resistance in ourselves, as if we are not supposed to be saying these things. And yet the trick we must learn if we are going to deal effectively with shadowy issues is never to go halfway and then get paralyzed with fear or "morality." We must always go further, deeper.

No sex without violence. That is our taboo principle. A fool might take this idea as a vindication of rape, brutality, and sadomasochism. Most "good" people are likely experiencing a degree of shock at reading such smut in a nice astrology book. But please go further: "violence," in the Martial sense, takes many forms. *It goes without saying that physical violence has absolutely no place in any healthy sexual relationship.* It kills trust, and without trust love dies. The same can be said of emotional violence. But there is another kind of violence: *honesty.* Honesty— when it hurts to say it and it hurts worse to hear it. Honesty that confronts a person's precious defense mechanisms and cherished lies.

A couple has contracted that uniquely modern disease: drifting apart. He's deeply involved in his career. She's getting into astrology in a big way. Nominally they are supportive of each other, but deep down there are angers and fears. Naturally their sex life has begun to reflect the distancing that's taken place in their marriage. One night it all boils over. All their "goodness" flies out the window. All the tension that's built up between them gets released in one incendiary fireball. But they hang in there. The fight is ugly, but honest. It takes time and they both bleed, but the conflict finally gets them down to the truth. She's afraid that, in light of his worldly success, he's losing respect for her. He's afraid that, in light of her interest in astrology, she's thinking of him as a psychological or spiritual cripple. It takes four hours of hell for them to rip away that numbing veneer of politeness that was eating away at the passionate heart of their marriage. But it's worth it. That night they make love, and it's the best sex they've had in months. Why?

Because in the world of healthy adults, *good sex and unchallenged defensive blockages are mutually exclusive.*

When someone you love martializes one of your planets, you can count on conflict developing there. This statement is not nearly so pessimistic as it sounds. You need that conflict. That planet is not as alert as it needs to be. There is something it fears to see, fears to learn, some truth "so terrible" that an awful lot of the planet's energy is locked up in defensiveness. When the healing begins, you'll probably feel for a moment as if your martializing partner has turned into your enemy, or at best as if he or she is misguided. Maybe there is misguidance. Maybe there is cruelty. That's possible. But maybe there's truth, too, a truth you'd rather not hear. Control your fear. Control your rage. Listen and judge. At worst you hear an untruth. That's not so bad: correct it. At best you restore to your partnership that dangerous, delicious, passionate edge of shared growth.

Should you find yourself in the martializing role, remember that whatever planet you touch in your partner is touching you too, right in your Mars. No matter what the identity of the other planet in the interaspect, your Mars is being stimulated. So take a moment to mistrust yourself. Passion distorts, usually by magnifying: the person who's merely in a bad mood, through the eyes of passion, becomes The Most Negative Person in the World. The one who's left his underwear on the floor becomes The Filthiest Pig Who Ever Walked the Earth. Reflect a moment before you speak. You probably see a truth, and you probably should share it, even if it won't be popular. But watch how you phrase it. Watch your tone of voice. Resist that hilarious, devastating one-liner that's sure to rankle. It might work beautifully in a comedy of manners; but it won't fly in the bedroom. No need to be overly gentle. But don't be foolishly extreme either.

Demi Moore martializes Bruce Willis's Mars, Venus, Pluto and Saturn, and he martializes her Sun, Venus, Mercury, Neptune, Ascendant, Moon and Saturn. If we use whole sign aspects, he martializes every planet in her chart, and every planet in her chart pushes his own Mars into more active manifestation. Perhaps this emphasized dynamic of martialization contributed to their eventual divorce.

MARS MARTIALIZES MARS
Flowing aspects: Mars, as the god of war, is inherently a prickly planet, so when we say that the Mars functions in these partners get along well, we need to recognize that this is a complex matter. There is definitely a lot of

206

wonderful stuff in this kind of link: lots of bodily passion, fierce loyalty to each other, the capacity to support each other brilliantly in crisis situations. There is also a way in which each warrior eggs the other one on . . . to war! This adds volatility to the relationship. And perhaps that is the inevitable price of passion.

Challenging aspects: Friction between the gods of war: the mythic imagery speaks for itself here. Mars is always connected with the touchy, flammable, even nasty side of human nature. With this tense interaspect, a simple, chronic element of annoyance exists between these partners. The truth is that each one fears the other's anger—and each deals with that fear by responding with preemptive anger to the sight or even the prospect of anger in the other partner. The results are predictable, but so is the shape of the answer. Each person needs to learn to say "I am scared" one more time . . . *before* launching the warheads.

MARS MARTIALIZES JUPITER

Flowing aspects: This merry connection between Mars and Jupiter has a robust, jovial air about it. The Jupiter partner has an expansive impact on the Mars person's vigor, erotic enthusiasm, and general animation, while the Mars person challenges the Jupiter person to stretch further, trust himself or herself more, and to ask for more from life—and especially from the relationship. There is a feeling of high animal spirits about this connection, and that's a precious ingredient in the physical side of love.

Challenging aspects: There's friction here which can definitely lead to hot sparks flying into the tinder box. In bad moments, the Mars person perceives the Jupiter person as operating in high-handed, superior kinds of ways—and that perception infuriates the Mars person to an unreasonable degree. Meanwhile the Jupiter person sees the Mars partner as petty, nasty over trifles, and chronically peeved, which may lead the Jupiter partner to preach at the Mars person—and we know how the Mars person will react to that! This is a silly loop of ego-driven behavior. Each person should call it what it is, humbly recognize his or her own part in the stupidity, and learn to laugh at it.

MARS MARTIALIZES SATURN

Flowing aspects: These two planets are the bad guys in traditional astrology, but it's a bum rap. Mars is connected with anger, but also with desire and erotic delight. Poor Saturn is often saddled with notions of frustration and heaviness—but it's also the planet of commitment and maturity. With Mars getting along so well with Saturn, there's wonderful astrological support for this couple's being able to work through personal differences in a spirit of respect and reasonableness. Then there's the gravy: Saturn promises to sustain the sexual passion that drew them together in the first place.

Challenging aspects: The bad guys in traditional astrology again—and with their tense interaspect, the partners need to stay alert to dangerous dynamics between them. In a nutshell, the Saturn partner may unwittingly turn the Mars person into a time-bomb by cunningly controlling and undercutting his or her anger, sexuality or general rambunctiousness. Of course, then the water just builds up behind the dam, with obvious results—and one less predictable one: post-explosion, the Saturn partner would retreat into his or her own darker Saturn dimensions of coldness, control and distance. That retreat then loops into re-igniting the Mars person's fury.

MARS MARTIALIZES URANUS

Flowing aspects: Since both Mars and Uranus have short fuses and tend to egg each other on, we can expect that colorful moments abound between these partners. The interaspect certainly isn't fundamentally about peace, but there's a playful spirit of teasing and rivalry here that keeps the interaction lively. In the long run, both people will experience markedly more adventure and surprise in their lives due to this zesty chemistry, provided they're careful not to hide their more tender sides behind a facade of lusty comradeship that leaves no room for love's softness.

Challenging aspects: Both Mars and Uranus are edgy, and in these two charts, the two planets tend to annoy each other—a touchy situation. Superficially, this combination tends toward outbursts that are more smoke than fire, and don't usually last very long. More deeply, though, the partners need to be aware of the *attrition of trust and ease* that can arise in the kind of relationship in which an explosion might happen at any moment. Getting to the roots of the friction is helpful, and basically here they are: the Uranus partner's need for freedom and space is something that the Mars person needs to accept more graciously, while the Uranus partner needs to improve his or her skills at remaining emotionally present when the Mars person has a gripe.

MARS MARTIALIZES NEPTUNE

Flowing aspects: Animal passions (Mars) and mystical propensities (Neptune) are trying to link here. Even though there is a supportive connection, that sacred sexual fusion is not always an easy goal to reach. Still, these partners feel its magic calling them. Deep, sustained eye contact and a freedom from any prim physical inhibitions are the indispensable keys to tapping into this treasure of an astrological connection. Tantra, in the framework of commitment, may be helpful.

Challenging aspects: Neptune is the Mystic and Mars is the Warrior, so these two planets don't start out with much natural sympathy. In this couple, their friction is exaggerated by a tense aspect, so there's potential for trouble here—and some tricks for minimizing it too. The Mars person needs to be careful of the unbridled, unconscious expression of animal enthusiasms, which might fry the Neptune partner's tender, and often hidden, psychic and emotional sensibilities. Meanwhile, the Neptune partner can help both of them by scrupulously weeding out any spirit versus flesh dichotomies that might have insinuated themselves into his or her character or beliefs.

MARS MARTIALIZES PLUTO

Flowing aspects: Both Mars and Pluto link vigorously to libido, and with these partners, the two planets are cheerleaders for each other in that department. There is simply a fierce passion here, a kind of "chemistry" that can help these people get through the threadbare patches that are part of any relationship. More deeply, the soul-searching spirit of Pluto provides them with an impulse to delve more and more deeply into one another, and each new layer of nakedness, once attained, is a great driver of their mighty appetite for connection. The Mars person needs to prepare to have many primal fears uncovered.

Challenging aspects: Mars and Pluto are the most war-like of the planets, and here they are poised in a relationship of mutual antagonism. Obviously, this part of this relationship must be handled with deep self-awareness, lest vicious rows and ominous undercurrents take a terrible toll on trust. The Pluto partner has real insight into the Mars person's fear issues, but must learn to temper the expression of those insights with humor, diplomacy, respect and prudent timing. Otherwise, he or she simply triggers natural defensiveness in the Mars person. Meanwhile, the Mars person has a right to defend himself or herself, and not everything the Pluto partner thinks about the Mars person's "case" is valid. At the same time, the Mars person benefits from recognizing his or her exaggerated prickliness in the relationship.

JOVIALIZATION

PLANET: Jupiter.
AS GIFT-GIVER: To brighten.
  To uplift.
  To expand.
  To cheer.
AS THIEF: To flatter.
  To intoxicate.
  To overextend.

Faith is one of those pretty words, like love, that tends to get blurry when you hold it up close. What does it mean? One might have faith in a sound investment or in a particular spiritual teacher or even in a rickety set of stairs. What are the common denominators? Certainly faith implies confidence. That's part of the picture. But faith is more specific. It connotes a quality of confidence that extends beyond strict reason, as in the case of religion—or rickety staircases.

With faith comes lightness. A burden is lifted from our shoulders, shared with whatever entity inspires our faithful feelings. With that easing of responsibility, joy arises, and joy's sister: humor. We laugh. We smile like a bride. And like the bride, we look forward to our future with a heady mixture of triumph and delight.

The planet that has astrological dominion over these emotions is Jupiter, the proverbial king of the gods. Naturally, throughout much of astrology's history, these Jupiter energies—faith, joy, humor, success—have been viewed as positive contributions to any birthchart. Jupiter was a so-called good planet, and anything it touched was blessed. Or so went the theory. The truth is more complex. Not negative, just more complex.

Faith. Joy. Humor. A feeling of invincibility. They're all thoroughly wonderful as *feelings*. But reality sometimes has other plans. A kid got his driver's license a year ago. Now he wants to find out how fast his SUV can take that curve. His Jupiter circuitry is cooking—just before he rolls the car and kills himself. That's the dark side of the "lucky" planet: unrealistic overextension, too much optimism, all the reality-denying, shadow-fleeing excesses of what's sometimes called positive thinking.

Jupiter helps us to see opportunity. It puts us in a state of consciousness in which we are hypersensitized to positive possibilities and deem ourselves worthy of claiming them. That's its gift. The hook is that sometimes Jupiter has to get us half-drunk on expansive, world-conquering emotions before we get the message. And those emotions are dangerous.

When you jovialize someone you love, think of yourself as that person's cheerleader. Should you jovialize a friend's Scorpio Moon, for example, then your task is not merely to cheer her up, but rather to help guide her toward real Scorpionic victories, to assist her in seeing new possibilities in her efforts to penetrate the heart of the psyche, which is a basic Scorpio Moon process. Maybe you take her to a lecture by a famous novelist and thereby encourage her to discover a creative outlet for her pent-up psychological intensity. Maybe you introduce her to astrology.

Maybe you tell her jokes. Seriously—humor can be a potent agent in opening the deeper reaches of the mind. Woody Allen, a great clown of the modern era, is a Sagittarian with Jupiter and Mercury both conjunct his Sun. Those three planets all form a sextile interaspect to Diane Keaton's Aquarian Moon. Thus, as she opened her heart to him in their glory days, he not only jovialized her experimental instincts (Aquarian Moon), but also mercurialized them and solarized them. Together, Woody Allen and Diane Keaton were masters of slapstick, but as a team they also used humor to pick the lock on a number of often painful, taboo subjects: insecurity, sexual vulnerability, fear of aging, psychotherapy, betrayal, ethnicity, and so on. That represents jovialization at its best: the ability simultaneously to brighten and to deepen your partner's perspective, especially regarding topics previously full of threatening impossibility.

One of the hazards of being human is that we tend to take ourselves awfully seriously. Should you be jovialized by someone close to you, let your partner teach you humor, even if it seems to be at your own expense. Humor opens the door to greater gifts. Try to get the joke, knowing that if you do, you'll also get a lot more. That friend or lover has an instinctive grasp of your highest potentials. He or she knows how you've been *underestimating yourself.* Your resistance to the humor is a measure of your attachment to narrower perspectives moored in darker, more hurtful periods of your life.

The Thief twists the process of jovialization, pushing his or her partner into foolish excesses or premature, ill-founded efforts. Flattery figures

211

prominently in the Thief's strategy. So do humor's shadows: teasing and destructive mockery. Often the most damaging aspect of jovialization arises when the partner feels bound to say only positive things, encouraging you, in the name of "supportiveness," to perform brave, bold, foolish acts.

Keep an eye out for the Thief, but enjoy the rest. Jovialization—bringing out the hidden best in someone who's sharing your life—is high on the list of reasons why love is worth the effort it takes.

Director Steven Spielberg jovializes Kate Capshaw's Sun, Ascendant and Pluto, while she jovializes his Sun and Uranus. Think of her comic scenes in *Indiana Jones and the Temple of Doom:* pure Jupiter slapstick!

JUPITER JOVIALIZES JUPITER

Flowing aspects: The easy connection between these two Jupiters implies that these partners bring a lot of encouragement, support and inspiration to each other. They also seem to enhance each other's plain dumb luck. The bugaboo lies in the fact that they tend to overextend and say "yes" to too many things. Unchecked, that could lead to superficiality and glitz taking a toll on the core depths of this bond, or to getting spread so thinly that it leads to exhaustion.

Challenging aspects: The tense connection between these two Jupiters implies that while these partners bring a lot of encouragement and support to each other, it may be misplaced and quixotic at times. The core of that problem is that together, this couple can display a distinct tendency toward overextension and saying "yes" to too many things, and possibly toward aggravating any tendencies toward ego inflation in either one of them. Their dreams may also be in practical conflict.

JUPITER JOVIALIZES SATURN

Flowing aspects: The Jupiter person's dreams and aspirations benefit from the Saturn partner's steadying hand, and his or her ability to point out potential pitfalls or overlooked fine print. Meanwhile, the Saturn partner's natural caution is tempered and informed by the Jupiter person's faith and encouragement. This is a classic indicator of *effective teamwork.*

Challenging aspects: The Jupiter person's natural enthusiasms exist in a tense relationship with the Saturn partner's caution and maturity. While they can sometimes benefit each other through enhancing awareness of each other's blindspots, the traps that must be avoided are the tendency for the Jupiter person to feel that the Saturn partner is raining on the parade too

212

often, and the Saturn person's feeling chronically pressed into a kind of parental, boundary-setting role.

JUPITER JOVIALIZES URANUS
Flowing aspects: Serendipity: that's the word for the happy cross-fertilization of the Jupiter person's dreams and the Uranus partner's creative genius. These two are unstoppable together, once they start jamming. We can count on the Jupiter person for an exciting vision, and leave it to the Uranus partner to come up with the twists that turn it into a masterpiece.
Challenging aspects: If these partners are operating in an closed, isolated system, they can come up with some spectacular blunders together. There are tendencies toward inflated answers that don't work, and "breakthroughs" that wind up costing a fortune. The key here is sobriety of judgment, waiting periods before serious action is taken, and above all, good advice from trusted friends. In saying all that, we must not lose sight of the fact that there is some real genius released when these two put their heads together. Trouble is, it's mixed in with the more dangerous stuff.

JUPITER JOVIALIZES NEPTUNE
Flowing aspects: The Neptune partner's dreams—both literally in the sense of night-dreams and figuratively in the sense of inspirations and fantasies—offer incalculable, almost supernatural support to the Jupiter partner's deepest hopes and strategies. Meanwhile, the Jupiter partner's humor and faith deepen the Neptune partner's spirituality in precious ways, encouraging him or her to claim opportunities that feed the soul.
Challenging aspects: Illusions are always charming until the bill arrives. With this couple, it's not that the relationship is an illusion. Rather, once their dreams start to interact, there can be such a rapid cycle of inflation, over-extension, and general escalation of all bets, that initially good, modest ideas turn into lofty card-castles which soon topple. So these people should take one step at a time, remember Murphy's Law, and check out their plans with grounded friends before they bet the house.

JUPITER JOVIALIZES PLUTO
Flowing aspects: Few qualities are more inspiring than the ability to face life's darkness squarely and still keep the faith. These partners bring that strength out in each other. There is a certain innate pluck in the Jupiter

person. It blends in a lovely, precious way with the Pluto partner's clear-eyed ability to look into the heart of darkness. Together they produce a kind of spiritedness that's greater than either partner could sustain alone.

Challenging aspects: Is the cup is half full or half empty? Clearly, both principles are true—and worth knowing. These two need to be wary of polarizing into the Jupiter person's being the optimist and the Pluto partner the pessimist, or the Pluto partner as the psychologist, and the Jupiter person the one who "just wants to be happy and get on with life."

SATURNIZATION

PLANET: Saturn.
AS GIFT-GIVER: To crystallize.
 To focus.
 To confront.
 To discipline.
AS THIEF: To repress.
 To control.
 To frustrate.

Saturn is the astrological bogeyman. The planet of death. The lord of solitude. Or so say the traditionalists. Sepharial, an early twentieth century British astrologer, writes: "Saturn gives delays, impediments, defects, secrets, fatalities, falls from position, misfortunes, melancholy moods, chronic hurts, sorrows, disease, and hurts to women and children. It makes the native independent, unhappy, secretive, cautious, jealous, miserly, and governed by habit."

Not exactly date bait, right?

You'd get no disagreement from Professor A. F. Seward, "the world's foremost astrologer" (if not the world's most modest), circa 1915: "Saturn's influence . . . causes its subjects many reverses, usually in middle life. Much of their trouble coming through marriage and love affairs."

Unsurprisingly, the old school astrologers' dark view of Saturn carried over into synastry. The ringed planet's interaspects were perceived as baleful influences upon marriage, prophetic of estrangements, emotional coldness, and the early demise of one of the partners.

Out of this tradition of horror and gloom, a singularly odd perception is currently arising. In modern times, more often than not, strong Saturn

214

contacts are the best markers of long-lasting partnerships. Again and again we see it: the birthcharts of a couple that holds together through thick and thin, slogging through the swamps and toasting the good times, are stitched together with a network of Saturnian links.

Any marriage, and most friendships for that matter, sooner or later comes upon stressful times. Such tension is inevitable whenever two monkeys are stuck in the same small cage. Years ago the practical and social pressures that kept marriages intact were far more pervasive than they are now. Those pressures were a double-edged sword—negatively, they kept many couples bound together in a semi-homicidal emotional wasteland throughout their adult lives, all as a result of a mistake they made as teenagers. Positively, that pro-marriage social pressure helped many a couple survive the bumpy places in the road. Now, with the taboo largely removed from divorce, couples who stay together must *choose* to stay together, actively and consciously. With the door to "freedom" wide open, each lover must willingly accept the limitations inherent in a vow of partnership. In hard times, sustaining such a decision takes a big dose of the healthiest kind of Saturnine energy: *self-discipline.*

Saturn the Gift-Giver offers *mature commitment.* Saturn's message is that, while love is certainly an emotion, it is also more than an emotion. It is a promise to act in a responsible, open, honest way, no matter what kinds of tension are in the air.

Should someone you love saturnize a planet in your birthchart, you might not enjoy the feeling at first. Like a fine brandy, that contact typically must be given time to mature before its full flavor emerges. Your partner confronts that part of your own character, challenging it to mature, impelling that planet to make a mammoth push toward its mature potential. Often Saturn suggests a specific, concrete plan for that push, helping to crystallize and focus the energies of the contacted planet. Subjectively you may experience saturnization as an apparent effort on your lover's part to control you or even repress you. Is that true objectively? Possibly—that's the Thief's way. But even if the process is the work of the Gift-Giver, you might still sometimes experience those bad feelings. For all our fancy talk, no one really *likes* to grow—especially the kind of growth that carries us from the delightfully vague world of dreams into the painfully limited world of reality. That particular transition is Saturn's specialty. Retrospectively, you may appreciate the results of saturnization, but they can take time to appear, and meanwhile the process itself is tiring, frightening, and often thorny. Typically it even feels unnatural, since in a way our saturnizing partner is asking us to become someone other than the person we already are: someone wiser.

Saturn, subjectively again, fills us with feelings of hunger. Like the proverbial carrot at the end of the stick, it holds before us a sense of what *could* be. Should someone saturnize your Mercury, for example, that person pushes you to speak and think more clearly and rigorously, pointing out inconsistencies in your ideas, holes in your logic. Should someone saturnize your Venus, he or she might similarly confront you regarding your romantic ideals, sexual assumptions, and intimate behavior. Should someone saturnize your Sun, then the authenticity of your entire way of being in the world is called into question. In all cases, if you accept reality and make a disciplined effort to change yourself, you've received a Gift.

On the dark side, the Thief can turn all that inspiration into frustration and self-criticism. How? By setting *impossible standards*. Never satisfied, always demanding, the Thief tantalizes, frustrates, and ultimately depresses whatever planet it contacts.

If you saturnize someone, scrutinize yourself. Be careful you're not the Thief. All of us are frightened sometimes. All of us live in a world we cannot control, dependent for our survival upon seemingly random forces we can barely influence—like the whimsies of warmongering politicians or the statistical reassurances of the people behind your local nuclear power plant. Those out-of-control feelings *scare* us. Therein lies the glitch: as a result of our natural fear of what we can't control, we might unconsciously seek to overmanage some zone of experience more under our direct influence—like the decisions of somebody we love. That's where the Thief gets in. We displace our legitimate, but frustrated, urge to be in control of our own experience, twisting it into a compulsion to keep another human being under our thumb.

Should you saturnize someone who trusts you, study your motives. Are you trying to keep an unnecessarily tight rein on that person's behavior? Are you emotionally invested in keeping your partner safely predictable, in his or her "proper place?" Have you recognized his or her inalienable right to navigate independently in this mysterious world? If not, then the Thief is under your skin, using you.

Carl Jung and Sigmund Freud, the co-developers of psychoanalysis, worked well together for many years, pushing each other's work to new levels of passion and depth. Such shared accomplishments alert us to Saturn contacts between the men. Clinching our guess, we observe how their

216

relationship soured once Jung, the younger man, began to diverge from Freud's party line regarding the nature of the human unconscious. Jung's sense of being "squashed" and Freud's feelings about Jung's "disobedience" or "betrayal" all point toward the activity of Saturn the Thief. When we look at their birthcharts, we discover that Freud saturnized Jung's Jupiter and Saturn through trines, and, most tellingly, his Mars through an opposition. Turning the viewpoints around, we also learn that Jung saturnized Freud even more powerfully. Jung's Saturn trined Freud's own Saturn. It also contacted Freud's nadir through a conjunction, his Venus through a sextile, and his Sun, his Uranus, and his Mercury through square interaspects. Thus, these two men, virtual studies in saturnization, illustrate for us the best and worst of what this contact can mean. And perhaps ironically, despite their personal falling out, Saturn won in the end: their names, in history, are now forever married. At one level, at least, their relationship endures.

SATURN SATURNIZES SATURN

Flowing aspects: This easy, supportive connection between two Saturns is a sleeper. Its real value creeps up slowly, over a period of years. Gradually, the couple realizes that together they've forged mighty empires of the heart, painted masterpieces, and scaled daunting mountains of difficulty. There is little that they might not accomplish together in their quiet, relentless way.
Challenging aspects: While each partner has needs for solitude and independence, they are going to have to work very consciously and respectfully toward establishing effective ways for those needs to be met. The clash between their practical, responsible sides, or between their blind spots and blockages, could lead to a logical, agreed-upon "devil's bargain" in which they both pay too high a price in terms of their right to privacy, alone-time, and their own pet projects.

SATURN SATURNIZES URANUS

Flowing aspects: The Saturn person's practicality and groundedness enhance the Uranus partner's genius and inspirations, while the Uranus mate returns the favor with innovative solutions to various pragmatic dilemmas that the Saturn person faces. Together, they can create a uniquely powerful combination of dogged hard work and mind-boggling breakthroughs that mow down whatever stands between them and where they want to go.
Challenging aspects: Careful, conservative thinking along tried-and-true paths (Saturn) is a precious heritage. So are inspiration, paradigm shifts, and

breakthroughs (Uranus). In the context of this relationship, with the tense aspect between Saturn and Uranus, it's important that the Saturn person not get too identified with practicality and the Uranus person with innovation. If that polarization happens, this relationship could get as tedious as a political talk shows.

SATURN SATURNIZES NEPTUNE
Flowing aspects: Neptune is dreamy and Saturn represents hardheaded pragmatism, so the combination isn't a natural one. Still, in the case of these partners, the planets are supportively disposed toward each other. The bottom line is that when the couple allows a cross-fertilization of the Saturn person's practical instincts and the Neptune mate's visions and dreams, the combination can be a winning team.
Challenging aspects: Neptune's dark side is flaky unrealism. Saturn's is a kind of bleak, despairing sobriety. For these people, the trick lies in making sure that they don't twist themselves into a polarized situation in which each person comes to represent one of those dark sides, resulting in a pointless argument that strips each one of part of their humanity.

SATURN SATURNIZES PLUTO
Flowing aspects: When these partners set out to accomplish something, even against long odds and with formidable opponents, they're a tough team to beat. There is a hardheaded, determined quality in the Saturn person, and it is enhanced by a down-and-dirty sense of the ways of the wicked world in the Pluto person. This happy link between Saturn and Pluto is just itching for something into which to get its teeth. Hint: better find it a project, or its teeth might strike closer to home.
Challenging aspects: There is a gritty, dogged intensity evident here. This couple can slog its way through many obstacles, even though technically there is a challenging aspect between Saturn and Pluto. The key here lies in each partner's making sure that the couple always has some worthwhile external battle to fight, perhaps for some good cause. Otherwise, the Saturn-Pluto connection might start chewing on more convenient targets: namely, the couple itself.

URANIZATION (accent the first syllable)

PLANET: Uranus.

AS GIFT-GIVER: To individualize.

To liberate.

To surprise.

To revolutionize.

AS THIEF: To disrupt.

To shell-shock.

To frazzle.

To deprave.

Those of us in midlife now, when we were kids, were taught to pronounce "Uranus" like this: "yer-AY-nus," with an accented long *a* on the second syllable. In late January 1986, when the Voyager probe flew by the planet, the newscasters all agreed to a different pronunciation: "YER-in-us." Astrologers have been known to use both pronunciations, but many use a third: "yer-AH-noose."

This linguistic mess is hardly a major moral issue—but it's certainly a delight to anyone who understands the astrological significance of the planet. As synchronicity would have it, if you so much as open your mouth to utter the name of this planet, you have a Uranian experience: you must think for yourself—and no matter what your choice, somebody is going to accuse you of mispronunciation.

If Uranus could talk, its message would be, "Why don't all you people think for yourselves? You can pronounce my name *any way you want!*"

All of us are subjected to overwhelming social pressures, squeezed into prefabricated roles, with prefabricated opinions, tastes, lifestyles, even thoughts. Men are still taught not to cry. Women are half-trained to cry perhaps too easily, and then half-trained to feel ashamed and weakened for doing so. We are all encouraged to equate happiness with success and success with money. Each society is different, but ultimately the same in terms of creating this *consensual reality*. Only the customs vary. The essential process—socialization into cultural norms—is universal.

And that's why God made Uranus.

This is the planet of rebellion. It refers to the ability to break rules. To question authority. To crack the mold into which culture tries to pour our lives.

Uranian energy is, above all else, exciting. It fires us up, puts a sharp edge on our senses, accelerates the mental processes. Also, for reasons that are difficult to comprehend logically, this planet brings in long shots.

Someone buys the right lottery ticket and wakes up a millionaire. Another person is transferred to Iceland. A third unexpectedly inherits an estate in Australia. Despite the fireworks, the key to understanding Uranian energy is to recognize that the planet promotes *individuation*, the effort to become truly one's self. The long shots appear to function as "cosmic matching funds" that support and amplify the core Uranian process, helping us to move into more unique self-expression.

In intimacy, uranization is a giddy feeling, not for the faint-hearted. The rug is pulled out from under the uranized planet. Everything is questioned. Idols fall. Comforting certainties evaporate.

A woman comes from a strict, puritanical background. A man appears in her life who uranizes her Venus. He pushes her to rethink her sexual mores, asking her to separate what she feels from what she's merely been trained to think. Another man is a nonviolent Quaker. A woman appears who uranizes his Mars. She makes him angry—and forces him to rethink his position on aggressive behavior. Does he abandon his Quaker ideals, become abusive and violent, simply because someone's Uranus happens to contact his Mars? No—not unless he's been hiding those kinds of feelings behind a thin facade of pacifism. She merely encourages him to go beyond the Quaker position that he has learned and to replace it with direct personal experience, independent analysis, and absolute honesty. She might have no idea that that's what she's doing, but those are the effects.

If you uranize someone, remember that conventionality is not simply a destructive, limiting force. It is also a stabilizing, even deepening, influence. Very few individuals are so inherently strong and wise that they'd be better off had they been left alone in the jungle at an early age. Life is full of quagmires and puzzles. For a million years, men and women have been mapping them, passing their wisdom down the line of generations. That wisdom is far from perfect, but most of us can benefit from using it until we gradually develop better, more individualized answers. In uranization you might push your partner too fast, exciting him, pressing him to claim a level of freedom he is currently unprepared to handle responsibly. The woman from the puritanical background might find herself unintentionally pregnant. The Quaker might humiliate himself by hitting the woman who uranized his Mars. In either case the uranized individual might then act regressively, fleeing into safer territory in shocked response to the frightening, perilous Uranian freedom.

Should you find yourself strongly uranized in an intimate relationship, get ready to move into uncharted territory. You've found a partner who is going to push you, cause you to ask dangerous questions, encourage you to stretch toward the limits of your true individuality. To hold up your end of that exciting process, concentrate on keeping your balance. Be willing to doubt everything you've ever taken to be true, but at the same time, be wary of giddiness and blind, bulletproof enthusiasm.

Let's look at Freud and Jung again. Freud's Uranus conjuncted Carl Jung's Moon, while Jung's own Uranus sextiled Freud's Moon and squared his Sun. This solar and lunar uranization is a central element in the synastric bond between the two men. Each stimulated the other's Uranian capacity to crash through the post-medieval picture of how the human mind operated, and pushed themselves—and the world—into the era of modern psychology. Pierre Curie uranized his wife's Mercury through an opposition; the corresponding intellectual breakthroughs led to a Nobel Prize. Illustrating the long shot dimension of Uranian activity, a woman was born on the Carribean island of Martinique in 1763. A fortune-teller looking at her birthchart would have noticed a conjunction of Venus and Mars on her midheaven and predicted "fame through marriage, but troubles there too." Along came a man named Napoleon, uranizing that configuration through a sextile. He married her, and for a while she was empress of France.

URANUS URANIZES URANUS
Flowing aspects: This happy connection between the Uranian placements in these partner's birthcharts implies a pronounced tendency toward egging one another on in terms of individuation. In other words, the longer they remain together, the more they become themselves. That's ultimately a welcome evolution, but the hitch is that a lot of people around them will interpret it as the two of them getting stranger and stranger.
Challenging aspects: The troubled, frictional connection between the Uranian placements in these birthcharts implies a pronounced need to be hyper-aware of each other's legitimate requirements for autonomy and "space." Never let a difference in ages get confused with different levels of authority or even wisdom, especially in an intimate relationship!

URANUS URANIZES NEPTUNE
Flowing aspects: There is a natural ease between the Uranus person's respect for individual autonomy and the Neptune partner's mystical, spiritual

inclinations. They can support and inspire each other in these departments, and probably will.

Challenging aspects: There is tension between the Uranus person's need for objectivity and the Neptune partner's mystical, spiritual inclinations. If they listen to each other in a spirit of openness and respect, each can benefit from the dialog. If they don't, it can become one of those arguments that makes the angels weep.

URANUS URANIZES PLUTO

Flowing aspects: Life is chock full of taboos: things we're not supposed to mention, feelings and drives that aren't "psychologically healthy" or "normal." With the easy connection between Uranus and Pluto here, this couple can discovered early on that one of the great delights of their bond is their capacity to look at almost anything together, even at things that would shock half their friends.

Challenging aspects: Beneath our calm facade of normalcy seethes the wild ocean of the unconscious mind with all its drives, needs, and dark imaginings. Sharing insights into those parts of ourselves is close to the center of the meaning of the word "intimacy," and this couple is innately pretty good at it. The trouble is that unconscious material tends to burst forth explosively between them, as if each one has a kind of unpredictable detonating effect on the other one's darkest side. This relationship promises to be a wild ride, not for the faint-hearted.

NEPTUNIFICATION

PLANET: Neptune.
AS GIFT-GIVER: To inspire.
  To uplift.
  To sensitize.
  To enchant.
AS THIEF: To confuse.
To dissipate.
To weaken.
To glamorize.
To deceive.

You're lying in your bed at night, drifting off to sleep. Suddenly a jolt runs through your body. You've caught yourself falling asleep. Where were you three seconds before the jolt? Space. Spirit. The unconscious. Or, as a saxophone player we used to know once put it: "backstrokin' in the Sublime."

Whatever your personal answer, the astrological answer is "Neptune." This is the planet of consciousness itself. Pure being. Whatever you choose to call that spaciousness that stares out through your eyes: that's Neptune.

Neptune figures prominently in the charts of saints (and drunks), visionaries (and dreamers), mystics (and people who stare into the television set for six hours every night of their lives). *Self-transcendence* is the common denominator. Usually that's taken to be a positive attribute. That's half the truth. The other half lies in recognizing the hallucinatory, fog-bound pit that lies directly beneath the fragile human ego.

Psychoanalytic theory places great emphasis upon the child's struggle to emerge from that Neptunian pit. Or, to use proper theoretical language, it emphasizes the infant's struggle to differentiate ego from unconscious. As a result, mainstream psychologists look askance upon any "regressions" into the blurry Neptunian state.

Mystics take a different view. To them, the elemental purpose of living is to explore that mysterious inner landscape and to make peace with it, even merge with it.

As astrologers we must recognize that the Neptunian coin has two sides: mystical rapture and oblivion. Our primary difficulty, strange as it may seem, lies in learning to tell one from the other. The crux of the problem centers on an old, misunderstood word: glamour. Nowadays "glamour" has become a cheap label. To call a woman glamorous is to praise her, faintly, as if to say, "You're beautiful . . . in a tacky sort of way." We might even be tempted to think that "glamour" is a modern word, since it seems so inextricably woven into magazine culture. Actually the roots of the word "glamour" are ancient, linked to the Celtic traditions of fairies, wizards, and magic. If a leprechaun needed a horse, he might "cast glamour" over a bucket of stones. To the hapless farmer, those stones would then appear to be priceless gems—and an eminently fair trade for his swaybacked mare. Glamour, in other words, is the capacity to make something appear to be other than what it actually is.

Each one of us actually *is* other than what we appear to be. But what exactly are we? That's Neptune's message: "You're not an ego—you're a *consciousness*, and that's far vaster and more exciting." Glamour gets in and wreaks havoc when, instead of melting ego for a while, pulling back its curtain and glimpsing those shimmering inner terrains, we misread Neptune's message and seek merely to glorify ego through inflated, unrealistic fantasies about ourselves. The perfectly competent postal clerk fancies himself to be a rock star. He leaves his job and his family and winds up down and out in L.A., screwed up on cocaine. The housewife from Nebraska imagines herself to be a movie star and winds up in the gutter next to the postal clerk. The New Ager gets into meditation and fancies herself a channel or a shaman.

That's the dark glamour of Neptune, the one we must avoid unless we want all those mainstream psychologists saying "I told you so."

In synastry, neptunification can be ecstasy. It can also sensitize every nerve in your body and then kick you hard in the stomach. If someone neptunifies a planet in your birthchart, that part of you feels enchanted, lifted to a new level of vision. It also likely feels disoriented, as if the waiter has been more zealous than you had imagined in keeping your champagne glass topped off.

All of us, in the process of living, get a bit crusty. Habits develop. Walls go up. We need to be reminded of that softer, gentler, more magical place buried beneath the rituals. Why? If only because that Neptunian region is the true source of life's happiness. Think about it like this: no matter how fortunate you might be in every outward sense, it's still possible that you might be sad. And conversely, no matter how ill-starred your life might seem, it is still possible that you might be far happier than the more outwardly fortunate person. Happiness, in other words, is in Neptune's domain: consciousness itself, not circumstance. If someone neptunifies you, he or she touches that part of you that lies behind all the dramas of life's surface. He or she goes right to the heart, bypassing your crust—and bypassing all your defenses too.

If you find yourself neptunified, especially in the early stages of intimacy, be careful. Try to keep a clear fix on reality. You might not be seeing your partner clearly, despite the warm feelings you're experiencing. You might instead have a super-clear fix on some romantic ideal you've been carrying around in your unconscious. Neptune requires balanced judgment. Perhaps the most practical rule of thumb is that when neptunified, go slowly. If the partnership has a sound basis, it won't disappear overnight.

Should you, on the other hand, neptunify someone who's important to you, try to create an environment of gentleness and support for that person.

More specifically, consider what planet in his or her birthchart your Neptune touches, and recognize that you have the capacity to nurture the development of that function in an almost magical way. Your lover, for example, might have a Sun-Saturn conjunction in his fifth house. His identity (Sun) is dependent upon establishing some kind of self-expressive, creative outlet (fifth house), but he was born with a frustrating sense of inadequacy and blockage there (unconscious Saturn) that can only be overcome through application, effort, and persistence (conscious Saturn). You neptunify that configuration. What should you do? Follow your heart—but what comes out might resemble this scenario: look right into his eyes, open your heart, lock souls, and tell him that you see a poet in there. That's it: direct, soul-to-soul contact, bypassing everything else.

Elizabeth Taylor has a Scorpio Moon in the second house. She feels (Moon) a Scorpionic hunger for a profound, dramatic sense of connectedness with a mate, perhaps complicated at times by feelings of personal insecurity (second house). The late Richard Burton, her longtime lover and husband, solarized her Moon. That interaspect alone is enough to account for the intense reactions they apparently created in each other, as he drove her Moon into active manifestation, and she, in lunarizing him, flooded his awareness with emotion. But Richard Burton also had a prominent Neptune, lying conjunct his Ascendant in his first house, correlating with his infamous alcoholism. That powerful Neptune formed a close square to her Scorpio Moon. Thus he neptunified her as well as solarized her, filling her heart (Moon) with other-worldly emotions and a sense of soul-contact. But did she perhaps see a perfect man in him, only to feel cheated again and again as his humanity asserted itself?

NEPTUNE NEPTUNIFIES NEPTUNE
Flowing aspects: With the partners' Neptunes working together this way, they share a lot in terms of basic mystical or spiritual values, and also in terms of the ways their imaginations work. If they make time to sit quietly together, rather uncanny psychic links begin to evidence themselves—each partner will know what the other one is thinking before he or she says it.
Challenging aspects: These partners' basic mystical or spiritual selves put the inner universe together very differently. Also, their imaginations work according to different laws and aesthetic principles. If they make time to sit quietly together, they'll "get the joke"—which is that they're both right and that each one corrects the errors and excesses of the other.

225

NEPTUNE NEPTUNIFIES PLUTO

Flowing aspects: For technical astrological reasons, this aspect is extremely common, so it would be wrong to draw too many unique conclusions about this couple from it. Basically, there is a happy convergence of spiritual and psychological values here, as if there is an assumption that one cannot possibly grow spiritually without doing psychological work, and vice versa. And, at least for most of the people currently aboard planet Earth, that's true!

Challenging aspects: A silly, destructive conflict can erode the health and sanity of both partners, and their best strategy is to treat it like poison ivy: in other words, just avoid it. The conflict arises when the Neptune person attempts to give the Pluto partner spiritual advice about the Pluto partner's personal, psychological journey, or when the Pluto partner returns the favor by psychoanalyzing the Neptune person's religious or philosophical beliefs.

PLUTONIFICATION

PLANET: Pluto.
AS GIFT-GIVER: To penetrate.
To reveal.
To transpersonalize.
AS THIEF: To tyrannize.
To corrupt.
To horrify.
To darken.

Pluto stares right through you.

Pluto asks you, "How much time do you spend thinking about what you're going to eat next? With whom you might get to sleep? How much money you have? What the other monkeys think of you?"

Most of us, if we have the courage to answer honestly, answer embarrassingly. For most of us the "big four"—food, sex, money, and power—are mightily fascinating subjects.

Then Pluto laughs in your face. He shows you galaxies, burning quasars, eons of time. He calls you a microbe on a dust mote. He tells you that your whole life is a joke. And then he walks away.

What answer can we make? How can we defend ourselves against Pluto's chillingly empty analysis of our lives?

226

One answer is to make no answer. To simply accept the elemental pointlessness of existence. Down that road lies despair, though one of the stops along the way is existentialism with its emphasis upon life as the "theater of the absurd."

Maybe we have a better answer for Pluto. Maybe we say, "Wait a minute—yesterday I sent a hundred dollars to the Sierra Club. Show me a monkey anywhere who would do that."

In sending money to the Sierra Club—or in undertaking any similarly selfless action—we *transpersonalize* ourselves, that is, we become identified with a set of motives and needs that have absolutely nothing to do with the monkey in us. And in so doing, we shrink the power of the monkey to define us, and thereby offer Pluto a smaller target for his icy barbs.

Altruism. A sense of mission. A feeling of transcendent purpose. These are the Gifts of the high Pluto. What stops us from moving in those precious directions that give meaning to our lives? The answer lies in our deepest wounds. The shame we carry. The lies we've been told. The tragedies, great and small, we've endured. How much of our energy goes into holding the darkness at bay? How much potential love, creativity, and loftiness do we waste on maintaining our denials? Answering those kinds of questions honestly takes a lot of Plutonian courage. But even then we haven't gone far enough. One ingredient is still missing: compassion. We hold all that hurtful material in the depths of our unconscious souls for one reason: it would shatter us to do otherwise. There is so much we are simply too fragile to face.

When someone plutonifies a planet in your birthchart, that part of you is going to be pushed hard. Challenged. Asked to face its own shadow. How are you kidding yourself in that area of your life? What are your most treasured lies? If you can tolerate that kind of scrutiny, then your plutonifying partner offers more: a way to lift that planet to a new and higher level of meaning, a way to transpersonalize it, help it serve a purpose in the larger world—which in turn helps you by offering that uniquely Plutonian feeling of *cosmic legitimacy*. Nietzche's famous dictum is relevant here: "That which does not destroy me makes me strong."

A woman has a Cancer Moon in the eighth house—she has introspective, nurturing instincts (Cancer Moon) that are locked into an exploration of a realm of the unconscious characterized by many social taboos (eighth house). Her response to the configuration is less than optimal. She becomes moody and preoccupied with her own emotions, hungry for sexual fulfillment (eighth house), and yet intimidated by the vulnerability that real intimacy creates. She's fascinated with the idea of death (eighth house again) but shrinks from the unpleasantness of its actuality, perhaps slipping into morbid fantasies (Cancer Moon).

A man comes into her life who plutonifies her Moon. Like a theater-goer in a horror film, she reacts to his message with both hands covering her face—but one eye peering between spread fingers, glued to the screen. He points out her self-absorption. He picks apart her rationalizations. He's intuitively keyed into all her defenses. With his help she faces a part of herself that in the harsh light of the Plutonian perspective is intolerably wasteful and absurd, given life's brevity.

This Plutonian facing of the shadow is only the first part of the process. The second part is to lift the contacted planet toward some transpersonal expression. Perhaps her new love encourages the woman to volunteer in the local rape crisis center. Perhaps she becomes involved with a hospice, helping people who are dying. Both of those activities involve playing a nurturing role (Cancer Moon) in an environment fraught with taboos (the eighth house). In either case her Cancer Moon is plutonified, lifted from mere self-indulgent moodiness and fear into the higher Cancerian world of active nurturing and healing.

Is plutonification always so glorious? Not at all. Perhaps the man simply horrifies her with his intensity, driving her deeper into her shell. How? Maybe by dumping the illnesses of his own Pluto on her, corrupting her spirit with cynicism and bitterness.

Perhaps he does worse: perhaps he tortures her with truth, penetrating her defenses, but doing so without compassion, seeking only to assassinate her character and undermine her dignity. Perhaps he tyrannizes her, power-tripping and guru-tripping and psychology-tripping her until their relationship looks like a case study in spiritual fascism.

If you find yourself plutonifying someone, start by trying to remember the last time anyone complimented you on your halo. If it's been a while, then be scrupulously careful of preaching to your partner. You've probably got some valuable insights into the shadowy side of the planet you're plutonifying. Don't overestimate them! That planet in turn is stimulating your own Pluto, and therefore whatever tendencies you have toward taking on too much authority in another person's life are being emphasized. So go lightly—honestly and confrontively, but humbly too.

228

Be sensitive also to the notion that a half-truth that someone really hears and uses is vastly more helpful than a whole truth so threatening that it is rejected. In plutonification, one can cut too close to the bone and only stimulate the development of even more elaborate defense mechanisms in the partner. There is a fine line between a truly transpersonal urge to help another human being and a merely self-aggrandizing urge to appear uncannily wise and penetrating. Cross that line and you've walked right into the lair of Pluto the Thief.

The nineteenth century pro-slavery politician Stephen Douglas was a charismatic speaker and wielded powerful influence. His support of slavery was so repugnant to Abraham Lincoln that Lincoln felt compelled to make a public stand against him. The famous Lincoln-Douglas debates that followed pushed Lincoln into national prominence and ultimately into the presidency. Douglas's Pluto opposed Lincoln's midheaven (public destiny), unwittingly plutonifying him into characteristically altruistic action.

Abraham Lincoln and his wife, Mary Todd Lincoln, also illustrate the dark side of Pluto in a particularly poignant way. He plutonified her Saturn through a conjunction and her Mars through a square. These are challenging configurations, involving the two malefic planets of medieval astrology. Their marriage was a tempestuous one, and this plutonification is sufficiently thorny to account for that fact. Was there something of Mary Todd Lincoln's urge to control everything (Saturn) and her own unconscious violence (Mars) that Abraham Lincoln was helping her face? And when he was assassinated while sitting next to her in the theater, did she glimpse a brutal example of the seeming pointlessness of our existence, the legacy of the Thief?

PLUTO PLUTONIFIES PLUTO

Flowing aspects: Pluto moves very slowly, so people born within a couple of years of each other always have the conjunction interaspect. For that reason, we should be wary about making too much of this particular aspect. It does often encourage a kind of ease about being honest with each other, and very frequently it also suggests a sense of having shared secrets—a phenomenon we always observe among young people of similar ages, with their secret codes and private in-jokes, as well as the eternal assumption by each generation that it has invented sex.

Challenging aspects: The tension that exists between these partners' Plutos suggests a need to proceed very diplomatically and cautiously whenever either person feels the need to bring up the other one's "psychological profile." Both partners are touchy with each other in such situations—plus each is particularly prone to errors of exaggeration in analyzing the other one's true unconscious profile and motivations.

Where is Nodalization?

We have not included a section on "nodalization" because the nodes are *points,* not planets. While they are living parts of the psyche, as the planets are, they don't have specific "natures," the way planets and the Ascendant do. Instead, they draw their natures from the sign-house-aspect matrix they occupy. As such, this kind of interaspectual reasoning doesn't really work for them—although we can often get tantalizing hints about the past-life connections between people by considering interaspects between one person's planets and the other one's nodes.

CHAPTER FOURTEEN: YOUR PLANETS, MY SKY

Lois is a graduate student in philosophy, a reserved, calm young woman with a taste for books and rumination. Six months ago she discovered Mike, and she's laughed more in those six months than she has since she was a little girl. She's not taking the petty wars of academia so seriously. Her increased enjoyment of life shows in a more relaxed teaching style, and she's full of new ideas for her doctoral dissertation.

Mike's Sun falls in Lois's fifth house, the house of love affairs, playfulness, pleasure, and creativity. That is, if *his* sun were placed in *her* chart, that's where it would fall. At the end of Chapter Twelve, we discussed how to recognize these configurations. Now let's learn to interpret them.

Mike has become bored with the monotony of his life, habituated to a routine existence. Now he's realized that there's a world of ideas and experiences that he's never explored before. Since he met Lois, he's rediscovered his curiosity and is happily indulging it—at the library, at lectures, movies, concerts, and in conversations with this fascinating woman that last until two in the morning. He feels as though Lois let him out of a cage, and he tells her so—he's even talking more intimately.

Lois's Sun lies in Mike's third house, stimulating his appetite for communication, perception, and the exchange of information. She *solarizes* (brings out, emphasizes) that part of his life. We introduced those interaspectual terms—solarization, lunarization, and so on—in regards to aspects between the *planets* of one chart and another in Chapter Thirteen. The terms work in helping us understand the impact of the placement of one person's planets into the other person's *houses* as well. This is another fundamental device in synastry. It helps us see the impact that each person has on the other's *circumstances and behavior (houses)*. This procedure is called *transposing* one person's planets into the other's houses.

Mike and Lois are, of course, imaginary people. Let's discuss how this technique works in reality by considering the charts of Eleanor Roosevelt and Franklin D. Roosevelt.

Eleanor Roosevelt's Moon lies at nineteen degrees and thirty-four minutes of Cancer. FDR's eleventh house begins at twenty-six degrees and six minutes of Cancer. Eleanor Roosevelt's Moon falls in FDR's tenth house, and its lunarizing themes are felt in that area of his life.

What if FDR's eleventh house had begun at twenty degrees of Cancer instead? Then even though Eleanor Roosevelt's Moon would have been in

FDR's tenth house mathematically, we would have read its lunarizing themes primarily in FDR's eleventh house. Why? Because the cusp of a house is a very sensitive zone. Like the event horizon around a black hole, a cusp pulls a planet forward. It may technically be in the preceding house, but if it's within approximately a degree and a half of the cusp, read it as being in the following house.

Pay particular attention to the houses affected not only by each partner's Sun, but also by the Moon and Ascendant. Where your Sun falls in your partner's houses, you *solarize* that house. Where your Moon falls in his chart, you *lunarize* that territory.

In house transposition, we consider not only the primal triad, but also all ten planets and the Ascendant. With so many factors involved, more than one house is always accented in transposition. The houses that receive the most impact from your partner's planets are the areas of your life that are most affected by him or her. Like it or not, you'll spend more time wrapped up in the affairs of those houses if you share your life with this person. Your mate will be like an actor in the theater of that house, beckoning you on stage. One strange dimension of this fact is that your partner might not intend this effect all, might complain of it, and might not have any obvious personality characteristics that would explain it.

Suppose that your lover puts six planets in your third house. We know that, like Mike in our example at the beginning of this chapter, your third house activity will be increased—you'll talk more, become more curious, experience more chaos and wild cards in your life, even if your partner is stolid, silent, and alphabetizes his CD collection. Third house *behavior* is what changes, quantitatively. How does it change in quality? The natures of your partner's planets falling in your third house tell you *how* your experience changes. Refer to Chapter Thirteen, "Interaspects," to see what the venusification of your third house, for example, might be like.

We can sum up what we've learned in two simple principles.

*   In transposition, the more planets that are transposed into a house, the more the behavior and activity of that house increases.*

*   The mood or tone of the changed behavior is indicated by the nature of the transposed planets.*

Let's try an example. Someone who venusifies your third house may enhance your verbal creativity, increase your eloquence, and improve your writing style, even if all you've ever written is grocery lists. On the other hand, this person may make it difficult for you to assert yourself verbally and

232

speak unpleasant truths—Venus is conciliatory too. Someone who uranizes your third house may spark your originality, helping you to tear up those grocery lists, forget your writing group's criticism—and finish your novel your own way. Or you may develop a case of foot-in-mouth disease around such a person, blurting out inappropriate comments. Third house behavior is increased in both examples, but the tone of the behavior varies with the planet involved, Venus in one case and Uranus in the other.

Let's discuss the transposed houses one by one. Remember: the house is the *lesson*, planets are *teachers,* and signs are *methods.* Imagine that you are reading about a classroom (house) visited by new teachers (planets), not your own. Will these newcomers inspire you to learn more? Will they coach and enlighten you, sharpen and amplify your experience of that house? Or will they behave in incomprehensible ways, prevent you from learning at your own pace, or exhaust you with propaganda? The choice, at least in part, is yours.

THE TRANSPOSED FIRST HOUSE

Traditional Name: House of Personality.
When Healthy: Enhanced personal style. Strengthened will. Improved poise. Increased sense of control over one's self and one's direction in life.
When Confused: Blurred, false, or missing sense of identity. Awkwardness, lack of self-assurance. Overly controlling or aimless behavior.

The first house is the mask you wear in the world—we use that term for the Ascendant, but the whole first house is symbolically synonymous with the Ascendant, which is really only its cusp. Think of it as astrological clothing. Clothing is superficial, but it's absolutely necessary in our culture, used not only to protect and cover the body, but to signal something about the role we play, our job, our mood, our essence. We learn that certain styles and colors are becoming to us, and others aren't. Think of your Ascendant as your astrological energy wardrobe, a personal style that you project to the world. Certain behavior patterns facilitate your interactions with those around you or give you confidence and make you feel comfortable.

When your first house is strongly affected by your partner, a new "wardrobe consultant" has entered your life, and the impact hits more than your clothes. The Ascendant is how we *act*, the filter through which we express ourselves. We could call it our window on the world, and the person who affects it is a window washer—or a window smearer.

Prepare to be made more aware of your behavior patterns, both healthy ones that need encouragement, and embarrassing ones you're ready to outgrow. Why do you sit in the back of the room during lectures? Why do you banter with the popcorn vendors at the movies? Why do you carry a list to the grocery store and stick to it? Why don't you walk down every aisle in that grocery store to see if looking at the shelves will remind you of forgotten items?

How did you feel about reading those questions? Intrigued? Amused? Irritated? Thrown off balance? When you're with someone who bombs your first house, you'll feel all of the above and then some. You will find yourself examining your personal style more than before.

How will you react? Perhaps you overcome your shyness or break your bad habit of dominating the conversation when nervous. Perhaps you'll develop more flair and self-assurance—or perhaps you'll decide you're a hopeless nerd and refuse to budge from your fetal position, unless it's to break a Ming vase. Perhaps you'll get into ridiculous fights over where you part your hair or the way you laugh. But perhaps you may need to.

Why? When someone puts planets in your first house, your style can be enhanced and made more self-aware—but you should watch out for attempts, conscious and unconscious, to force you into shoes that don't fit you. The Ascendant is the way in which we have to behave if we are to feel sane and effective in the world. That behavior can be improved, but it can also be distorted by a powerful first house transposition, especially from a partner with a strong ego.

If you have a strong influence on your partner's first house, realize that you must tolerate his or her mask. It's not phony; it's how that person needs to present himself or herself. You can point out ways in which that behavior might be changed, but you shouldn't try to eradicate it. You must tolerate the essence of the person's style, rather than mock or malform it—unless you want to live with someone who feels psychologically naked around you all of the time and will eventually improvise defenses, or fight back, or leave. Don't question every move your partner makes, and try to see the humor in all masks.

Woody Allen's Sun, Mercury, and Jupiter are conjunct and fall in Diane Keaton's first house. He solarized her style, even literally, since the Annie Hall look became a fashion after that movie's release. We could also say that he mercurializes and jovializes her style, giving her roles as high-strung, talkative (Mercury), giddy clowns (Jupiter). Keith Richards's Pluto in Leo lies in Mick Jagger's first house, and Richards has certainly played a part in the development of Jagger's Leonine rock-and-roll mask and the cultural icon it's become.

THE TRANSPOSED SECOND HOUSE

Traditional Name: House of Money.
When Healthy: Increased self-esteem, based on who one is, rather than what one has. More efficient management of material resources.
When Confused: Decreased self-esteem. Preoccupation with status symbols and financial security to prove self-worth. Fear of personal or material risk.

Your friend Jennifer is telling you the history of her love life. Andrew always made her feel like a worm. He cut her down in subtle ways. When she noticed the pattern and dumped him, he even told her she'd never amount to anything without him. Bob was different. She felt really secure around him at first, because he was so sensible and down-to-earth, but after a while she got tired of his obsession with brand names, mutual funds, and being seen in all the right places. Chris was a thoroughly nice guy, good-natured and gentle, but always broke and always hitting her up for a loan. Finally she found Daniel, her husband. "He makes me feel like the most gorgeous, fascinating, capable woman in the world, like there's nothing I couldn't do. And my life has really stabilized since we've been together. I never thought I'd be able to buy a house."

Did Jennifer just have a string of bad luck until she met Daniel? Maybe, and maybe not. These four men all transposed a substantial number of planets into Jennifer's second house. One undercut her self-image; another improved it. One was a drain on her resources; another supported them.

When your second house is heavily influenced by your partner, it can be one of the most painful of contacts, carrying great psychic costs. This person can undermine your self-esteem, constantly bringing you face-to-face with how worthless you think you are. It may not be said out loud, but an examination of the events in your life since you've been together can reveal a persistent pattern of your crippling devaluation by yourself and your partner.

235

Don't run away before you consider the corollary: A person who affects your second house can also be your partner in one of the most life-enhancing relationships you'll ever have, wonderful for your morale, and for your outer resources as well as your inner ones. If you want a cheerleader, your best backer and your biggest fan, someone to encourage you to develop your untapped potential, someone who'll see potential you never dreamed of, look for someone who activates your second house.

How that house is activated depends on many things: the maturity of the two people involved; their honesty; their willingness to work together; to be honest when necessary and gentle when appropriate; and, perhaps above all else, their own self-esteem.

If you energize your partner's second house, be truthful and careful. You are a kind of astrological bellows that can inflate or deflate your partner's sense of personal worth. Don't commit the cruelty of encouraging nonexistent talents. Don't sharpen your claws on your mate just for the pleasure of the exercise, either. You can give your lover a wonderful gift: in a culture where low self-esteem is something like the psychological equivalent of the common cold, you can help improve your lover's confidence. But remember that you are holding a double-edged sword, and you can also inflict more than the usual share of misery on your mate by your ability to devalue him or her, to strike right at the heart of his or her sense of dignity. If you have a strong influence on your partner's second house, you should memorize one of the Buddha's observations: Before you say anything, ask yourself, "Is it true, is it kind, and is it necessary?"

Paul Newman's Jupiter and his Ascendant-Mercury-Venus conjunction fall in Joanne Woodward's second house, the latter configuration on her Saturn-Venus conjunction. Newman has reviewed (Mercury) some of Woodward's dance routines (Venus) and added steps (Mercury) for her film (Ascendant-Venus), certainly a second house, fan-and-cheerleader activity. Woodward's Sun, incidentally, lies in Newman's second house conjunct his Moon, so in their case, second-house transposition works in each direction, with each partner supporting the other's confidence in concrete ways.

THE TRANSPOSED THIRD HOUSE

Traditional Name: House of Communication.

When Healthy: Open-mindedness and non-judgmental perceptiveness enhanced. Curiosity stimulated. More information and experiences gathered. Communicative abilities strengthened.

When Confused: Increased dogmatism. Confusion, "disinformation," lessened ability to distinguish and maintain one's own point of view. Scattering of energy, overscheduling, time wasting, disorganization.

An extraterrestrial visiting the earth would ask a lot of questions that might never occur to you. When we check books out of the library, why use a card when it would make better sense to trade in a book of our own for the duration of the loan? Why do young boys look at their shoes when they're talking to girls? Why does your political system work the way it does—wouldn't it make more sense if the person who got the most votes *always* won?

A partner who activates your third house arrives in your life and presents you with an encyclopedia full of questions about the world around you, and with an extra set of antennae to soak up possible answers and new experiences. The affairs of this house include its traditional name, "communication," but its definition is wider than speech and writing and intellectual activity. This is the house of perception, observation, and of gathering information—not just the house of deduction and sorting information. Someone who transposes many planets into your third house can throw open new windows on the world for you. A mate who influences your third house can broaden your horizons, diversify your perceptions, expand your experiences, arouse your curiosity, challenge your assumptions, and sharpen your wits.

He or she can also bewilder you, bias your opinions, wear you out with endless talking, censor you or your sources of information, thereby weakening your reality testing, and exhaust you with the increased pace of your life. His or her world view may be imposed on yours, and you may feel brainwashed.

If your third house is energized by someone you love, be prepared to reevaluate some of your most deeply cherished notions. Enjoy the new experiences, but be willing to accept some confusion and some shifting in your world view. Unless you're so wise that you can no longer learn anything, it will probably be good for you. But reserve your right to think for yourself.

237

If you stimulate your partner's third house, you offer him or her the estimable pleasure of never being bored. Be careful of appointing yourself teacher, however, and respect his or her opinions when they vary from yours. It's possible to share the same facts but have different interpretations of them.

Author Simone de Beauvoir's Uranus-Mercury-Sun conjunction falls in existentialist writer Jean-Paul Sartre's third house. They met while both were studying for advanced degrees in philosophy (Mercury) and maintained a lifelong, unconventional (Uranus) professional and personal relationship. De Beauvoir is probably best known for a landmark feminist work, *The Second Sex*, published in 1949, but also wrote novels, memoirs, and essays, some on Sartre. She solarized this writer's third house and also mercurialized it, encouraging his work and analyzing it for others, and their relationship had a Uranian flavor.

THE TRANSPOSED FOURTH HOUSE

Traditional Name: House of the Home.
When Healthy: Increased self-understanding. Heightened sense of "rootedness" and security. Positive domestic emphasis.
When Confused: Entrapment in unresolved psychological dynamics from one's personal history. Extreme withdrawal; psychological isolation.

The furniture in this house is the furniture in your head. The fourth house is subjective, internal, and complex. Think of its central activity as the search for roots: the psychological roots of home and the biological family. Someone who has access to this part of your nature has a hand on the door to your personal unconscious—and to the skeletons in your closet.

The atmosphere of the parental home in general can be described by the contents of the fourth house, and sometimes it seems to refer to one parent more than the other. A partner who energizes your fourth house can invoke that atmosphere, bringing up mother issues or father issues in your life. Be aware of the fact that this person's presence in your life may hook you back into old family behavior patterns. Your partner's gift to you may, in fact, be precisely the illumination of those issues, which can lead to your resolution of them, because you can't change something that you don't know is happening.

238

Someone who energizes your fourth house can hold a key to your self-understanding, helping to heal old wounds, contributing to the feeling of security that comes from being reconnected to your true self. A mate who transposes several planets into your fourth house makes a good companion on journeys of inner exploration, and probably a pretty good roommate as well, although that word doesn't go deep enough. You may remember from Chapter Six that the arc of intimacy begins in the fourth house. This is the house of hearth and home—and, everything else being equal, it's easier to create a home with someone who energizes your fourth house.

Such a person can also help drive you crazy, uprooting you in every sense of the word, rattling the skeletons in your closet, locking you into the painful repetition of scenes from your childhood. You can withdraw from the partner, from the world, from your own sanity.

Like it or not, when your lover activates your fourth house, he or she is deeply under your skin, and material from that subjective layer of the unconscious stirs and moves, demanding attention. You can react by reconnecting your inner and outer selves, or by watching passively as they drift further apart.

If your fourth house is strongly affected by your mate, you don't have to earn a Ph.D. in psychology, but you had best spend some time understanding what sort of family dynamics influenced your childhood, and how you may or may not be repeating these patterns with your partner. The self-knowledge you can attain with such a person is priceless. Your lover is automatically fluent in the language of your innermost heart, your dreams and visions. If you want to know yourself and to be deeply known, you have found a good traveling companion.

If you stimulate your partner's fourth house, it's wise for you to have some basic psychological knowledge, too, and for the same reasons: so that you don't unwittingly become cast in a drama that your partner may need to recognize and release. Be very careful about the unconsciously manipulative effect you can have on your mate. You should also be wary of the way your partner might look you straight in the eye, but see his or her mother or father. What you stir in that person goes back to childhood and is therefore not always a model of adult rationality. You're entrusted with something close to the core of this person's being, and that fact should produce something like reverence in you. Be a good steward. You can contribute to a profound sense of belonging and identity in your mate, and that goes beyond the traditional nesting interpretations of this house.

Truly illuminating illustrations for the transposed fourth house are rather difficult to obtain, since we're not on a fourth-house level of closeness to the people in our examples. Freud's Moon fell in Jung's fourth house. Books have been written about their relationship; an extremely brief version is that they split over the question of the unconscious, which Jung thought was a source of wholeness and wisdom (the intuitive Moon), and Freud thought was the container of material that needed repressing (Saturn). Nineteenth-century French poets Paul Verlaine and Arthur Rimbaud had a brief, turbulent affair, terminating with a drunken Verlaine wounding Rimbaud with two shots from a revolver. Each put Neptune (fantasy, illusion, poetry, intoxication with the Spirit or spirits) in the other's fourth house. Verlaine's Saturn also fell in Rimbaud's fourth house. Did that placement contribute to the adolescent, in revolt against the world, seeing Verlaine as an authority figure (Saturn)?

THE TRANSPOSED FIFTH HOUSE

Traditional Name: House of Children.
When Healthy: Creativity stimulated. Enjoyment of life enhanced. Childlike spontaneity encouraged. Increased ability to fall in love—with life, with a person, with a creative act.
When Confused: Insistence on living in the present, at the cost of future plans or the relationship itself. Inability to delay gratification, childishness. Prima donna behavior, self-dramatization, acting out. Infatuation.

How would you like to be a child again?

Chances are that you have mixed feelings about that question. The child-related issues of the fourth house revolve around childlike feelings, needs, and fears. The fifth house has more to do with childlike self-expression and spontaneous, playful behavior. It would be wonderful to go back to the days when you had a sense of wonder for new experiences and new people, when it was easier to play, to laugh, to love, when your imagination was more active. On the other hand, childhood had its drawbacks, among them the eerie feeling that time dragged on forever, that you had little control over your life or future, and that you were a frustrated captive in a country bordered with incomprehensible "thou shalts" and "thou shalt nots." Childhood is an egocentric, self-indulgent time, partly because the boundaries of the world aren't, understandably, much bigger than those of the self.

A partner who affects your fifth house by transposition can put you back in that childlike place, with all the beauty and delight—and regressive self-indulgence—possible when the house of creative self-expression, love affairs, and joy is stimulated. Are you ready to fall in love, playfully, headily, breathlessly? Your romantic ideal may well be met by someone who activates this house. Do you want to have more fun, to forget about Monday morning and just enjoy a relaxing, silly, non-constructive weekend? Would you love it if someone encouraged you to drag that unfinished novel out of your filing cabinet, enroll in a pottery class, and get your camera out of the closet? Would you like to be able to reach out and connect with people more easily? Then you would benefit from a mate and dear friends who energize your fifth house.

On the other hand, someone who stimulates your fifth house can also pump up all your childish, irresponsible behaviors, feeding the part of you that wants what you want when you want it, regardless of what it might cost you: your best interests, your future plans, your integrity, your primary relationship. More is needed for a long-term commitment than your fifth house romantic ideal. Someone who affects this area of your chart can give the hungry child in you a voice, a microphone, and center stage, encouraging a "play now, pay later" mentality.

If your partner affects your fifth house by transposition, enjoy the relationship! Here's someone who is easily able to make you laugh and to spark your originality. But take care that he or she doesn't contribute to your *childish*, rather than *childlike*, behavior.

If you energize your mate's fifth house, you can act like a tonic or a Muse, enhancing play and creativity. There need to be positive reasons for staying in a couple, and you can supply plenty: life is more fun with you. Take advantage of your direct line to that person's smile muscles. You can also invoke the sappy romantic in your partner, now and twenty years from now.

But if that sappy romantic demands that life always be as magical as your first month together, you may need to disillusion him or her, gently. A similar dynamic exists with your ability to release the child in your mate. Encourage that child's spontaneity, but don't encourage it to tyrannize the adult by demands for constant attention or instant gratification.

Bess Truman's Mars-Sun conjunction falls in Harry Truman's fifth house, and the dynamic of that marriage was a playful one (fifth house). Edward VII and Wallis Simpson each placed the Sun into the other's fifth

241

house; theirs is a famous (solarized) romantic (fifth house) story. Kate Capshaw's Saturn, Sun and Mercury fall in Steven Spielberg's fifth house.

THE TRANSPOSED SIXTH HOUSE

Traditional Name: House of Servants.

When Healthy: More confidence in one's competence and skills; increased recognition of them by others. Greater sense of responsibility and ability to mentor and be mentored. Improved understanding of one's strengths and weaknesses.

When Confused: Decreased confidence in one's abilities; lack of understanding of one's faults or virtues. Poor mentoring. Lack of clarity about one's "job description," due to preemption by partner or to insufficient recognition for one's own skills. Earning love by performing tasks, or refusal to assume enough responsibility.

The fundamental issues of the sixth house are competence, usefulness, responsibility and the transmission of knowledge or lineage. The sixth house contains echoes of the second; its questions are similar. What use am I? What can I do well? Am I recognized for that or not? How does that make me feel about myself? But it also offers concrete ways of improving ourselves in those areas.

If your mate makes a strong impact on your sixth house, prepare to ask yourself those questions more often, and prepare to have some good answers.

Helen's Sun falls in Barry's sixth house. They meet at the small college where Helen teaches American literature, when Barry does a human interest story on the revamped English department for the paper where he's a part-time reporter. The rest of the time he writes fiction. So does Helen. They fall in love.

What effect could Helen's Sun have on Barry's sixth house?

One scenario looks like this: Helen reads Barry's material and praises its originality, characterization, dialogue, and immediacy. She lists famous writers whose work resembles his, delighting and encouraging him. She also points out that he gets so lost in his characters' heads that he has trouble stringing a plot together, suggests authors to read for role models, recommends an editing service, gets him into a writers' group that refers him to an agent, and wonders why he doesn't try his hand at a play like *Spoon River Anthology*, where characterization rather than plot is essential. Barry takes these comments to heart and his work takes off. He wins first prize at a drama festival, and there's talk of a Broadway production.

This is the wonderful side of sixth-house transposition. Helen has given Barry affirmation of his writing ability, confidence in what he does well (characterization and dialogue), understanding of where his skills need improvement, and practical help and mentoring in improving them. She has encouraged him to take his talent seriously and to take responsibility for developing it, leading to recognition from others.

Darker sixth-house scenarios are available, too. Helen could just as easily have read Barry's material, compared him scathingly and unfavorably—and accurately—to the geniuses whose work she teaches, and advised him to stick to the newspaper. He might have found that his faith in his ability to write a news story was also shaken. He might have decided that he'd better study *all* of the authors that Helen had to read for her Ph.D., before he wrote another word of fiction. Demoralized, he might have quit the paper, given up writing altogether, and found another line of work, while at night he humbly helped Helen grade papers and wished he were more talented. How lucky he is that Helen saved him from spectacular failure. How kind of her to let him ghost-write her articles. But of course part of him resents the demoralization to which he consented and takes passive-aggressive revenge by failing to live up to his other responsibilities in the relationship.

If you stimulate your partner's sixth house, you are not necessarily his or her teacher or mentor, but your influence can lead to that person's mastery of whatever skills are most personally meaningful to him or her—or to their substitution with empty busywork. Criticize constructively, and don't make indiscriminate assignments. And deal as delicately as you can with the paradox inherent in this house transposition: as a lover, you must treat each other as equals; and yet circumstances will dictate that you are also in a position to critique your partner as would a teacher.

If your mate transposes several planets into your sixth house, make sure you have a good grasp on the abilities that are personally meaningful to you, and be prepared to resist efforts to draft you into other areas. Be prepared as well for some review of those skills that can lead to their improvement. Be careful not to accept or reject new possibilities without thought. Neither of you should have to expend efforts to receive love, and neither of you should carry all the load.

Mary Shelley, author of *Frankenstein*, transposed her Mars-Sun-Uranus conjunction into poet Percy Bysshe Shelley's sixth house, conjunct his

Mercury. Her Venus-Mercury conjunction also fell in Shelley's sixth house on his north node. Their common passion for (Mars) and genius in (Uranus) literature (Mercury) was a major part of their marriage and extended to a circle of friends (Venus). Jimmy Carter's Mars falls in Rosalyn Carter's sixth house. She attended his cabinet meetings (sixth house), causing some controversy (Uranus) for him and undoubtedly some stress and challenge (Mars) for herself.

THE TRANSPOSED SEVENTH HOUSE

Traditional Name: House of Marriage.
When Healthy: Improved ability to relate on an equal basis. Relationships become open-ended and mutually supportive. Emotional depth of partnerships enhanced, increased intimacy.
When Confused: Blurred sense of identity, overidentification with partner or attempts to dominate partner. Projection. Unequal relationships. Too many relationships, leaving no time for self. Dependency or fear of dependency; fear of intimacy.

House of Marriage. House of Open Enemies. Will you love or hate someone who affects your seventh house by transposition? Your reaction may not approach either extreme, but we can guarantee that it won't be indifference. A person who lights up this house commands your attention, calling it away from yourself (first house) to the not-self (seventh).

If your mate or friend energizes your seventh house, realize that in one sense he or she represents something you need and are drawn toward. That feeling of identification, that sense of oneness, is essential for committed love, and your mate can bring you that feeling. Appreciate the depth of that connection to your heart, but don't lose yourself in it.

Traditional astrologers say that you'll marry someone whose planets fall in your seventh house. Is that true? Maybe, maybe not. This is the house of intimacy, and formal marriage is only one kind. In the best of all possible worlds, you will feel a sense of spiritual kinship with someone who illuminates this house, and probably instantaneous affection. You are natural allies, partners, buddies. You have business together, perhaps metaphorically, perhaps literally. Such a person makes it easy to forget about yourself and identify with him or her.

244

If that sounds like the basis of a great relationship, you're right. If that sounds like trouble, you may also be right. The problem with forgetting yourself is that sooner or later you have to remember yourself again. A person who energizes your seventh house can give you something like amnesia, robbing you of the sense of your own identity and leading you to sacrifice your legitimate concerns.

What happens then? You don't have a romance, you become a parasite. In the darkest scenario, you may realize it, but be too frightened to do anything, terrified that if your partner goes, what little sense of identity you retain will go, too. Perhaps you fight back by trying to dominate the relationship, locking your transposed seventh house into a battle of "open enemies." Or you may make genuine, sustained efforts to sort out your own wants and needs from those of your mate, and to compromise rationally so that both sets of requirements are met, allowing each of you to enjoy the feeling of completion and fulfillment that a transposed seventh house can bring. Your lover can then seem like your long-lost other half, finally found. And that's a wonderful feeling, especially when you don't have to pay your identity for it.

Keep working. Think of your partnership as a sailboat whose steering requires constant attention as the boat yaws from starboard to port. The sailor's phrase, "One hand for yourself, one hand for the ship," is applicable to the transposed seventh house: keep an eye on your partner's needs and an eye on your own, too.

Another side effect of the transposed seventh house can be an increase in the sheer number of new people that you meet. Make an effort to welcome your mate's friends into your life and be ready to cultivate new acquaintances together. If you're starved for companionship, you'll love this. But if your social schedule already makes you fantasize about a year on an isolated island, you may need to take steps to keep the schedule under control.

If you stimulate the seventh house of someone you love, transposing many planets there, your partner can feel a selfless concern and tenderness for you that is hard to match elsewhere. Don't take advantage of it and try to turn him or her into your clone, or you can activate the house of open enemies instead. You deserve resistance if you try to preempt someone's identity.

Zelda Fitzgerald's Sun-Ascendant conjunction fell in F. Scott Fitzgerald's seventh house, and his Jupiter in her seventh, accenting their feelings of closeness and connectedness. Seventh house transpositions frequently occur in couples and friendships: Kurt Russell's Moon falls in Goldie Hawn's seventh house; Bruce Willis's Ascendant falls in Demi Moore's seventh house; Melanie Griffith's Mercury, Venus and Jupiter fall in Antonio Banderas's seventh house, and John Lennon's Ascendant fell in Yoko Ono's seventh house.

THE TRANSPOSED EIGHTH HOUSE

Traditional Name: House of Death.
When Healthy: Feelings intensified. Psychological sophistication increased. Improved ability to imprint on or bond to partner. Healthy sexuality. Acceptance of death; openness to the occult or religious feelings.
When Confused: Neuroses intensified. Morbid self-absorption. Sexual blockage. Denial of fear or death or of transpersonal dimensions of reality.

The House of Death, at least in medieval astrology. But a person whose planets fall in your eighth house is not necessarily someone who helps you write your last will and testament. There are all kinds of death symbolized by the eighth house. Physical death, and questions about what part of the human spirit might survive it. Death of the sense of separateness, sometimes available through sexual merging; the Elizabethans called orgasm "the little death." There is the death of sexual innocence, and there are also psychological deaths, as previously cherished self-concepts are shattered and fall away.

This is the house of the instincts, survival instincts, sexual instincts, and other feelings that arise from profound layers of consciousness. We confront the bedrock of our psyches in this house—or are confronted with it, either by our lovers directly or through the feelings and circumstances we experience with them. Maybe we understand ourselves better; our former self-image dies. Perhaps what we have discovered sets us free, or perhaps it overwhelms us, scaring us so badly that we run from further insights and from anyone who might evoke them. Refusal to look at the truth about ourselves is another kind of death.

The other side of this house is *rebirth*: birth of enhanced self-understanding, of a deeper capacity for intimacy, of a stronger, wiser spirit. Someone who affects your eighth house offers you those possibilities, but you will not make them real without the willingness to face yourself honestly and to acknowledge your feelings, drives, moods, and instincts. If

246

you're hiding from yourself, a mate who transposes planets into your eighth house has the key to the closet where you keep your skeletons, whether you like it or not. You'll deal with them, or they will deal with you.

John's Sun and three other planets fall in Mary's eighth house. Within days of meeting him, Mary finds herself telling John all about her teenage bout with anorexia, something she has never discussed with anyone but her therapist. Perhaps she realizes she needs to do more work on resolving the issues underlying her former eating disorder, goes back into therapy, and feels better. Perhaps her talk with John was exactly the catharsis she needed, no more and no less. Instead, perhaps she's terrified by the feelings their conversation has stirred up, and she runs away from John and has a relapse. No way to tell how she'll react. All we know is that John's impact on her eighth house puts Mary in touch with that part of herself. How she handles it is up to her.

Is that the only way John affects Mary's eighth house? Probably not. His presence in her life also results in Mary's spending more of her time considering her sexuality, what it is and what it isn't. Perhaps she'll find John attractive and perhaps not, but his influence directs more of her attention to sexual issues. If Mary commits to John, she will also find herself more preoccupied by thoughts and feelings about death, the survival of consciousness, and other transrational subjects. Again, whether those topics disturb or fascinate Mary depends on her, not on John.

If you energize your mate's eighth house, you can make an unforgettable impact on him or her, physically, emotionally and psychically. Make sure it's not psychological dynamite; you're not necessarily your partner's therapist, nor should you be, although you can help bring those skeletons up to the light of day.

Elizabeth Taylor's Sun-Mars-Mercury conjunction lies in the late Richard Burton's eighth house, increasing the passionate intensity in their marriage. Van Gogh's Midheaven-Mars-Venus conjunction, and his Sun, fell in Gauguin's eighth house; their relationship certainly exposed Gauguin to some of the more turbulent aspects of the eighth house. So did Monica Lewinsky's association with Bill Clinton, and her Moon falls in Clinton's eighth house.

THE TRANSPOSED NINTH HOUSE

Traditional Name: House of Long Journeys Over Water.

247

When Healthy: Increased openness to new experiences. Well-considered, but flexible, world view. Reflection upon values and the meaning of one's life. Cross-cultural experience.

When Confused: Loss of one's belief system, without positive replacement. Rigid defensiveness of personal philosophy. Intolerance, dogmatism. Boredom. Nihilism.

What is the meaning of life? What are you doing here on this crazy planet? Why do you *bother* living?

Did you have your reply ready? Could you have jumped onto a soapbox and delivered a speech? If you've got life all figured out, you may not appreciate someone who energizes your ninth house. But if you don't have all the answers and you don't mind new questions, you'll love that person.

You might expect someone who lights up your ninth house to call you from the airport with two tickets to Easter Island. That's entirely possible. But there are mental journeys as well as physical ones. You could also spend an evening together in your living room poring over an Easter Island picture book, looking at the giant statues gazing out to sea, speculating about why they were built and what happened to the builders. Your conversation could take several interesting twists. Were the statues idols? Why do religions create icons? Is the urge to create linked with the capacity to feel awe? Do *you* do anything creative? Have you ever played with modeling clay? Well, it just so happens that your friend has some out in the car . . .

And you spend the rest of the evening up to your elbows in clay and new ideas.

Be prepared to stretch with someone who transposes your ninth house. Let go of your viewpoint on the world, because you're about to be handed a telescope, a microscope, and a kaleidoscope. Allow your perspective to change. Welcome experiences that are foreign to you, whether you have them in another country or with people whose nationalities and natures are different from yours. This house is also known as the house of higher education, religion and philosophy. A partner who stimulates your ninth house can educate you, in the broadest sense of the word. You are led to question your pivotal values—another term for religion, really—and the principles by which you live.

You might feel like Galileo did the first time he saw the moons of Jupiter. You never again see the universe the same way.

On the other hand, you might understand how cult members feel when someone is brainwashing them. The horror of it is that you might allow that to happen. A mate who energizes your ninth house may consciously or unconsciously substitute his or her world views for yours, or trigger dogmatism in you as you try to defend your own. We could all be wiser than we are, and it won't hurt you to try someone else's beliefs on for size. But if they don't fit, don't keep them—and if they do, then stretch to include them. The delicate line you are walking is to avoid defensiveness and understand your mate's ideas first, before you reject them out of hand.

If you affect your partner's ninth house, don't proselytize. Your influence can give your mate a smorgasbord of experiences and a renewed sense of wonder at the fascinating complexity of life. Life with you will not be boring. Your presence may help your mate open up to entirely new ways of thinking. But that doesn't mean that you're on a divine mission to convert the savage. Also, if your partner's birthchart indicates an above average requirement for reflection or solitude, realize that you are increasing the pace of his or her life and understand that need for time to process new thoughts and activities.

De Beauvoir's Jupiter and Neptune fell in Sartre's ninth house, with her Neptune conjunct his. It's interesting that a tenet of existentialist philosophy (ninth house) involves becoming conscious (Neptune) of one absolute given, the simple fact of one's existence, rather than one's essence or the possible meaning of that existence. The late Linda McCartney was a vegetarian and an animal rights activist, along with her husband Paul. With that shared philosophy we would expect ninth house transpositions: Paul's Mars and Pluto fall in Linda's ninth house, and Linda's Saturn, Uranus and Jupiter fell in Paul's ninth house.

THE TRANSPOSED TENTH HOUSE

Traditional Name: House of Career.
When Healthy: Public identity reflects total self; meaningful work; sense of mission.
When Confused: Inauthentic social role; narrow attachment to status.

Follow someone around for a week. Find out all you can about that person without a face-to-face meeting. Talk to colleagues, neighbors. Do a search on the Internet. Sift through garbage. Look up credit records and tax returns and voter registrations. Unless you found something really naughty in the garbage, at the end of that week you have constructed a working description of that person's tenth house: the public identity, the role in the culture; status; reputation; what he or she stands for; what others know about him or her, without personal acquaintance. The surface of the life, in other words—where the soul interfaces with society as a whole.

When your mate's planets stimulate your tenth house, they stimulate your public identity and expand the amount of time you spend dealing with it. Run for public office. Work in the drive to forbid the polluting toxic waste dump proposed for your area. Marry someone of another race—and thus become a public symbol whether you like it or not. Move into an upscale subdivision—or a downscale ghetto. Play in a band on the weekends. These are all tenth house activities—there are many ways to establish your public myth in the minds of others, even without trying. The trick is making sure that the myth isn't too far from reality. Be wary of a relationship promising status, power, and notoriety if the nature of that status, power, and notoriety is irrelevant to you personally.

You are a painter, and a good one, and your oils have achieved some local recognition. People are prodding you to send slides to New York City. Dealers are sniffing around your studio. Along comes a friendship with an art critic who has connections in the city. Sounds wonderful, right? Yes, if your heart and soul are expressed through those paintings, and if it's important to you to have them recognized. No . . . if you've decided that you've learned all you can from painting, and now you're obsessed with photography. Don't avoid the art critic if other factors in the relationship seem right, but don't be bamboozled into hauling those canvases to New York. Invite the critic into your darkroom instead.

If you energize the tenth house of someone you love, you can help this person gain recognition and affirmation for being herself. In the medieval sense, you can act as a king-maker who helped a monarch gain his birthright. But first you should understand exactly who your mate is, what he or she values, where the core of the identity lies, so that you don't put an impostor on the throne. A relationship with someone who is maintaining that uneasy balance with the outside world is like loving someone who's living under a false identity. It strains both of you, with diminished room for authentic intimacy.

Aristotle Onassis's Mercury-Ascendant-Sun conjunction fell in Jacqueline Kennedy Onassis's tenth house; one result of their marriage was to make her even more a subject of public scrutiny than before. Director Roberto

Rossellini's Sun, Mars, Venus and Jupiter all fell in actress Ingrid Bergman's tenth house. As well as affecting her career (tenth house), their affair was considered a great public (tenth house!) scandal in the late 1940s and early 1950s, drew a lot of criticism, and caused Bergman to be ostracized in Hollywood for a while.

THE TRANSPOSED ELEVENTH HOUSE

Traditional Name: House of Friends.
When Healthy: Enhanced sense of purpose. Clarified goals. Relationships and contacts that support our aims. Improved strategic sense. Useful alliances. Effective networking.
When Confused: Loss of purpose. Confusion about direction in life. Hesitance about commitment to anything. Associates who waste our time. Pointless social over-extension.

House of goals. House of friends. House of the future. What do you want to be doing five years from now? What sort of person do you want to be? What kind of lifestyle will you have? What will you have accomplished?

Are you taking steps to get there?

Do you have any help? Who's supporting you? Where are your allies?

All of these issues are raised in a relationship with someone who transposes planets into your eleventh house. The person may or may not bring them up, but the nature of the interaction will be such that you will ask yourself these questions, whether your partner does or not.

Jane has been ice skating since she was four years old. She's training for the next Olympics. Her coach transposes a cluster of planets into Jane's eleventh house. So does her best friend, who wants Jane to quit skating, devote herself to ballet, which she's also been studying since she was small, and move to New York with her to audition for ballet companies. Jane's boyfriend Philip also affects Jane's eleventh house by transposition. They sincerely love each other, and he's supportive of whatever choice she wants to make. They've been involved for over a year when Jane gets pregnant. Now what?

The choice is Jane's. Her career, her residence, her marital status, her pregnancy, her decisions, all belong naturally to Jane. People who stimulate her eleventh house force her to define her goals and make choices, sometimes helping and sometimes hindering her, but in the long run those choices, and

251

the responsibility for their consequences, are Jane's and Jane's alone. She takes her friends' needs and viewpoints into account, and probably even solicits their views, but in the end, it's she who decides.

Someone who energizes your eleventh house brings you face-to-face with what you want to do with the rest of your life. They put those questions on center stage for you. You are like the horse in the proverb; your mate leads you to the water, but you have to decide whether you want to drink. You choose the goals and move towards them yourself. Perhaps your mate supports you or perhaps not, but his or her presence in your life catalyzes your making those decisions—or backing away from them.

Not to choose is also a choice. Refusal to commit to a specific future still creates a future: drifting, time-wasting, aimlessness, daydreaming about what you're going to do one of these days.

Goals are seldom reached alone. The traditional association of this house with friends has some validity, if we substitute for friends the notion of associates—like-minded others, colleagues, or simply those who have similar goals. A mate who energizes your eleventh house can bring those kinds of people into your life, helping you create a network, a support system, of people all moving in the same direction. On the other hand, if you've allowed your mate to make your choices for you, or if you've made none at all, someone who affects your eleventh house will still pull a lot of people into your life—to help you waste your time and distract you from your essential lack of purpose.

If your lover activates your eleventh house, plan to spend some time considering what you want to do with your future. Discuss your thoughts with your lover. Listen to the feedback, but make up your own mind. If you stimulate your mate's eleventh house, have that same conversation, but do more listening than talking. Do you know what your mate really wants? Are those goals ones that you can support without sacrificing your own? Look at your mutual friends and acquaintances. Are those associations positive for everyone involved, or are they merely taking up your time?

Keith Richards's Saturn falls in bandmate Mick Jagger's eleventh house, adding the potential of practical strategies (saturnization) to Jagger's attainment of his goals. Humphrey Bogart and Lauren Bacall's Moons fell in each other's eleventh houses, adding to shared feelings and a similar vision of their future. Yoko Ono's Venus and Saturn fell in John Lennon's eleventh house, and John Lennon's Venus fell in Yoko Ono's eleventh house. Their marriage undoubtedly brought her professional contacts (eleventh house) and helped bring her art to a wider audience, and changed the direction of both of their lives.

THE TRANSPOSED TWELFTH HOUSE

Traditional Name: House of Troubles.
When Healthy: Enhanced ability to transcend the smaller self and sense the eternal. Increased openness to spiritual, psychic or meditative experiences. More willingness to let go of ego attachments and identifications.
When Confused: Blurred sense of identity; mental and emotional confusion; increase in escapist, self-destructive, numbing behavior; "bad luck," as attachments are forcibly stripped away.

Wendy believes in prosperity consciousness. One assumption she has about people is that if they're hurting for money, it proves they don't love themselves enough, because we all have the right to abundance as God's children. Wendy isn't Scrooge, nor is money her highest value, but prosperity consciousness still permeates her myth of herself and the world.

Wendy meets Thomas while contributing to a charity drive that he directs. Five or six of his planets fall into her twelfth house. She quickly recognizes that Thomas is more conscious, more open, more loving and happier than she is. Yet Thomas is chronically broke. He devotes his time and energy to administering organizations that give to the poor, and he keeps almost nothing for himself. To her credit, Wendy is intrigued by Thomas and makes an effort to get to know him better. Thomas doesn't talk much about his beliefs, but she learns from one conversation, and a lot of observation, that he regards the love of money as an attachment that would hold him back spiritually.

Poverty isn't inherently holy—our example could just as easily have been Thomas's encounter with a prosperity advocate. Maybe he's attached to "holy poverty." The point of the story is that someone who energizes your twelfth house comes at you from your blind side, undercutting your myth of yourself and the world, presenting you with new perceptions that invalidate your premises.

How do you react? At a lower level, we react badly, disliking the person who pulls the rug out from under us and kicks away the props that support our ego. It can be an enormously stressful and unsettling encounter. But there is rich potential in it too. Someone who activates our twelfth house walks into our life saying, "Where you have put your treasure, there your heart is also." We are forced to look at our attachments and our rigid identification with our egos. Ego itself is not the problem. If we didn't have egos, we couldn't function here. It is our *identification* with our egos, our *attachment* to our egos, our *thinking that we are no more than our egos,* that can be problematic. If we are willing to grow and to acknowledge our higher selves as well as our egos, someone who affects our twelfth house by transposition strikes a spiritual, mystical chord in us. If we're not, we feel more as though he or she slammed a grand piano lid shut on our fingers.

In a minor relationship involving twelfth house transposition, that's as far as it goes—we expand our consciousness and partially release an attachment, or we shut that person out and make an attempt to explain them away. But if we are in a serious connection with someone who hits our twelfth house in a big way, it's serious business. The fortune-teller would say that such a person will bring you misfortune. Truth is, with such a person, the deal between the higher selves reads something like this: this thing to which you are overly attached—in the course of this relationship, you will either release your dependency on it, or you agree that it will be ripped from your life.

Is that a misfortune? Judge for yourself.

If your mate affects your twelfth house by transposition, and you want to avoid the preceding scenario, be willing to question yourself. All of us are playing a role in the world: our personalities, our outer selves. Do actors worry about what will happen to their wardrobes, or to the stage setting when it's struck at the end of a play? They know that they are the creators; they are what is real, while the play and its characters is a creation that comes and goes, interesting while it lasts and worth acting well, but not what is truly most important. Be willing to look at the "character" your outer self portrays, and how much you define yourself through transitory, outward conditions. Learn to identify yourself with your inner being, your higher self, and then your character's costumes and props and speeches, although necessary to function in the world, will become less important. You will feel more free—and that sense of *engaged detachment* from life, and the buoyancy that accompanies it, are the gifts pressed into your hands by a partner who stimulates your twelfth house.

If you activate your lover's twelfth house, remember: you are not his or her guru. Your presence in your mate's life can facilitate confrontation with that level of reality, but you are not there to force that growth to happen according to any scripts of yours. Your effect on your mate's life is to lessen

254

his or her *exclusive identification with his or her outer personality.* That influence can frighten your partner, and with good reason. We all need to have an outer self that functions effectively in the world; complete lack of one spells insanity. Don't try to strip your partner of his or her personality.

Kenneth Starr's Mars-Venus conjunction falls in Bill Clinton's twelfth house, and Clinton probably felt as if the rug was being pulled out from underneath him by the Starr report. Jimmy Carter's Venus-Neptune conjunction lies in Rosalynn's Carter's twelfth house conjunct her Sun-Neptune; this transposition undoubtedly has something to do with the shared faith that is part of their marriage. We were struck by the number of artistic collaborations with twelfth house transpositions; creativity can flow from the twelfth house source. Mary Shelley's Jupiter fell in Percy Bysshe Shelley's twelfth house; Elizabeth Taylor's Pluto and Jupiter fell into the late Richard Burton's twelfth house, and his Moon in her twelfth. Antonio Banderas and Melanie Griffith transpose their Moons into one another's twelfth houses, while Kate Capshaw's Jupiter falls in Steven Spielberg's twelfth house.

CHAPTER FIFTEEN: PUTTING IT ALL TOGETHER

Ever been confused by love? Ask a hundred people. You'll get ninety-nine positive responses and maybe one demurral from someone with a bad case of testosterone poisoning. Forming a lasting bond with another human being may be one of life's most rewarding experiences, but it can also push us toward our mental and emotional ragged edges. In the secret world of intimacy, common sense is half-suspended. Logic is bent, rules are changed. It's beautiful and perplexing.

In synastry, astrology offers us a *metaphor* for love. It offers a symbol—a streamlined representation of a phenomenon too complex for the mind to grasp in any other way.

How do we benefit from using such a metaphor? By allowing it to simplify and schematize for us the essential dynamics of a partnership. What do we gain? Clarity. And what does that clarity cost? A high price—to gain clarity we must invariably sacrifice some of the truth. The further we delve into the realm of symbols, the more we put distance between ourselves and the immediate reality of living.

The astrologer's task—your task now—is to find a point of balance. On one hand, we have life with its boundless spider web of infinitesimal details. On the other hand, we have astrology: a few dozen symbols trying to represent that spider web. Go too far in the direction of the symbols and your interpretations become either trivial and misleading ("Leos are never happy with Scorpios"), or so heady they become vacuous, disconnected from everyday experience ("Your asteroid Eros is in a bi-novile aspect to the midpoint of his Mercury and Jupiter. You stimulate him erotically to speak exuberantly at a theoretical level.") (Client: *"Huh?"*)

Go too far in the other direction, away from the symbols and back toward life, and what happens? Astrology's simplifying, clarifying diagram falls away, leaving you just as confused as you were before you bought the astrology book. Then the same old fights re-emerge, punctuated with new phrases . . . "your infuriatingly patriarchal, domineering Saturn" . . . "your fawning, vague Pisces Moon, which can never take a consistent position!"

Balance is the answer. Take in as much complexity as you can, then stop. Find your own comfort zone. Astrology is flexible. Tailor it to your personal needs and mental strengths. Keep freedom and personal choice in it. Keep one eye on reality. Keep the other eye on all those interaspects and house transpositions. But never let the symbols overwhelm you. When you start to feel perplexed, back up. Flex astrology back toward simplicity, even if that means moving temporarily into generalizations. Then go forward again, adding the details and subtleties that make synastry come alive.

Let the symbols speak to your heart, in other words. And if your heart has trouble with four-syllable words, limit the symbols to three-syllable words for a while. How? Read on. That's what the rest of this chapter is about.

I'll Never Be Able to Figure All This Out

Unless you're the kind of person who can solve calculus problems in her head while reciting long Shakespearean passages in Swahili, you probably haven't remembered every detail in the preceding chapters, let alone figured out how to get them all working in concert. Synastry is complicated. It had better be! After all, it's trying to mirror human love.

He: intimacy-hungry with many eighth house Libran planets. She: private and solitary, with Saturn a key player in her birthchart. His Moon sextile her Sun. Her Uranus conjunct his Venus in the fourth house. Each of these factors and dozens more must be analyzed, understood, and fitted into the larger scheme. And you must accomplish that task without ever losing your sense of the big picture.

Who can succeed? Maybe nobody. Our brains have limits. Perfect understanding of even a single birthchart is probably beyond us. In synastry we face two such birthcharts, plus their interactions. The mind boggles.

How You Can Succeed Anyway

There are two guidelines that guarantee success in synastry despite the density of the astrological information. One we've already briefly considered: whenever you start to get confused, simply retreat back to a simpler level of astrological analysis.

Guideline Number One: *Accept the fact that no human intelligence can successfully correlate all the details in a synastric interaction. Proceed by starting with the simplest levels of analysis. Add layers until you feel mental strain. Then stop and work as deeply as you can with what you have. At all costs, keep your heart engaged!*

In other words, don't push too hard. It doesn't work. There's no sense diverting so much energy into the purely analytical parts of your brain that you starve your intuition. That happens easily, and it makes for a sadly common phenomenon: dried-out, pedantic astrology.

The second guideline, outlined precisely throughout the rest of this chapter, is to follow an orderly, step-by-step procedure in your analysis. Otherwise the resulting tidal wave of undigested astrological ideas will surely wash away your concentration, leaving you with one of those slack-jawed stares you saw on the faces of the kids in the back row of algebra class.

Guideline Number Two: *Plan your attack! Make an outline and stick to it. By absorbing specific, predefined interpretive strategies, you can rightly judge the order in which to ask yourself questions, and you can put the answers into a coherent comprehensible pattern.*

A vivid overview of two Sun or Moon signs, profoundly understood and clearly presented, is vastly more helpful than a confused, disorderly gloss of buzz words describing dozens of more obscure interaspects. That realization is the core of the first guideline. Throw in guideline number two—a systematic approach—and you'll likely discover that you've been underestimating your interpretive powers.

Staying on Top of the Symbols

A systematic approach: that's the key to staying on top of synastry's flood of information. It's a lot like playing jazz: to succeed, you must learn to improvise within a structure. In jazz, that structure is a pattern of musical chords. In synastry, it's a logical sequence of astrological questions. Each must be answered in the correct order. Miss a step, and you'll blow a sour note.

In the preceding chapters we've been looking at the astrology of intimacy from a theoretical perspective. In the remainder of this chapter, we leave the world of theory and enter the realm of everyday astrological practice. With the knowledge of theory you've gained, you are like a budding jazz musician. You know your scales. You know what notes fit each chord. You can tap out complex rhythms. You have some mastery of your instrument. Now all you need is a melody! That is, a structure within which to play and thereby to explore and expand your skills.

Just as there are an infinite number of possible melodies, there are probably an infinite number of ways to organize an astrological analysis. In the pages that follow, we don't mean dogmatically to exclude other methods, and we certainly don't mean to stifle your own creativity. Our aim is only to offer a practical, effective interpretive system that has worked well for us. With a fair understanding of the details we've already covered, coupled with the following procedural outline, we guarantee that you'll be able to provide yourself and your friends with insightful, comprehensible astrological interpretations. This, in other words, is *our* melody. Maybe later you'll compose your own.

The Grand Scheme

Clear off a tabletop. Get out your collection of felt-tip pens. Put a bright light nearby. Turn on your telephone answering machine. And make a pot of tea. Settle down. You'll be here a while. Don't expect anything to happen quickly. You're going to have an exciting experience, but it won't be exciting in the shock-a-minute way of the latest Hollywood blockbuster. More like the excitement of watching the dawn unfold a perfect morning glory.

Your first step is to gather up your tools. Maybe you've run all the printouts you need on a computer or ordered them through the mail or online. Maybe you're one of the diehards who's still doing the work by hand. In any case, here's what you will need:

1. A copy of each of the two birthcharts, with their own aspect grids.

2. A document listing all the interaspects—either a synastry worksheet or one of the synastry grids available on all the major forms of astrological software.

3. A document listing all the house transpositions—again, that could be a synastry worksheet you've made yourself, or one of the various printouts available.

A pleasant visual alternative to number 3 is a "biwheel" printout of each birthchart, with the other person's chart displayed around it in the outer wheel—that makes for a quick, intuitive reference in terms of house transpositions.

Now you're ready to begin to squeeze meaning out of that chaos of symbolism.

How? Start with:

Guideline Number Three: *Put aside everything but the two birthcharts. Look at them one at a time.*

Every human being is different. That's one of the reasons life—and astrology—is so fascinating. Since we're all different, each of us brings different needs and expectations into intimacy. Don't miss those differences!

260

Use the birthchart to help you understand the individuals, independently of each other.

Miss this step and you'll start projecting your own stuff onto your poor clients, falling into the insidious trap of imagining that what's important to you in a relationship is equally important to everyone else. Not all women need their partners to be politically correct. Not all men need their partners to be thin. You might find it perfectly natural if your lover never wears anything but blue jeans and a sweatshirt—but let his or her religious sentiments diverge one inch from your own and sparks fly. That's fine. Just don't let those personal predilections blind you to the fact that the world is full of honorable people who couldn't care less about their lover's religion, but for whom a fashionable style of dress is a critical ingredient in maintaining the electricity of a sexual bond. *You've got to let each of those people start out as mysteries to you!*

We'll demonstrate this with F. Scott and Zelda Fitzgerald in the following chapter, but here's the outline of the procedure:

Pick one of the birthcharts. Start your analysis by looking at the "primal triad:" the Sun-Moon-Ascendant blend. Use the formula we introduced in Chapter Two to turn that blend into a single sentence based on fundamental archetypes. This person, for example, may be the *Storyteller* (Gemini Sun) with the soul of the *Hermit* (Capricorn Moon) wearing the mask of the *Shaman* (Scorpio Ascendant). Think about the sentence. Get a feel for it.

Now think about it at a deeper level. Behind the exoteric character description implied in that sentence, what is its deeper, esoteric soul-meaning? *Why,* in a purposeful, evolutionary universe, would this being manifest as a storyteller with a hermit's soul and the mask of a shaman? Through that Gemini Sun, we recognize an evolutionary intention to absorb a tremendous amount of fresh, even shocking experience in this lifetime—and a corresponding soul-discomfort at being bored or fenced in. The Capricorn Moon adds that some of the experiences this spirit needs in order to nourish itself arise only with tremendous effort and sustained self-discipline, and that the full digesting of these experiences depends on fairly protracted periods of solitude. With the Scorpio Ascendant operating as the interface between this soul and the outer world, we see a socially obvious attunement to the wavelength of human reality where serious, strong, emotional realities exist. This soul feeds on intensity and contact with the taboo—and quickly feels like the proverbial fish out of water in conventional, superficial social situations.

261

Add the house positions of the Sun and Moon. Where is this Storyteller's life happening? In the house of career? In the house of marriage?

Now mix in some planets. Is there a planet forming a conjunction with one of those primal triad factors? Is Neptune, the planet of mysticism, fused with that Hermit's soul? Now that Hermit is a mystic too—if he doesn't slip into some form of escapism to numb that overwhelming sensitivity. Is Mars, the god of War, fused with that Shaman's mask? Then we are probably looking at a particularly *scary* Shaman, whether or not that's his intention—what's that going to mean in terms of intimacy? Are there many planets grouped in a single house or sign? Then we have yet another focalized area.

Pay particular attention to Venus and Mars. They aren't inherently more important than other planets, but they play pivotal roles in love and sexuality. In synastry we accord them special attention.

Look at Venus. What sign does it occupy? That tells you what best fills this person with warm romantic feelings—what supports the simple *liking* which allows the harder evolutionary work to be sustained and tolerated. What does this soul need in a mate in order to maintain long-term interest in the bond? What are his or her evolutionary intentions in terms of partnership? And how does this person go about radiating attractiveness?

Now consider Mars. What sign shapes its action in this birthchart? The red planet offers you insights into the more passionate dimensions of the individual's character. What fills her with desire? What turns him on? How does he or she go about actively pursuing the object of his or her fancies? And what fears might complicate love in this particular evolving psyche?

If you need a deeper review of Mars and Venus, go back and scan Chapter Five.

Next, check the *arc of intimacy*: houses four, five, six, seven and eight. (If you need a review of those houses, turn back to Chapters Six through Eleven.) Any planets there? If so, they are keys to this soul's intimacy puzzle. Maybe there's a planet or two in the fourth house. Peel away the layers of the onion—just whom is this person revealed to be, deep inside, once the deepest kind of clan bonding has unfolded? What family of origin themes need to be understood before a truly new home could be formed with another adult? What kind of home would be appropriate and right for this person?

Does he or she face any lessons in the area of emotional spontaneity, love-play, or expressiveness? Is there significant business to be finished with other souls? Are there planets in the fifth house, in other words? What resources do these fifth house planets offer? How can their energies be misapplied?

Now move on to the sixth house: what about issues of responsibility and self-sacrifice, so essential to any kind of ongoing commitment? What issues must be faced with absolute humility? And what about this person's mentors? Whose help is necessary if this person is to become fully human? To whom, if anyone, does he or she owe a similar gift?

Planets in the seventh house? Here, in the traditional house of marriage, look for portraits of specific soulmates whom the person is destined to meet—and *needs* to meet, for evolutionary purposes. You'll see vivid descriptions of the lessons he or she needs to learn if those bonds are to prove productive and harmonious. Are there issues for this soul around trust and interdependency? What blind spots, inherent to this being's nature, must be corrected through surrendering to external help? Always remember that for most of us the lion's share of our seventh house partners are people with whom we actually don't fall in love or experience sexual energy—our spiritual friends usually outnumber our lovers here.

Planets in the eighth house? You've revealed the formula for sexual electricity or chemistry. What opens this soul to those half-incomprehensible, transformative erotic emotions, so sweet and compelling at first, that strip us naked, revealing our deepest wounds? What can we say about the character of this person's *natural mate*? What "journey into the dark" stands between him or her and actually creating the reality of lasting love?

Is your head spinning?

If it is, then perhaps you've gone far enough. Maybe it's time to remember guideline number one: don't strain yourself. You may only have scratched the surface of the birthchart, but you were scratching a vein of gold. Just from the questions we've covered, you've learned a lot. You've gotten a sense of the *person* behind that chart, and that's enough to satisfy the requirements of guideline number three, at least for starters. One of the things we hope you'll notice when we get to analyzing the Fitzgeralds' charts in the next chapter is how much we leave out. Accept the fact that for practical reasons of time and human limitations, a lot has to be left out of every interpretation. Take comfort in that! Just like jazz, sometimes it's the notes you *don't* play that really make the song.

Pour yourself another cup of tea. Take a breather. Let all that you've just discovered coalesce into a feeling for that chart. Can you visualize the big picture? Are you resonating with that person the way you might still be resonating with a movie character as you walk out of the theater? Or with an old friend five minutes after you hang up from a coast-to-coast phone call? Is your *body* feeling that birthchart, in other words? If so, you're doing fine. If not, then back up. Start over again . . . "the Storyteller with the soul of the Hermit wearing the mask of the hypnotist"—let it sink in.

Why are we being so warm and fuzzy here? Why all this emphasis upon subjective reactions? For one simple reason: as you move on to the next steps in your synastry analysis, you need temporarily to store all these ideas about the first birthchart. To keep them on ice for a while. There is no way to do that purely intellectually. There's too much information. As you move into the next phase of your interpretation, you run the risk of forgetting half of what you learned in phase one. *But human consciousness can organize vast quantities of information for storage in the form of emotional impressions.* That's basically how we remember people—and it's a good way to remember birthcharts too.

Maybe you're a more advanced astrologer, with more than an elementary knowledge of birthcharts. If so, then go further in your astrological analysis. Consider each planet, the aspects it forms, the house and sign it occupies. Guideline number one is not meant to be an endorsement of laziness, only a realistic recognition of limits. Push those limits! Go as far as you can in unraveling each chart. Just remember to assess yourself every now and then. Are you getting lost in details? Have you begun to lose the overview? Has the center of gravity shifted away from your heart, into your head?

Whether you are capable of world-class birthchart interpretations or a neophyte barely able to recall a few archetypes and key words for each sign, the process is essentially the same. Look at the birthchart. Learn what you can. Understand it. Feel it. And know your limits.

When you're done, put the first birthchart aside. Take another sip of tea. And repeat the process with the second birthchart.

At this point, if you've played your cards right, you've internalized the essential spirit of both birthcharts. If you're a beginner, such understanding might seem an elusive goal. Don't let that daunt you. Be persistent. Once you couldn't read a stranger's face. You didn't know *that* symbolism. Now, after a few years' experience, you can probably do a fair job of picking out the crazies and the energy-vampires at a glance. Astrology is the same. Give it a little time, and those hieroglyphics will communicate just as much to you as any zoned-out gaze or hungry leer.

With the two birthcharts unraveled individually, you are ready to proceed to the second major phase of your synastry analysis: watching them interact.

Guideline Number Four: *After you have absorbed the two birthcharts independently of each other, consider the interaspects they form between them.*

Look at your computerized synastry grid or the worksheet you've filled out. There are dozens and dozens of interaspects. How will you ever soak up all that information? Once again, take refuge in guideline number one: you probably *won't* grasp each and every one of those interaspects, and that's okay. You don't really need to pay attention to all of them. The more of them you can absorb, the deeper and more precise your synastry analysis will be. But even if you absorb only a few, you can still do useful, accurate interpretations. The trick lies in figuring out which of the interaspects are essential to your understanding of the partnership and which ones are merely fine-tuning.

Start strictly with the interaspects formed by the Sun, the Moon, and the Ascendant in each chart. These are absolute bedrock—and are generally present in long-lasting relationships. Jack's Moon squares Jill's Ascendant. Their Suns form a trine. Jill's Moon conjuncts Jack's Sun. Don't feel a sense of doom if you see challenging aspects here—nowadays, they can just easily mean passion, intensity, and aliveness in the relationship. The one fortune-telling rule that actually still seems to work pretty often is "no aspects, no action." If nothing is going on between the two primal triads, the survival of this relationship is going to depend on lots of space, independence, and tolerance for separate lives.

If you're fuzzy about the details of interaspect analysis, you may want to reread the chapters "How Birthcharts Interact," and "Interaspects."

Next, stretch out beyond Sun, Moon, and Ascendant to include planets. How does Jack's primal triad impact upon Jill's birthchart as a whole? Does his Sun, for example, form an aspect to her Venus? That is, does he solarize (emphasize; bring out) her Venusian qualities of attractiveness, affiliativeness, and warmth? Now consider the specific nature of the interaspect. Is it a square? That is, does that solarization occur through a tense, perhaps annoying process in which Jack applies friction to Jill's Venusian circuitry? Or is the aspect formed between his Sun and her Venus a harmonious trine? Then solarization occurs in a flowing way, with his identity (Sun) naturally enhancing (trine) her qualities of natural grace and affection (Venus).

265

Remember that at this stage, you are strictly concerned with the aspects that one person's Sun, Moon, or Ascendant make to the planets in the other person's chart. Jack's Mercury may square Jill's Saturn, for example, but it wouldn't have come up yet. Consider each primal triad interaspect to the other person's planets, one at a time, until you've covered them all. Then reverse the process, considering how Jill's primal triad fits into Jack's planetary patterns.

At any point in the process, if you start to feel overwhelmed, you need to back up—strategically. If Jack's Sun, Moon or Ascendant makes a *conjunction* with any of Jill's planets, it could really be a disaster to ignore it. After that, pay attention to interaspects in the following order: oppositions, squares, trines, then sextiles.

Perhaps you feel comfortable with your understanding of those critical interaspects. Great! Now it's time to go beyond the primal triad, putting particular focus on Venus and Mars and their planetary aspects. Maybe Jill's Saturn opposes Jack's Venus. That would be important—her need for solitude might feel like an emotional snub to him sometimes. She could see him as needy and he could see her as cold. That could be a big mess—or a relatively simple challenge in the communication department.

Staying on top of interaspect analysis can get hairy at this point. How do you know which planets to emphasize and which ones you can safely ignore? Two rules of thumb will guide you:

* *The more prominent the planet in the individual birthchart, the more seriously you take its interaspects—and of course an interaspect between a prominent planet in one birthchart and a prominent planet in the other chart would be pivotal.*

* *When in doubt, focus on aspects in this order of descending importance: conjunctions first, then oppositions, squares, trines, and sextiles.*

Keep going until you begin to feel that telltale strain. Maybe you felt that strain as soon as you considered the first interaspect. Time for another cup of tea! Relax. Go slowly. Remember that gut-level understanding of a single interaspect is worth a lot more than skimming many of them superficially.

If you're straining, then your wisest strategy is to reduce the number of interaspects with which you are working. But resist the temptation to eliminate the Sun, Moon or Ascendant from your considerations. They're always critical, even when you're just using whole sign aspects—anyone with the Sun in Aries is going to create feelings of being squared in someone with the Moon in Cancer!

With the rest of the planets, an effective way to narrow your field of inquiry is to focus more attention on the conjunctions, oppositions, and squares, as we mentioned earlier. Another way is to tighten the orbs of the interaspects. Maybe Jack's Mercury lies in twelve degrees of Cancer, squaring Jill's Mars in five degrees of Libra. For the square to be perfect, Jill's Mars would of course have to lie in twelve degrees of Libra, exactly ninety degrees from Jack's Mercury. As it is, the interaspect is seven degrees away from being precise. By considering only interaspects within, say, two or three degrees of exactitude, you drastically reduce the number of planetary relationships. More importantly, in narrowing your orbs, you systematically throw away your pennies before you throw away your nickels and dimes. You're left with only the truly pivotal interaspects.

Watch what we do with the Fitzgeralds in the next chapter—the majority of their interaspects won't be discussed specifically. We find it more effective to go deeply into the truly pivotal ones.

Maybe you've gotten a feel for every interaspect in the synastry grid. Maybe you've only felt a glimmer of understanding for three or four of them. Either way, the secret of success in synastry lies in customizing your approach to the symbols, making sure it fits your level of skill and experience—and is tractable enough for your intuition to remain active. If you're not overextended, you're doing fine and you're ready to proceed to the next step in your analysis.

Guideline Number Five: *After absorbing the interaspects, move on to considering house transpositions—where the planets in the first chart would fall if placed in the houses in the second chart, and vice versa.*

Where would Jack's planets lie if they were placed in Jill's birthchart? That is, which houses would they occupy? If Jack has Jupiter in 19 Scorpio and Jill's Ninth house begins in 15 Scorpio, then *his* Jupiter lies in *her* ninth house. What does that mean? In this case, he jovializes (expands; encourages) her ninth house qualities of adventure and philosophy.

If the reasoning behind these house transpositions is unclear to you, please review Chapter Fourteen, "Your Planets, My Sky."

How do you work with house transpositions in practice? You can eyeball it and fill out a synastry worksheet. You can also order computerized printouts that show the data—although be careful here! If Jill's ninth house cusp had been at 20 Scorpio instead of 15 in our example a few lines ago, then a computerized printout would have dutifully indicated that Jack's Jupiter fell in her eighth house. The psychic reality of their experience is that his Jupiter is conjunct her ninth house cusp, being only one degree away. If you are using computerized calculations, be wary of that glitch. House cusps have orbs—when a planet is with a couple degrees of one, its action is thrown forward.

The easiest way to see house transpositions is to use the biwheel option. Put Jack's planets around the outer rim of Jill's chart, and vice versa. What you have then is a pair of charts that graphically indicate exactly where and how each person stimulates experience and growth in the other one. Then all you have to do is look.

Ideally the astrologer would consider each house transposition separately and in detail. With some experience, that ideal is attainable, although it's probably overkill. The quantity of information available here is not so vast as what we uncover in the webwork of interaspects. Still, feel free to invoke guideline number one—you don't need to comprehend every house transposition in order to do effective interpretations. Even with only a few of them understood, you can have a solid grasp on this step in your synastry analysis. As with interaspects, the trick lies in knowing which house transpositions are really essential to understand, and which ones are secondary. If you start simplifying in a random way, you might mistakenly throw out the key that could unlock the secrets of the partnership. Sun, Moon, and Ascendant—once again, these primal triad factors are pivotal. Novice or otherwise, begin your house transposition analysis there. Where does Jill's Sun lie in Jack's chart? Where, in other words, does she solarize his life? You can safely assume that the issues, experiences, and pitfalls of that existential arena (house) will be pushed into greater prominence in Jack's life, so long as he remains close to Jill.

The transpositions of the Moons are next on our list. Here the process is lunarization—where does Jack introduce a deeper element of emotion, imagination, and creativity in Jill's life? Where does he nurture her, and where might he run the run the risk of infantilizing or smothering her?

Jill's Ascendant impacts upon one of Jack's houses. Here she pushes the affairs of that part of his life into more active behavior, helping to shape their self-expressive style, often adding confidence and flair. Her Ascendant may lie in his third house (communication). Maybe she encourages Jack to write or simply to speak more freely and comfortable. Maybe she helps him find his "voice." Jack of course ascendantalizes Jill in return, perhaps stimulating her eighth house through that transposition. Then, among other effects, he helps her express her sexuality in a more confident, colorful way.

Two Suns, two Moons, two Ascendants: six house transpositions. If you've considered all of them and gotten an impression of how they operate, then you've fulfilled the minimal requirement in this phase of our synastry analysis. Maybe that's enough. Once again, monitor yourself for mental strain. If you're comfortable, try going a little further. We've emphasized the importance of avoiding overextension. Be just as wary of underextension! Maybe you can take your house transposition analysis a step further.

Which planet should come next? There is no rigid answer. The rule of thumb, again following the same principles we met in interaspect analysis, is that the more central a role a planet plays in the individual birthchart, the more important is its role in synastry. Jill's Mercury might be very powerful, lying in its own natural sign, Gemini, and ruling her Virgo Ascendant. Knowing that it falls in Jack's seventh house (intimacy; partnership) is a critical piece of information. On the other hand, Jack's Mercury might play only a bit part in his birthchart, lying unaspected in Taurus in the backwaters of his twelfth house. In any but the most detailed of synastry interpretations, its house transpositions can be ignored.

In general, Venus and Mars should receive attention. They're important in intimacy questions, regardless of how obscure they might be in the individual birthchart.

If you're uncertain about the specific meanings of any of the planets, review the chapter on interaspects. As you've probably detected, the logic behind all the basic interaspectual processes—saturnization, uranization, neptunification, and so on—is exactly the same for house transpositions. Just remember that the planet now affects an entire house rather than upon another planet.

A practical tip: pay special attention when more than one planet is transposed into a single house. Jill might, for example, transpose Mercury, Venus, Neptune, and her Sun into Jack's seventh house. While each planet has particular meaning, the message you need to receive loudly and clearly is that she's *bombing* his house of marriage. Then you add the subtleties by considering each planet's separate significance.

Time for Another Trip to the Teapot

There is a cunning little demon running around in your head who hates astrology and doesn't want it to work. He would like nothing better than to ensnare you in a quagmire of details. He'll gladly grant you a profound understanding of how Jack's Jupiter fits into Jill's twelfth house in a loose sextile to her Mercury—provided you pay the price of forgetting that their Ascendants are conjunct and their Suns form a square aspect. Even better, that demon would like to cancel out the *human understanding* you could have gotten from those birthcharts—that bottom-line sense that Jack is conservative and bookish, while Jill is preparing for an assault on the town's jalapeño-pepper-eating crown.

That's why there is so much emphasis on the teapot in these instructions. It's up there with the ephemeris and the computer, high on the list of astrological tools. At this juncture in our synastry outline, you're as busy as a starving lizard in a swarm of mosquitoes. Don't get so busy you lose perspective. Are the two people becoming living characters in your mind, like Frodo Baggins and Gollum, or Humphrey Bogart and Lauren Bacall? Do you sense patterns of friction and enhancement, of joined purposes and cross-purposes, just as you might when sitting with two close friends? If those feelings are there, then you're ready to advance to the next step.

Whole-Brained Astrology

Imagine that Madonna, Miss Manners, and the Lone Ranger got stuck in an elevator together. What would happen? We don't know either, but like you, we immediately smile when we consider it. Those personalities are vivid ones. Most of us have a feeling for each of them, a sense of their values, their styles, what makes them tick. We can't help but giggle when we imagine the situation that trio would create—the possible alliances, the inevitable ruffled feathers, the comic misunderstandings, the truces.

Madonna. Miss Manners. The Masked Man. Something inside you has registered ten million minuscule details about each person and automatically converted those details into a feeling. That's the form in which your psyche stores its impressions. Mention the names, and instantly a kind of emotional summary of each person is called up. It works with cultural icons—and it works with a thousand times more richness and depth with your friends and families.

270

The juxtaposition of those three disparate characters in the incongruous circumstances of a stalled elevator instantly feels funny to us. Still, the purpose behind our invoking that image is a serious one. We want to demonstrate that in reacting to that scenario, your brain accomplished something quite remarkable. In a few milliseconds it successfully correlated three complex and unrelated bodies of information and placed them in an alien context. It also instantly began generating models of all the possible outcomes of their interaction. And in its spare time, your brain took a moment to make an aesthetic response: it decided that there was something funny about this particular alignment of information.

What's more amazing, you didn't need to be Albert Einstein to get the joke. Almost anyone familiar with the basic mythology of our culture would react that way virtually instantaneously.

Astrology is mental work and it takes some intelligence to get anywhere with it, but when people lament that "astrology is too hard for them," what they're probably really saying is that their approach is wrong. They're trying to do something with their conscious intellects that really calls for the use of their whole brain/mind/soul system. Walking is hard too—if you try to do it on your fingertips.

Guideline Number Six: *The astrological symbols serve only one purpose: to convey a body of information to the heart where it can be felt, interpreted, and returned to conscious awareness in the form of compassionate insight.*

The heart does most of the work. But you won't have to teach your heart anything new in order to have success with synastry. Why? Because your heart's already had many years of training. Every time it's loved or hated, laughed or cried, it's learned something about how to breathe life into the astrological symbols.

No effective astrologer can bypass the intellect. To be truly whole-brained we have to engage intelligence as well as emotion and intuition. That astrologer has done the homework, learning by rote all the details and procedures of this ancient technology. But that astrologer knows *why* he or she went to all that trouble. Once the language of astrology is absorbed, the heart can work its magic, plugging astrology into a storehouse of wisdom and experience far too variegated and complex for intellect to encompass.

Practice, of course, is the key. It took your heart a while to learn to decipher the messages sent by a glance or a change in the tone of a voice. Astrology, although just as rich, is less familiar. You've got to stick with it a while, giving the symbols time to mesh with your own inner vocabulary. Friends are a gold mine here. You already have an emotional reaction to them. Now all you have to do is peer at them through the filters of their charts. That's one good way to learn to associate the human feelings you already possess with astrological structures.

Another productive strategy is to study the birthcharts of well-known people. You may understand in an abstract way that the fifth house has something to do with pleasure—but when you discover that the childlike and naïve Marie Antoinette had her Sun and Moon there, your understanding takes on new dimensions. When she was told that the peasants had no bread, she famously said, "Then let them eat cake!" Many historians believe that her remark was not a callous one—her life-circumstances (house symbolism) had been so defined by the luxurious world of Versailles that she actually thought she was making a helpful suggestion.

Stick with it. Go slowly. Never be embarrassed to retreat to simpler levels of astrological analysis. Don't be intimidated by the labyrinthine intellectual complexity of the system. Even professional astrologers base their interpretations on a few simple, bedrock feelings about a birthchart.

Give astrology time, trust yourself, and before you know it, you'll find yourself getting misty over the way your lover's Venus makes that delicate sextile to your weary Saturn, just as if he or she had sent you a love poem. When that happens, your heart has learned the most ancient language the earth has ever known. And you can call yourself an astrologer.

CHAPTER SIXTEEN: THE FITZGERALDS

Few couples in history have managed to embody so perfectly the spirit of an age. The Roaring Twenties are forever mirrored in the colorful, tragic lives of Zelda and F. Scott Fitzgerald. When they met in 1918, he was the classic dashing young lieutenant, while she was the beautiful eighteen-year-old Southern debutante. From the beginning, Scott expected literary fame and its attendant fortunes. Although his plans were thwarted for a while, by 1920 he had published his first novel, *This Side of Paradise.* Shortly thereafter he married Zelda, and together they came to epitomize the manic high living and cosmopolitan chic so characteristic of that glamorous decade.

Flitting between New York, Paris, and the French Riviera, they drank and spent and partied, often to excess, but always with a quality of style and charm that for a while kept them one step ahead of the shadows that lie down those roads. Of that period in their lives, F. Scott Fitzgerald later wrote, "I remember riding in a taxi one afternoon between very tall buildings under a mauve and rosy sky; I began to bawl because I had everything I wanted and knew I would never be so happy again."

Those words proved prophetic. If the Twenties showed the Fitzgeralds on top of the world, the Thirties showed them devoured by the very shadows they had managed to elude for so long. Scott's heavy drinking developed into full-blown alcoholism; Zelda became schizophrenic. They separated, although their love for each other never died. Reading their letters, one gets the impression of Greek tragedy: two lovers, given a taste of paradise, then pulled apart, battered, and broken by elemental flaws in their own characters. Four days before Christmas 1940, F. Scott Fitzgerald died of an alcohol-related heart attack. Seven years later, Zelda died in a fire in the sanitarium where she was interned. She was buried by his side.

Figures Four and Five on pages 149 and 150 show the Fitzgeralds' birthcharts. Immediately the astrological energies that attracted them to each other are apparent. Quickly scanning, we discover that Scott's Sun in early Libra formed a nearly precise sextile aspect to Zelda's Sun, in early Leo. A stimulating sextile also linked their Moons: his in early Taurus, hers in early Cancer. Zelda's Ascendant and Mercury fall in Scott's seventh house, and her Sun is within three degrees of his Leo Descendant—hence his instant fascination with her. Intensifying the sexuality of the bond, we discover that their Mars placements were virtually identical, both around the twentieth degree of Gemini. Throughout the good years of their marriage they had an almost legendary enthusiasm (Mars) for staying up until dawn simply talking to each other (Gemini). Their passions, in every sense, were on the same wavelength (conjunction).

Let's start with Zelda's birthchart. Who was this woman? What was her soul seeking to learn or resolve in this lifetime, quite independently of Scott? After we've absorbed the message of her chart, we'll do the same for her husband. Then we'll have a deeper look at their interactions.

Zelda Fitzgerald

One glance reveals a pronounced duality in Zelda's birthchart. On one hand, we find the Sun and Ascendant in demonstrative Leo, trined by an ebullient Sagittarian Jupiter and an iconoclastic fifth-house Uranus. On the other hand, we see a feeling-oriented Cancer Moon conjunct gentle Venus, bolstered by the sensitive qualities of a twelfth-house Sun.

She's the *Performer* (Leo Sun) wearing the mask of the *Performer* (Leo Ascendant)—but with the soul of the *Invisible Woman* (Cancer Moon).

To that simple formula, we add two planetary conjunctions involving the primal triad. With Venus conjunct her Moon, the archetypes of the *Artist* and the *Lover* were grafted onto her soul. Mercury conjuncts her Ascendant; thus, her outward style was mercurial—quick, bright, communicative, and probably rather "wired."

In her early years, Zelda dealt with these astrological ambiguities in much the same way that adolescents everywhere typically do: she simply repressed the more problematic side of her psychological equation. In her own words, "When I was a little girl I had great confidence in myself . . . I did not have a single feeling of inferiority, or shyness, or doubt, and no moral principles."

The tension between the Performer and the Invisible Woman in Zelda would ultimately contribute to the madness (twelfth house shadow) that destroyed her. In Zelda's own words, "It's very difficult to be two simple people at once, one who wants to have a law to itself and one who wants to keep all the nice old things and be loved and safe and protected." To Zelda's words "loved and safe and protected," we might add the Leo word "noticed."

The fourth house relates to the family of origin, as well as to the inner life. She had Jupiter in Sagittarius there, trining her Sun, and she was born into advantageous circumstances that filled her with a family mythology of high expectations and a sense of being bullet-proof. In Montgomery, Alabama,

274

Zelda was an enviable figure: a judge's daughter, a lovely, popular debutante. Her Performer's need for applause was satisfied. When she met and married Scott, their glamorous New York life met those same needs admirably—at first. But as Scott came to be increasingly lionized as a major literary voice, Zelda's Leonine need for attention was thwarted. The resultant competitiveness between them is often cited as a central factor in the painful years that followed their spectacular rise. We'll explore the astrological dimensions of that competitiveness in great detail later in this chapter.

The Sun is literally the gravitational center of the solar system. Symbolically, it is the gravitational center of the psyche too. That's always true—and particularly so with Zelda, because, with Leo rising, the Sun is also the ruler of the ascendant. Thus "getting her act together" (Ascendant), as well as maintaining basic vitality and sanity (Sun), depended absolutely on a strong response to the evolutionary challenges of both factors shaping her Sun: Leo and the twelfth house. Let's consider those two pieces separately.

Exoterically, Leo is the Lion—the king of the beasts. One associates that imagery with natural authority and presence. True to the symbolism, people carrying major Leo emphasis in their charts generally radiate star quality: an aura of poise, confidence, and "bigness." Esoterically, though, what is such a soul *learning*? The evolutionary intention revolves around recovering a sense of feeling comfortable, safe, and accepted—the polar opposite of what one would expect, looking at them. From a karmic perspective, whenever we see this much Leo energy in a person, there is a very strong implication of a specific kind of prior-life trauma: being at the receiving end of *persecution, shaming, and negative projection*. Thus, the outward Leo appearance of confidence isn't matched inwardly. The soul is attempting to recover its sense of joy, inclusion, trust, and spontaneity. What we see outwardly are simply the *tools* it is using for that job.

Some things are invisible because they are so dim—faint stars in distant galaxies. Other things are invisible because they are so bright, like the face of the sun. Zelda was so blindingly bright that knowing her well would not have been easy. Behind her Performer aura was an ambiguity: the desire to be seen and appreciated mixed with an unconscious, reflexive fear that revealing her true self would lead to attack and destruction. She came into this world to address that wound through the Leo strategy of authentic—hence risky—*creative self-expression* before an appreciative audience. That appreciative audience was a critical ingredient: it would counter the darker effects of prior life shaming and attack.

In this more penetrating evolutionary light, Zelda's self-protective Cancer Moon—the crab inside the shell—is actually quite consistent: the mood of that configuration is one of cautious self-protection, and typically we also see that self-protectiveness extending into protectiveness toward others. That's a beautiful expression, but it can also correlate with the behavior of being attracted only to the walking wounded: hiding behind the shell of the Mother.

Further amplifying the centrality of creative self-expression to Zelda's evolutionary intentions, we see two planets in her fifth house. With Uranus there, her *individuation* depended upon honoring her inner artist, however strange or threatening to convention her revolutionary Uranian imagination might become. Saturn adds its usual element of challenge here—her fear of her soul being seen had to be addressed through the classic Saturn strategies of self-discipline, relentless determination, and a sustained drive toward excellence. Think of that Leo energy again.

The second major symbol shaping Zelda's Sun is the twelfth house, implying sensitivity, both emotionally and psychically. This also markedly enhances her creative imagination, supporting and amplifying the centrality of that theme. In common with all true mystics (twelfth house), Zelda came here to learn something about *non-attachment.* The deal she made with God was basically this: *"If I do my inner meditative, creative, visionary work and thus remember why I am really here, my twelfth house Sun will mean only sensitivity toward the inner landscape. But if I get attached to this world, if anything becomes more important to me than this deep remembering of my true nature, then You will take that thing away from me."*

Zelda, in other words, was playing for very high stakes.

There is a stellium—three or more planets—in her eleventh house. Beside her Cancer Moon, we also observe Venus in Cancer there conjunct the Moon, plus Pluto, Mars, and Neptune in Gemini, along with the south node of the Moon.

Before we look at the fact that the eleventh house is so loaded, let's think about that Venus. We know Venus is always important in synastry. Here it's also very important in her chart as a whole, since it's lined up with the Moon and thus deeply connected to her soul. In Chapter Five we learned that, from an evolutionary perspective, Venus in Cancer seeks *to form relationships that help develop and heal one's inner world of feelings. These*

276

relationships must be as safe as possible, involving profound, lasting commitments by gentle, nurturing partners—in stark contrast to prior life dynamics in which the soul was driven to take refuge within a psychic shell.
Already, that the interpretation echoes the deeper meaning of Zelda's big Leo focus. We'll amplify those notions in some detail below when we look at the ragged karma indicated by the Moon's south node.

The house of friends is one meaning of the eleventh house. Typically, someone with it so powerfully focalized will find life unfolding in a wide social circle. That doesn't mean intimacy; more like shared destiny, group karma, and lots of networking. More importantly, anything in the eleventh house takes a while to find its feet—it's a house that tends to take off later in life. With half the planets in her chart in this single house, it's imminently clear that the work Zelda came into this world to do was simply not the work of a young woman. In a word, this is the chart of a late bloomer. But no such blooming is ever automatic. If Zelda didn't lay the right foundation in her younger years, we would see these eleventh house planets manifesting their darker sides.

In nutshells:

The Cancer Moon/Venus conjunction reflects a soul-intention to achieve, by roughly midlife, artistic confidence (Venus), self-healing (Moon), and the creation of a happy, stable home life (Moon-Venus conjunction in Cancer). Failing that, there would be moody withdrawal into the inner life (Cancer Moon) and considerable dependency on others (Venus).

The Pluto-Mars conjunction in Gemini reflects a soul-intention to achieve, by midlife, a heroic, healing descent into the most wounded dimensions of her psyche (Pluto), from which she would emerge with her courage and natural assertiveness restored (Mars). This would then animate her public (eleventh house) "voice" (Gemini). Failing that, she would become publicly identified as a wounded person (Pluto) characterized either by anger or by her role as a victim (Mars as Hunter; Mars as Prey).

Neptune takes on special importance here in the eleventh house in that it naturally rules the twelfth house, where her Sun lies. We can confidently affirm that by midlife, Zelda would either be committed to her inner, Neptunian work, which as we have seen is inseparable from her creative work—or she would go down the dark Neptune roads of escapism, tragic loss, and madness.

We keep coming back to the centrality of creativity in Zelda's soul-intentions. What *form* would the creative work take? It's often dicey trying

277

to be specific there—creative people are generally talented in more than one arena—but with all those Gemini planets and with Mercury conjunct her Leo Ascendant, there is a very strong emphasis upon language. Her destiny was inseparable from words. In her deepest essence, Zelda carried the archetype of the *Storyteller*.

One more symbol lies in the eleventh house: the Moon's south node, also in Gemini. The south node is the point that is most resonant with the *feeling content* of our karmic past. Through her powerful Leo emphasis, we've already recognized that Zelda was carrying persecution-based wounds from the earlier history of her soul. That's confirmed powerfully when we recognize that her south node is conjunct that explosive, potentially violent alignment of Mars and Pluto, and opposing Uranus. Mercury is the ruler of her south node, lying in Leo and conjunct her Ascendant. We've looked at that Mercury in her present life a bit already, but as the ruler of her south node, it also takes on karmic significance. We see Zelda in a prior life playing a leadership role (both Leo and the Ascendant), functioning as a Mercury/Ascendant "spokesperson." She was swept along by the passionate, angry will of the collective (eleventh house; Mars; Pluto), which elevated her as a *symbol of itself*. The Uranian influence suggests a role as a rebel of some sort, and adds to the general sense of the situation being wildly out of control. The Martial and Plutonian themes corroborate that, further suggesting tremendous passions, and probably elements of violence. The imagery is absolutely consistent with the brief, dramatic lifetime of a martyr—a kind of "Joan of Arc" figure.

Zelda was born more than a little traumatized, in other words. And vulnerable, as we all are, to echoing the karmic pattern in the present lifetime.

The north node of the Moon always shows the way forward. Lying in Sagittarius and in the fifth house, conjunct Uranus, it again emphasizes the absolute centrality of creative self-expression to Zelda's evolutionary intention. The soul-healing behavior (house symbolism) must be creative, and also simply *pleasurable*—those themes are always elemental to the fifth house. She is attempting to restore her faith in life (Sagittarius), and also to establish radical autonomy and immunity to social pressure and manipulation (Uranus) this time around, both as an artist and as a human being. Given the harsh realities of her karmic past, we must strive to absorb, seriously and compassionately, how important it was for her *to have a good time* in this incarnation. How else could faith in life be restored?

278

Those at least were Zelda's deepest soul intentions.

With our sense of Zelda Fitzgerald's birthchart established, we've honored her as an individual, separate from her husband. Let's do the same for him now, then consider some of the most relevant interaspects and house transpositions between them.

F. Scott Fitzgerald

Turning to F. Scott Fitzgerald's birthchart, we observe that his Sun lies in Libra, his Moon in Taurus, and that his Ascendant is Aquarius. Thus, he is the *Artist*, with the instinctual, sensual soul of the *Animal-Spirit*, wearing the mask of the *Genius* or the *Rebel*. No planetary conjunctions complicate his primal triad as they did with Zelda, but we deepen our understanding when we add that his Artist's Sun lies in the brooding, psycho-sexual eighth house, and that his Moon is on the third house cusp, emphasizing his emotional drive to express himself verbally.

His Aquarian Ascendant, always drawn to rule-breaking, is ruled by a ninth house Uranus—and always remember that the ruler of the Ascendant is the ruler of the chart, and thus its house position always provides a revealing clue about *where a person's life is happening*. Look carefully at that Uranus, though: it's about seven degrees from the Midheaven. This ambivalent house position is not an uncommon interpretive situation, but one we must handle with some dexterity. It would of course be wrong to ignore the ninth house implications of his chart-ruling Uranus, but it would be equally wrong to forget its association with the Midheaven through that conjunction. The ruler of his Ascendant is really affecting two houses. Let's consider both of them.

Uranus is conjunct the Midheaven. That alone suggests a life very much dominated by a driven, wild-card sense of public destiny, emphasizing that the intentions of F. Scott Fitzgerald's soul for this incarnation involved affecting the larger community. Along with his Aquarian Ascendant, this Uranus implies that he is here to shake things up, break the rules and manifest genius, in some sense of that word. Some of the shake-up will likely revolve around publicly expressing or embodying Scorpionic material—levels of psychological honesty (Scorpio) that violate existing norms of behavior (Uranus).

But that Ascendant-ruling Uranus is also very clearly and centrally operating in the ninth house, implying that the scene of Scott's life will

279

include much experience of foreign cultures—or at least places that are exotic relative to his native Minnesota. His biography of course corroborates that simple prediction: Europe was a lot further away from America, psychologically, in those days. More centrally, a strong ninth house always indicates a soul-intention of gathering wide and varied experience: not only travel, but also learning, stretching boundaries, and adventure. Additionally, the ninth house correlates with belief systems: religion, in the broadest sense. What gave meaning to F. Scott Fitzgerald's life? Work (Saturn)—and the full, disciplined development of his own genius (Uranus).

Going more deeply, we find in Scott a virtual study in the planet Venus. It rules both his Sun sign (Libra) and his Moon sign (Taurus). That alone would place it in a dominant position, but Venus is also in its own natural sign, Libra. Furthermore, it's in a conjunction with Mercury—and Mercury is the natural ruler of the third house, where his Moon lies. What can this mean? Start with the obvious: Fitzgerald was one of history's consummate artists (Libra), his art (Venus) took the poetic form of language (Mercury), and it affected the larger world in a revolutionary way—there's that big Aquarian/Uranian focus again.

Always, in synastry, we take Venus very seriously. But, just as we did with Zelda's chart, we see a particular emphasis on the planet. As we learned in Chapter Five, with Venus in Libra, *the evolutionary intent is to form relationships that help develop one's ability to relate in sophisticated, romantic, courteous ways, with a constant focus on empathetic alertness toward each other. There is a strong reaction against prior-life experiences of sexual crassness or crudity in a partner.*

Amplifying and supporting the creative, romantic Venusian/Libran themes in his chart, we see a very busy fifth house. Neptune and Mars are there, in Gemini. The fact that the two fifth house (creative self-expression) planets fall in Gemini stresses the high probability of a *verbal* expression of that creativity. The Mercury/Venus conjunction and the third house Moon, as we've already seen, support that notion too. We've detected a powerful, recurrent theme in F. Scott Fitzgerald's chart.

But there's more to Venus than beauty. It's also the goddess of love. With the planet so central to his character, Scott undoubtedly radiated an intensely Venusian presence: warm, charming, magnetic, even seductive. That his Venus would more naturally manifest as a compelling *mating instinct*, rather than as simple flirtatiousness or sexual adventurism, is indicated through the placement of his Venus in the eighth house, along with his Libran Sun and his Mercury—not to mention the steady, stabilizing urges inherent in a Taurus Moon. Critically, his romantic, Libran love for Zelda was a central feature of his life. With his identity (Sun) motivated so elementally by the search for love (Libra), and destined to gather so much pivotal experience through the heterosexual male yoga of surrendering to one woman (eighth house), it is clear that Zelda's catalytic impact was a central theme of his life. Thus, although there is little evidence to support the allegation that "she wrote his books for him," we can fairly say that from the astrological perspective, he likely could not have written nearly so poignantly and truly without her. Why? *Because he wouldn't have been himself.*

Pluto lies in F. Scott Fitzgerald's fourth house, in Gemini. Where Pluto lies, there is always initially a life-shaping wound—and the implicit challenge to go down into the dark and heal it. The tools the soul brings into this world for that job are formidable: an instinct for delving (Pluto) into the psychological depths, especially areas that are conditioned by family dynamics (fourth house). Scott was a natural psychologist, as anyone reading his books quickly discovers. It's important to remember that in the 1920s, psychological language was not nearly as integrated into common sense as it is today. On the dark side, there is always a danger of what amounts to whining and self-pity with a fourth house Pluto, which can provide an excellent "excuse" for escapism, childishness, and irresponsible behavior. Tellingly, there can also be a *powerful, unconscious fear of creating a home*—which can correlate with rootlessness, lack of community, or self-sabotaging behavior in terms of truly consummating any relationship.

In typical eighth house fashion, the Fitzgeralds' marriage was psychologically profound—and often profoundly upsetting. Still, in 1925, Scott was able to write: "Zelda and I sometimes indulge in terrible four-day rows that always start with a drinking party, but we're still enormously in love and about the only truly happy married couple I know." And later, one sentence that captures so much of the dark side of his Libran eighth house spirit: "I left my capacity for hoping on the little roads that led to Zelda's sanitarium."

Jupiter lies in Scott's seventh house, in the last degree of Leo. "Lucky in love," says the fortune-teller. The facts of his biography might quibble with that assertion. Still, we can say that he would naturally be drawn to people who were characterized by jovial qualities: expansiveness, generosity of spirit, faith in themselves. Jupiter is also given to excesses and inclined to "party hearty"—those qualities would be evident in members of his inner circle too.

There's one more point to be made about his Jupiter: it lies conjunct the Moon's south node. More about that below, when we're ready to look at the karmic material more directly. We'll start down that road by going back to our simplest initial impressions of his birthchart, and looking at them more deeply.

Serenity, the highest realm of Venus, is the unconscious, spiritual goal that motivates the behavior of anyone with that planet strongly placed. At the most elemental level of evolutionary astrological interpretation, we observe that F. Scott Fitzgerald had reached a stage in the evolutionary cycle in which he needed to learn how to *establish and maintain inner peace.* Through the glass darkly, we glimpse something of the earlier history of his soul here: prior to this lifetime, he'd advanced in wisdom—but the process had shaken him to the core. Thus he arrived in this world rattled, and had reached a point in the evolutionary trajectory where his soul needed calming, integrative, reflective influences. An analogy would be the way that a couple might simply need to hold each other after a difficult discussion.

When it comes to re-establishing Venusian serenity, exposure to beauty and stable lasting love are good teachers, and Scott studied under them. But there are tricksters too, promising ease, but ultimately delivering agony. The abuse of alcohol is one of them, and he fell prey to its temptations.

Can we see alcoholism astrologically? Not reliably. We might see a predisposition toward the problem through Venusian and Neptunian emphasis, but ultimately the cornerstone of all helpful, even accurate astrological work pivots on the human capacity to choose among a wide range of possible behaviors. No astrological feature leaves us without options—or leads us inescapably toward the gin bottle. The same symbolism that can indicate a drunk can also indicate a creative visionary.

Still, the Venusian peace-seeking qualities of F. Scott Fitzgerald's birthchart suggest at least the possibility that he'd be tempted by anything that might numb him, including the desensitizing effects of drink. Echoing that idea, we see Neptune (altered states of consciousness) in his fifth house (pleasure), tightly conjunct an impulsive Geminian Mars. The red planet's explosive enthusiasms, coupled with Neptune's mind-altering proclivities, offered him many possibilities. One he often chose was a cycle of alcoholic benders, sometimes lasting for days. His Martial-Neptunian pattern of self-destructive drinking waxed and waned throughout his life and certainly contributed to his untimely death at the age of forty-four.

In a chilling line from his own notebooks, F. Scott Fitzgerald wrote his own sad epitaph: "Then I was drunk for many years, then I died."

The Moon's south node lies in Leo, conjunct Jupiter, in the seventh house. Discerning the karmic pattern out of which F. Scott Fitzgerald emerged requires penetrating scrutiny. On the face of it, everything looks copacetic—the node is in Leo, the sign of the king, conjunct Jupiter, the king of the gods. We're clearly looking at the karmic signature of one who was deeply marked by birth into the *aristocracy* in a prior life. That can of course be quite lovely—but with the south node of the Moon, we are always looking at *unresolved issues from the past,* and those, by definition, don't refer to situations where everything worked out well, at least from the evolutionary perspective. Pleasant, successful prior lifetimes may abound—but they don't emerge in a present-life birthchart as something requiring healing.

Let's dig for more clues. It's a seventh house south node, suggesting the *powerful influence of other people* upon him in that prior lifetime. The Leo south node is ruled by the Sun, which gives another hint: the Sun is in Libra, corroborating the civilized, sophisticated context of that lifetime. It's also in the eighth house, again emphasizing relational themes, and bringing in the strong sexual element. Sexuality is a fair guess with the seventh house, and an excellent one with the eighth.

Ominously, the nodes are squared by Uranus and Saturn. Planets square the nodes always suggest something that *blocked* or *vexed* us in the past, something left unresolved, haunting us, demanding resolution—a "skipped step," as Jeffrey Wolf Green puts it.

In that prior life, there was something "big" that was supposed to be accomplished and "stood up for" (ninth house; beliefs). It was also something rebellious: the Uranian piece. And it should have had a public dimension: Uranus's association with the Midheaven. But it didn't happen, or went badly wrong. What got in the way? Remember all the relationship symbolism: the answer is probably marriage—an "advantageous" marriage, in the typical traditions of the aristocracy. With Saturn squaring that south node, the marriage was likely a stultifyingly loveless one, but one that was backed up by many "Thou Shalt" and "Thou Shalt Not" proclamations—Saturn (patriarchal thinking) in the ninth house (religion). Remember our earlier reference to a present-life reaction against *sexual crassness or crudity* in a prior-life partner! The pressures of suppression built up (Saturn). Eventually the dam broke—Uranus tightly squares the south node—which in turn led to a *scandalous* (Uranus), *socially catastrophic* (Saturn), and very *public*

283

(Midheaven) explosion of *sheer, taboo erotic energy* (Scorpio Uranus, Scorpio Saturn).

We can't determine F. Scott Fitzgerald's gender in that lifetime, but due to the pervasiveness of the sexual double standard for the last five or six thousand years, it's easiest for us to make sense of this nodal story if we assume he was female—married off early in a sanctimonious and "appropriate," loveless way to a brutish partner, unable to endure it, succumbing to sexual "temptation"—and finishing life as a pariah, in public shame, perhaps even banished or exiled to another land (ninth house). The strong square of a Scorpionic Uranus to the nodes is consistent with that lifetime ending suddenly, perhaps through suicide or being put to death.

Remember: as we saw earlier, with his powerful Venus-signature, F. Scott Fitzgerald was born "rattled," and needing desperately to calm down. Now, through the south node of the Moon, we can understand the reasons for that shaken state in some detail.

The north node of the Moon lies in Aquarius in the first house. There is an overwhelming soul-desire here for freedom from the stultifying impact of social conditioning. That 's implicit in Aquarius. The first house can be understood to refer to a kind of "enlightened selfishness"—an emphasis on the fact that each soul comes into the world with a natural right to pursue its own evolutionary intentions, and a right not to worry unduly if it happens to upset other people's plans. In that prior lifetime, Scott had been a puppet. In this lifetime, there was a powerful intent to avoid that possibility happening again.

One final point—the planetary ruler of F. Scott Fitzgerald's north node is Uranus, in the ninth house near the Midheaven. Part of his intent for this lifetime was to express his iconoclastic Aquarian first house *beliefs* publicly, completing something akin to the higher work that was the "skipped step" from the prior lifetime. *Through the myth-making power of his art, he intended to alter the hypocritical social mores which had shattered his life in the prior context.* Cultural historians agree that the "roaring twenties" were a watershed in terms of sexual freedom, the liberation of women, and the debunking of puritanism. F. Scott Fitzgerald, for all his flaws and tragedies, was indubitably a driver of that social change, thus fulfilling at least this part of his evolutionary intention.

The Synastric Perspective

Sit for a minute and *feel* these two people: Zelda and Scott. We've let the astrological symbols speak. We've partly translated their primeval language into English. Now we need to let our hearts and intuitions absorb what we've learned.

In Zelda and F. Scott Fitzgerald, we see two highly sensitive, creative people, both with somewhat indrawn characters, both driven by primordial hungers into unnaturally extroverted manifestations. In Zelda's case, that hunger was the Leonine need for recognition and applause. In Scott's case, it was the Libran hunger for love, coupled with a compelling sense of outward destiny. The essential introspectiveness of Zelda's character is suggested by the Cancer Moon and her twelfth house Sun. In Scott, it is indicated by his Taurus Moon and his inward-probing eighth house Sun. Thus, despite the many differences between their birthcharts, we find distinct parallels between these two. Coupled with the striking interaspects and transpositions we briefly referenced at the beginning of this chapter, it is no wonder that they immediately fell in love. These two, if nothing else, were kindred spirits.

That they contributed to each other's destruction is also true.

In lasting relationships, the most typical astrological "glue" is a strong linkage between the two primal triads of Sun, Moon, and Ascendant. With Scott and Zelda, we're looking at epoxy! Her Leo Sun sextiles his Libra Sun and squares his Taurus Moon. (Remember to read those aspects "backwards" too: his Sun sextiles hers, while his Moon squares her Sun). Zelda's Cancer Moon sextiles Scott's Moon in Taurus. It also squares his Libra Sun. Her Leo Ascendant makes a square to his Moon and a sextile to his Sun. It also opposes his Aquarian Ascendant. All those interaspects are accurate within standard orbs of a few degrees. This is an unusually dense amalgam of interaspects at the primal Sun-Moon-Ascendant level.

A few lines ago we spoke of "epoxy" binding these two together. That by no means guarantees happiness—only that such couples don't break up easily, even when they perhaps should. The interweavings of these two lives were nearly total. The disconnected, private spaces typically present even in strong marriages were spookily absent.

Sun correlates with ego, and each Fitzgerald *solarized* (pushed; forced) the Sun of the other one through a stimulating, head-long sextile aspect. Scott also solarized Zelda's outward mask through the sextile of his sun to her Ascendant. This solar "pushing," as we saw in Chapter Eight, can be supportive or catastrophically premature, depending on the basic health of the planet being pushed. How healthy were their egos when they met? You can make your own judgement based on what happened. One thing is sure: whatever *ego-driven theatricality* and *self-importance* existed in either one of them was going to be greatly amplified through their contact with each other.

Moon correlates with emotional energies: moods, needs, fears. Each Fitzgerald *lunarized* (nurtured; emotionalized; sensitized) the Moon of the other one, again through a stimulating sextile. Lunarization always emphasizes emotional expression. Any adult will sometimes feel like hitting another one—but refrain. We all feel like crying sometimes—but instead we dry our eyes and solve the problem that's vexing us. This degree of "emotional repression" is absolutely essential to true adulthood, but when we're lunarized, it doesn't come as naturally. The Fitzgeralds brought out two qualities in each other: "the inner child" and plain childishness.

Scott's Libra Sun squared Zelda's Cancer Moon. This is another strong interaction, but a more jagged one due to the nature of any square aspect. His solar ego wanted peace, grace, and equilibrium, along with stable, meaningful love—and he had good evolutionary reasons for that, as we've seen. Zelda's Cancerian emotionalism undoubtedly rattled him, but when he snapped at her, she'd withdraw into her Cancer shell—which scared him even worse. Was this a damned-if-you-do, damned-if-don't situation? It certainly must have felt that way to both of them at times, but with enough understanding of each other's real needs and motivations, the problem would have been quite tractable. Each could adapt to the reality of the other, potentially.

Zelda's Leo Sun squared Scott's Taurus Moon—note the symmetry with the interaspect we discussed in the previous paragraph: again, we're looking at a square interaspect of Sun and Moon—one solar ego "bumping" the lunar emotional needs of the other one. In this case, Zelda's sanity (Sun) depended on being noticed, attended to and appreciated when she took the risk of expressing herself: that 's her Leo Sun. Scott's earthy, quiet and practical, productive focus (Taurus Moon), especially when he was writing (third house Moon) would tend to be oblivious to her "performances" a lot—and probably annoyed rather than appreciative when she pressed him to notice her.

With love, tolerance, and generosity of spirit, this problem too would have been tractable, had they thought about it consciously and humbly.

One hitch is that the Moon, by its very nature, doesn't think. It just feels and needs and wants. Astrological counsel, bringing unconscious material into the forum of conscious choice, could have potentially made a real difference here.

Turning our attention to house transpositions, we see Zelda's Ascendant and Mercury landing in Scott's seventh house, and her Sun so close to his seventh house cusp that it might as well be in that house too. Unsurprisingly, a big seventh house transposition is a very common pattern in relationships. Scott was naturally inclined simply to *like* Zelda, right from the beginning. More deeply, she had something he needed if he were to complete himself and fulfill his destiny—that wonderful, colorful Leonine sense of "theater." Since, as we saw earlier, there is so much in Scott's chart that suggests an emphasized need for the triggering impact of soulmates, we must pay particular attention to this house transposition. It would be significant for anyone, but especially so for an eighth house Libran with runaway Venusian energies.

We must also remember that what initially attracts us to our seventh house soulmates usually challenges and annoys us down the road. Just as we've resisted integrating that part of ourselves, we'll quickly enough have similar troubles with them. The threatricality that attracted Scott to Zelda at first, he would later come to perceive as her irritating "over-the-top" qualities. That's a natural part of the seventh house; it's then that the integrative work really begins.

Scott transposed three planets—Mercury, Venus, and the Sun—into Zelda's third house (communication). This configuration enormously stimulated her simple talkativeness, as well as her capacities as a writer. A good thing? Potentially, yes: we've seen that her soul was focused on creativity, and that with her Mercury-Ascendant conjunction, writing was potentially a good artistic outlet for her. But genius is a hard act to follow, and try as she might, Zelda was never able to achieve anything near her husband's literary success, financially or artistically. Would she have even tried, had not Scott so stimulated her third house? And would she have attained more of a sense of her own worth, had she not diverted so much energy into the medium of literature and *the search for recognition there*? These are difficult questions. Certainly Zelda was creative in her own right, and she did have a flair for language. F. Scott Fitzgerald, however, was one of the great voices of his generation. Head-to-head competition with such a talent is no formula for self-esteem.

Complicating this issue enormously, we also note that Scott's Taurus

287

Moon transposes into Zelda's empty tenth house, actually conjuncting her Midheaven. His nurturing effect on her career is the good news; his potential for triggering an infantile (lunarization) need for "fame" in her must also be noted. Lots of famous people don't have planets in the tenth house—we shouldn't assume that a lack of planets there precludes having an impact on one's community. What we can rightly assume is that such an impact will be a *side effect* of their simply being themselves—the "fame" happens incidentally, rather than being the result of a strategic campaign. Thus, while Scott did indeed have an evolutionary need to impact the larger world, Zelda did not. His lunarizing of her Midheaven could potentially distort that reality in her, especially given her Leonine need for attention. Implicit in all this is the distinction between art as a personal process of inner healing, and art as commerce and career. As any professional artist will affirm, success in one has little relevance to success in the other.

This line of reasoning brings us to consider carefully one of the most telling, driving interaspects between Zelda and Scott: their tight Mars-Mars conjunction in Gemini—the War God *martializing* the War God. Do we detect a theme here? Competitiveness is endemic to our species and not totally to be despised. Worthy opponents bring out excellence in each other, and are a fine cure for complacency. Even in the highest expression of the Fitzgeralds' intentions toward each other, this Mars-Mars alignment would spark that endless drive for higher ground, spurred in part by a desire to impress and even outdo each other. Clearly, though, such rampant expression of Mars-energy could potentially have a darker side. Their famous "four day rows" reflect it. One night Scott allowed Zelda to challenge him into making a series of dangerous high dives off the Riviera cliffs into the sea. What is going on in the mind of a wife when she encourages her husband to risk his life in such a stupid and pointless way? What is going on in the mind of a husband when he plays along with her?

More deeply, we can relate this martial dynamic to the house transpositions we were just discussing: Scott's solarizing Zelda's third house and lunarizing her Midheaven. Could he unwittingly press her into professional competition with him—competition on a distinctly uneven and unnatural playing field? That the playing field would be *verbal* and *intellectual* is clear—Mars lies in Gemini in both charts. Scott's is in the fifth house, correlating with creative self-expression among other possibilities. It's aligned closely with Neptune, emphasizing his imaginative powers. Zelda's Mars, on the other hand, lies in that packed eleventh house, linking it to the "late-bloomer" syndrome we discussed earlier—she would, if she did her inner work, find the power of her voice later in life. *But when Zelda met Scott, she was only eighteen.* Furthermore, Zelda's Mars was less than two degrees from Pluto—and that explosive conjunction was also linked through a wider conjunction to the south node of the Moon, implicating it in the emotionally unresolved, violent tragedies of her karmic past, *where speaking her mind led to disaster.* (Scott's chart shows the Mars-Pluto conjunction as well, but it's almost seven degrees wide, and linked to his south node through a more harmonious sextile, plus Pluto is separated even further from the node by being in a different house.)

One more piece of this complex puzzle leaps out: not only do the Fitzgeralds share that competitive Mars-Mars conjunction, but each of them also *plutonifies the other one's Mars.* Thus, even the darkest Martial denizens of their individual psychic underworlds would be invited to the table. Whatever unresolved issues either of them had around fear, anger, competitiveness, violence, the passionate side of sexuality—the basic Mars menu—would sooner or later be made manifest in this relationship. Any unresolved issues Scott had around his family of origin (Pluto in the fourth house) would be particularly susceptible to dark manifestation here. In a nutshell, they were practically guaranteed to bring out the worst in one another. Could there possibly be any good news in such a statement? Absolutely: the soul-agreement between these two beings was that they would come together in love to face these primal fears together—and fear is always the core issue with Mars-Pluto interactions. Together, they would do the journey into the dark. Together, they would attempt the soul-retrieval. Together, they would face the Beast.

For Scott and Zelda, the stakes were high and the game volatile. To succeed, neither of them would have to be saints, but they would each have to do a brave, humble, self-aware job of fulfilling the evolutionary intentions of their individual birthcharts. With that foundation, success in terms of this interaspectual Mars-Pluto complex would be almost inevitable. Without it: impossible.

Mars lies in Scott's fifth house, along with his Neptune. In Zelda's fifth house, we find Uranus and Saturn. So far we've focused on the creative and pleasure-oriented dimensions of that house. But as we learned when we studied the arc of intimacy, this is also the "house of love affairs"—and that means a lot more than courtship or fun. When this house is emphasized, there is a soul-intention to finish business that was left unfinished in prior lifetimes with other people. This work is serious, necessary, and must be honored. We emphasize that "finishing business" doesn't necessarily mean present-life sexual or romantic contact. It's really more about *releasing* the other person and *withdrawing our projections.* Accomplishing that aim does require social contact; it's never a question of simply avoiding the other person. In Scott and Zelda, we see a classic marital dilemma: two beings, married early in life, with outstanding business to be finished with other people outside the marriage. Natural human instincts make it hard to maintain the higher ground in these matters, but here's what that higher ground looks like: *fidelity to the marriage on the part of the fifth house person, and non-indulgence in jealousy on the part of the mate.* With the Fitzgeralds, that policy would have needed to go in both directions, since each of them played both roles: the married person and the person with a strong fifth house.

Remembering the Mars-Mars conjunction and its mutual plutonification, we see Scott under particular pressure in this "love affair" arena, since his Mars is actually in his fifth house. Would he succumb to the temptation to use his sexuality as a way of expressing rage at Zelda? One anecdote: Scott's flirtation with the dancer Isadora Duncan culminated in Zelda's hurling herself head first down a flight of stone steps. The raw facts of such a story speak volumes about what happens when Pluto invites Mars to take a walk on the dark side.

Let's cut to a question that underlies everything we're exploring: *Could an evolutionary astrologer have saved Scott and Zelda Fitzgerald's marriage?* It is tempting to react reflexively and say no. Perhaps that's the correct answer. The giddy, self-flattering "high" of their early years was blissfully addictive, and like most addictions, it led inexorably to a painful crash. But were there seeds of wisdom in this man and woman, even amidst the glorious fantasy of their first years together? Could the pain of their crash perhaps have watered those seeds with the tears of our ancient saviors: humility and desperation? Were Zelda and Scott bound to the nose-diving patterns of their biographies, or was the equilibrium between insanity's gravity and love's uplifting touch so delicate that a featherweight could have tipped the scales?

Naturally, these questions are ultimately unanswerable. No astrologer need wrestle with them. Our work in unraveling the synastric message is not to make prophecies, be they baleful or full of hope. Our work is only to help, only to offer a view of the higher road, and to point an incisive finger at the shadow in all its seductive guises. Beyond that, the two individuals themselves must choose their courses, together or apart.

Maybe an evolutionary astrologer could have helped Zelda and Scott. Maybe he or she, arriving at precisely the right instant, wielding the weight of a feather, could have upset the balance, planting seeds of mutual, compassionate understanding, informed generosity of spirit, and regeneration.

Again, we cannot know. But if astrology ever regains a place of honor among the allies of humankind, it will be because of individuals like you, reader, lying in bed wide-eyed late at night, struggling to find the words that might have made the difference.

Do such transformative words exist? Not if we believe in ironhanded fate. But perhaps "fate" is an empty concept, only a lie, only a device we use to hide from a notion a thousand times more awesome: that the featherweight that truly tips the balance of our lives is not mechanical fate, but rather our own innate capacity to make choices.

Maybe Zelda and Scott Fitzgerald, even deep in their pain and blindness, given a little help and a little hope, could have wielded that feather. No matter how true or how false that statement might be, if you're the type of human being who's cut out to be a evolutionary astrologer, you probably at least half believe it.

And for anyone who feels that holding out that kind of faith is like writing letters to Santa Claus, we quote a letter from Scott to Zelda. These words were written in 1934, in desolation, while she was in the asylum and he was trying—and failing—to ration himself to one ounce of gin per hour.

"The sadness of the past is with me always. The things that we have done together and the awful splits that have broken us into war survivals . . . stay like a sort of atmosphere around any house that I inhabit. The good things and the first years together . . . will stay with me forever, and you should feel like I do that they can be renewed, if not in a new spring, then in a new summer. I love you my darling, darling."

CONCLUSION: BORDER WARS

Many years ago we met a man who impressed us greatly. His name was J. C. Eaglesmith. He was Native American, a holder of the Sacred Pipe, a veteran of the ordeal known as the Sun Dance. A former marine who served in combat in Vietnam, he weighed maybe 250 pounds and most of it looked like muscle. In short, when it came to masculinity, he made the average tough guy look like your grandmother's knitting.

He stood before us at a conference, talking about "male" and "female" and what those words really mean. His eyes steady, his face impassive, he addressed us in his deep baritone. "I am half woman." A moment's pause, a hint of a smile, then: "My mother was one."

We all laughed. So did J. C. But what he said was true. Physically he is a man. But that just diagrams his plumbing. Once we recognize that a human being is far more than a mass of cells and bones, we enter the realm of mystery. And in that realm no one is as simple as a beard or a breast.

Humanity is realizing this, and it's knocking the stilts out from under a picture of the world that's held us in thrall for ten thousand years. "I am half woman." "I am half man." Those words represent a revolution just as profound as the discovery that the Earth is a sphere floating in the void.

Male and *female*. What do the terms really signify? Apart from anatomy, perhaps no one really knows. Women cry more than men, but why? Are women inherently more emotional or have they been trained that way? Men are more aggressive. Again, why? Testosterone—or training? No one knows. Nature and nurture are inseparable. What we intrinsically are blends seamlessly with what we have been taught to *imagine* we are.

Quagmires of social mythology surround us from birth. Winnowing the essential Self out of those quagmires is perhaps the core purpose of astrology. As we learn to decipher the birthchart, we recognize an individual's elemental nature and help free it from the deadening sinkholes of blind conformity.

Traditional astrology books, written in times when people were dogmatically certain about gender roles, often contain differing interpretations of the same configurations depending on the person's sex. "In the chart of a man, Mars in Aquarius means . . . " The problem is that there is no way, while looking at a birthchart, to discern whether that chart belongs to a woman or a man. They look the same. In their time, those Victorian astrologers may have been doing accurate work. But they may also have been mistaking whimsies of Victorian society for immutable laws of the universe.

The Moon, with its emotional sensitivity, has traditionally been viewed as feminine. The Sun, with its charisma and force, has been seen as masculine. But even proper, blue-haired dowagers in the garden club respond to the Sun, while their huffing, puffing husbands down at the Moose Lodge know the touch of the Moon. No human being is immune to the energies of any of the planets. If you're alive, you've got all ten of them in your chart.

Does astrology, arguably the truest mirror in humanity's possession, suggest that there are no psychic or spiritual differences between men and women? The truth is, astrology's rather mum on the subject. But it certainly implies that, whatever those differences might be, we've spent a lot of years and a lot of lives overestimating, exaggerating, and misdefining them. Every man has a Moon. Every woman has a Sun. One of the darkest skeletons in astrology's closet is the fact that astrologers were not the first to point out that awkward fact.

Perhaps there was a payoff, and not just for the astrologers. Perhaps this devil's bargain of parsing human consciousness into feminine and masculine functions served a purpose. A radical feminist might argue that this schism was men's way of disempowering women, keeping them dependent and weak. A radical masculinist, if there were any, might counter that women created the schism in order to shift an unfair, insufferable burden of practical responsibility to men, thereby condemning them to eternally shorter lifespans and elevated rates of suicide, alcoholism, and stress-related diseases. Meanwhile, the couch potatoes watching the debate on television might shrug and say, "That's just how God made us," then change the channel. Maybe they're right.

Still, we have that cryptic clue in the sky: the Sun and the Moon shine down on all of us, whether we start the morning with shaving cream or a choice of skirts. And if there's anything to astrology, then the Sun and the Moon resonate somehow in every one of us, unless we collude in the ancient deception.

How did this whole mess start? Let's go way, way back, long before cities, before agriculture, before the peaceful years of the Neolithic, back into the first ninety-nine percent of our species' history.

Men kill. Women cook. Men make war. Women make babies. It's an old, annoying line of reasoning, but let's look at it in a different way. Imagine killing! Forget codes of honor, waving flags, the stirring lies old men tell

294

young men—just imagine killing, destroying life, whether in violent confrontation or in hunting for meat. It's ugly, bloody, and disgusting, especially with primitive weapons. Something visceral in us all, regardless of gender, cries out against it. Yet conflict and hunting have been with humanity since the beginning. And the responsibility for those processes fell to men. Why? Because, obviously enough, men are bigger and stronger, and because women were busy elsewhere—more about that in a minute. Our question now is, *what did ancient man do with the pain that entered him when he killed?* What did he do with the sickness in his stomach? What, in other words did he do with his Moon?

He denied it! *The killer can have no Moon, not and still kill.* Man could not endure his Moon, so he thrust it upon Woman—let her be the one to quake and cry and feel.

Woman, meanwhile, found herself very young, or pregnant, or caring for infants. Or dead. Life was short and fragile. In a world where most children died in infancy, survival depended upon her ability to nurture. Imagine it! If you could go back in time, fifty thousand years before the beautiful caves of Lascaux or Altamira, and look into such a woman's eyes, what would you see? An animal? No: you'd see depth and soul and intelligence. A human being. And that human being faced a task that would put tears in the eyes of the bravest man. In the cold light of impossibility and endless death, she had to hold that infant in her arms and try to keep the spark of life glowing. How could she bear it? We are tempted to imagine that she hardened herself, but that idea doesn't stand up to scrutiny. *If primitive woman hardened herself, then she would have failed as a nurturer.* How can a hardened person return to a crying, dying child again and again? What would be the motivation?

Woman, no matter how bitterly difficult a life she endured, had to set aside her natural human selfishness and accept her lot as mother and healer. She needed, in other words, to set aside her solar ego. Woman had to love, lest humanity die. But what about the part of her that was just plain angry at her circumstances? What about the part of her that wanted to lash out at something—anything—as a primal release of rebellion and frustration? What about the part of her that hated her children for confining her? What about the part of her that hated her children for dying? Down the drain, down into the nightside of human awareness, into the Unconscious. *The nurturer can have no Sun—not and still endure the enormous self-sacrifice of nurturing.*

Woman surrendered her Sun, thrust it upon Man—let him be the one to have enough pride and illusions of glory to rage against nature's heavy hand.

295

Humankind has been "civilized" for about one half of one percent of its history. Our assumptions about "male" and "female" are vastly more archaic, lodged in the collective unconscious. To our ancestors it must have seemed that those scripts had been ordained by the gods, which is one reason most religions are such bastions of patriarchal thought, insisting that men mimic His Glorious Works while women make sure dinner is on the table.

That myth is dying. We who live today are witnessing the collapse of a gender myth whose roots are more primeval than memory. The *usefulness* of the myth ended long ago, back when men stopped spending most of their time hunting and fighting and women began living long and comfortably enough to do more than struggle with babies. But the myth has survived anyway, on momentum, right into the last century.

Good riddance? Yes, but let's not be too glib about it. There's a lot more going on here than women having careers and sleeping around, while men are allowed to shed a tear. No one's going to ride off into the sunset anytime soon, with justice done and the good guys back on the ranch. When men recover the Moon and women the Sun, the earth moves beneath our feet. Familiar ground shifts precipitously. Antediluvian energies, long fossilized, are released in a shattering detonation. That detonation will probably last another half a millennium.

Anger pours out—old, bitter anger, long repressed. It's the anger of our foremothers and forefathers who were nailed to the wall by those mythologies—the bitter anger of the female William Shakespeare whose voice was never heard, the vomiting anger of every soldier who saw a fearful reflection of himself in the eyes of his enemy just before he brought down the weight of the bloody ax.

Now, as the gender paradigms shift, we see that anger manifesting among women in the more vitriolic branches of feminism. We see it in blind hostility toward men, the crudely prejudicial idea that men are insensitive and brutish, incapable of love. On the male side, we see that same anger manifesting even more primitively in the rise of violent pornography, the exponential rise of rape, and the adolescent hoots that assail any woman who dares to walk down the street.

Perhaps the anger is inevitable, but anger is a cheap lens: it distorts anything we observe, magnifying hurts, diminishing complexities. Let's use a clearer microscope: compassion. Let's imagine for a moment that humanity has been doing the best it could. The primal man who shut down his feeling Moon in the face of the overwhelming fear and blood and death of his rough existence—was he wrong? The primal woman who sacrificed her solar creativity and individuality so that she could pour her life into insuring the survival of the next generation—was she in error?

If they were wrong, then humanity owes its presence in the world to their mistakes.

The problem is that the system worked too well. Like a neurotic spender with a brand-new credit card, we got hooked. Man projected his lunar side onto Woman. She projected her solar side onto him. Gradually, what originated as a practical psychological adjustment was no longer necessary or appropriate. But one point is sure: *life is twice as easy if you only have to face half of it.* Maybe *that's* the payoff. Maybe feminist rage and macho coldness are nothing but camouflage. Maybe it's laziness, not sexual politics, that lies at the bottom of the schism. That may be true today, but it didn't begin that way.

Like heroin in the ghetto, those gender projections can still make life easier. A man loses his job; no problem: his wife can carry all his insecurities and fears for him while he set about the task of finding another job. A woman's car breaks down; no problem: her husband can strain through the logic and bashed knuckles of repairing it. The practical world, in other words, becomes a male preserve. But women are not left out—the other side of life, the world of feeling and nurturing, is theirs, and they can feel superior there. Marriage in trouble? Woman feels the problem and helps Man talk about it. Man looking a little wan and flushed? Woman asks him if he has a fever and cajoles him into caring for himself. Child needs a kind word? Go ask mommy.

Today, many women are rediscovering the Sun. It heals them, makes them whole. They are finding their solar power: their self-reliance, their voice, their creativity, their ability to shape the myths, symbols, and future of society.

Meanwhile, men are beginning to rediscover the Moon. They too are healed and made whole as they reabsorb their own lost lunar capacity to love, to ask for help, to cry, to feel, to nurture.

That's the good news.

The bad news is that both women and men are terribly out of practice with their Suns and Moons. They don't know quite what to do with them yet. As this epochal reintegration takes place, there is a period of awkwardness. Like a blind man whose vision has been restored, the acquisition of these "new" solar and lunar functions causes both genders to spend a while bumping into things.

Women, as they claim the authority and self-reliance of the Sun, run the risk of becoming icy and dictatorial—picking up solar diseases, in other words. Unlike men, they have few role models and little tradition, even a flawed one, for dealing with those excesses. Some go too far and begin to lose touch with their Moons, unwittingly mimicking the madness of the men they revile. Others, more cautious, don't go far enough. They experience frustration, low self-esteem, and resentment as they fall short of the elusive solar ideals.

Men, meanwhile, have few traditions, role models, or mythologies to help them make peace with their lunar sides. They risk drowning in the mysticism and subjectivity of their new-found Moons, becoming narcissistic, overly attentive to their own issues, crippled by their "sensitivity." That, or they find themselves so submerged in lunar emotions and "needs" that their characters deteriorate. They lose that ancient kingpin of the masculine solar myth: their *sense of personal honor*. No longer can they maintain commitments, resist temptations, or fulfill responsibilities. Drowned in the Moon, they begin to lose their Suns.

And these are the men and women on the cutting edge, the ones who are actually wrestling with reintegration!

Naturally, among those most frightened by the collapse of the ancient system, a backlash arises. A family-values woman—motherly, asexual, obedient, vacant—dances in the *zeitgeist*. A good ol' boy—fearless, insensitive, efficient at the hunt—wrestles the imagined enemy. But increasingly those figures seem empty and quaint. In a few years they'll become comically nostalgic.

As humanity reclaims its solar-lunar wholeness, it is torn between an ill-defined, uncreated future and a burned-out past. We're a bit like a timid kid in her first week at an out-of-state college—tempted to go home again. But we can't. We've outgrown that possibility. Men are raising children, voluntarily going into psychotherapy, exploring forbidden "feminine" emotional territories. Women are flying in space, entering government, making their presence felt in science, art, and athletics. We can't go back, and we're not sure where forward is or what it looks like.

Compassion again. That's our clear lens. Three million years of habit is a formidable adversary.

What about those who have broken the archaic chain, who are no longer reciting lines from the ancient script? Certainly such individuals exist, at least in flashes and flickers, but their journey has only started. Releasing the old roles doesn't automatically create the solar-lunar future. How does that future look? No one knows. The possibilities are multitudinous. Will the old gender patterns endure in some modified way? Will men and women reverse roles? Will people feel free to be distinctly solar or lunar depending on their personal predilections? Is the future unisex? Where does gayness fit into the picture? What about the raising of children? Is it correct to assume that the optimal human being balances solar and lunar qualities evenly? Even if such balance is possible, does it follow inevitably that there would be no practical role divisions based on gender? What, if anything, do the words "feminine" and "masculine" ultimately mean, and how much do they have to do with one's physical anatomy?

Dogmatic answers to these questions abound, but dogmatism is just the shadow insecurity casts. The deeper truth is that no one really knows the answers yet, and that uncertainty frightens us. Humanity, as a species, is undergoing an identity crisis.

Can astrology help resolve that identity crisis? Yes and no. On the negative side, no birthchart can carry an astrologer beyond the limitations imposed by his or her prejudices and assumptions. Fatalistic astrologers look at charts and see inescapable fate. Depressed ones see impossibility. Psychological ones see psychology. Everything depends upon the pre-existing viewpoint of the astrologer, and no astrologer who is already convinced of the meanings of femininity and masculinity is likely to see much more than the vindication of his or her convictions.

But astrology can make a positive contribution to the healing of the schism in the human soul. It won't do that by giving us any ultimate answers, prefabricated and predigested. It will do it by helping us to find the answers ourselves. Astrology is, above all, a language. Like any language, its elemental purpose is to implement communication. Astrology's advantage over other languages is that it is optimized for the communication of psychological information. In other words, if you want to ask an electrician how to rewire your refrigerator, stick to English. But if you want to ask your husband or wife or lover about some hot-wired dimension of your relationship, the language of astrology is unparalleled. No other system of symbols can approach it for delicacy of nuance or laser-like penetration. There is no other way to be so absolutely, compassionately *objective* about one's self or another person.

Humanity today is in dire need of such a language. We have, in one sense, more than enough data: there are plenty of men and women in the world! Trouble is, all that data is locked inside human skulls. We need to mix it up, see how it settles out. We're dying for some conversation.

Conversation between men and women, perhaps spurred and sharpened by astrology, is a big part of the solution. But we must recognize that the schism between the sexes is a symptom of a deeper rift: the one that sundered *individual* psyches three million years ago, when men fled the Moon and women surrendered the Sun. The conversation, in other words, must originate privately, in the shadowy recesses of every modern mind. From there it proceeds into the world of intimacy.

Nor should the conversation stop there. The same rift that divides lunar-female and solar-male also splits the world into poets and rationalists, mystics and scientists, feelers and thinkers—half-wits all, with one half of human consciousness developed and emphasized, the other half banished to the shadows.

Rift or no, the planets spin above us impersonally, much as they did in the days of the Neanderthals. They pass through the same signs, make the same aspects, travel the same twelve houses. Midtown Manhattan or Olduvai Gorge, it makes no difference. Astrology, like death and food and love, is one of the human constants.

Or is it? Only partly so. Astrological forces interact with something less constant: human consciousness, with its endless creativity and changing social patterns. Rooted in nature, astrology may remind us of the archetypal outlines of sanity and wholeness, but within that outline humanity writes its own lines. Those who use astrological language today—especially those who practice synastry—must recognize the changing framework of ideas through which humanity perceives itself and makes sense of its sexuality. The planets may be constant, but men and women are not. Were a medieval astrologer to slip through a crack in time and try to establish a synastry practice in modern San Francisco, he'd be half crazy before he even figured out how to *talk* to people. He'd know astrology, but how to *apply* astrology to its primary task as a medium of communication in the modern era—of that, he would know nothing.

As our time-traveling astrologer got his bearings and began to practice synastry, he'd be shocked at our divorce rate. There was plenty of sex where he came from, both inside and outside marriage, but marriage itself was bedrock. Happy or otherwise, not much could shake it. Why? The answer lies with yet another seductive side effect of the gender schism between Sun and Moon: it had a remarkably stabilizing effect upon marriage. An artificial dependency was created between men and women, one that went far beyond their natural attraction. A woman simply could not survive alone; that at least was the myth. She could not support herself, protect herself, even think for herself. Similarly, a man on his own would fall, theoretically, into sickness, squalor, and moral decline. Who would see to his nutrition? Who would patch his socks? Who would prevent him from becoming an alcoholic? Who would sit in church and pray for his soul? Sun cannot live without Moon. Moon cannot survive without Sun. As long as one gender cornered either market, marriage left the realm of choice and entered the realm of necessity.

By gender-dividing the skills that are necessary to the maintenance of life, our ancestors—and in many cases our parents—created a phony *neediness* between women and men. Any astrologer who accepts that same division today is as out of place as our medieval time-traveler. In the old view, so many of the intimacy concerns that motivate modern people—personal growth, sexual fulfillment, keeping the magic alive—took a back seat to merely maximizing a couple's capacity to *tolerate each other's presence.* Strategic silences arose; lies were agreed upon; worlds were kept separate. In separation there was peace.

Stay together or die: that, in a nutshell, was the old reality.

Many modern astrology texts slavishly repeat those ancient principles, as if that formula still had widespread relevance. "Good" interaspects—trines and sextiles—are represented as positive omens for marriage. Why? *Because they are quiet!* Squares and oppositions are treated like bloody handwriting on the wall. How come? *Because those aspects indicate a pressing need for communication and evolution!* Sweet-tempered, oil-on-the-waters Venus had better shine brightly in the linkages between the birthcharts—otherwise the couple plays a perilous game: they face their clashes squarely without bailing out into the politeness and empty rituals of forgiveness. Dangerous business, if mere stability is our aim. And if solitary Saturn or confrontive Mars should rear their hideous heads in those birthcharts, then you'd better hope the bride knows a good lawyer.

Silliness. The first principle we must remember in recreating synastry for the modern era is that the realities that people actually experience exist at the interface of the archetypal astrological realities and the creative free-will inherent in human consciousness. No astrological configuration guarantees failure or success, perpetual antagonism or endless orgasm. Personal

301

commitment (a question of solar honor) and openness to personal growth (a question of lunar sensitivity) are the critical ingredients. Given enough of those qualities, any partnership can potentially operate in a satisfactory way, regardless of how the birthcharts are configured.

The second principle to remember is that *conflict* can be a positive force. Back when the consequences of divorce were so dire, honest, soul-penetrating conflict became taboo. It was too dangerous to tolerate. Inevitably conflict still developed, but it was released indirectly and symbolically in peevishness and irrelevant arguments. Men would "get" women by patronizing them—or hitting them. Women would "get" men with moodiness, psychological castration, and bitchiness. Solar weapons and lunar weapons. Such gambits release rage, but they never address the source of the rage. That source is left untouched, ready to explode anew whenever the ground trembles.

The majority of the people who come to us for astrological counsel today are women. The ratio is not as dramatic as it once was, maybe sixty/forty. But it's consistent. The majority of the men whom we see come to us open-mindedly, but most of them come only after having been encouraged to make the appointment by a woman.

The pattern is no quirk. Doctors, psychotherapists, most people in helping professions all report the same picture: women are more willing to ask for help than men are. The nurturers, in other words, know how to nurture themselves as well as others. Even in a field such as astrology, which because of its reputation selects for a clientèle that is more independent, iconoclastic, and just plain curious than the norm, women outnumber men. An administrator at the New York Open Center, a teaching forum receptive to controversial subjects, put it bluntly. She said, "The New Age is female."

Why? What's happened to the men? Gone fishing. Gone hunting. A significant proportion of modern males are still hooked into the solar-dominated mythology that allows no room for emotional interdependency or the exploration of life's lunar side. But as we've seen, the basis for that myth eroded long ago. It's been running on empty, running on momentum alone, for centuries. Men are breaking out of it, but not in such great numbers as women. The reason behind the pattern is extraordinarily simple: the reintegration of lunar and solar qualities is fundamentally a psychological change. The forces that propel it originate in the psyche; that is, in the subjective, lunar world. And who's been left in charge of the psychological dimension of life? Women! Naturally they'd be the first to *feel* that something was fundamentally wrong with the way we were living. Thus, feminism precedes masculinism. Reason would predict it, and history bears it out. Woman precedes Man into the subjective realm, just as surely as Man has preceded Woman into the objective realm of space flight, and for similar reasons.

Is astrology "feminine"? In the archaic view of the world, yes—in that mental framework, anything that pertains to the inward, emotive side of life is feminine. Poet Robert Bly, in his provocative essay "I Came Out of the Mother Naked," calls astrology "the great intellectual triumph of the Mother civilization." He postulates an era previous to the present patriarchal civilizations in which matriarchy held sway on earth. Astrology, with its "feminine" emphasis upon humanity's mutual interpenetration with nature, arose naturally in that intellectual climate, and was anathema to the later patriarchy with its emphasis upon objective conquest and control.

So the same tide that washes feminism into human consciousness also washes in an astrological renaissance, as well as a renaissance in other "feminine" arts, such as poetry, psychology, body work, and mysticism.

Some women seek to exclude men from the renaissance, as if access to the Moon were limited to those with wide hips and hairless faces. That's madness. Men, freed of the ancient schism, are creatures of Moon and Night just as naturally as are women. Astrology—and what some people still insist on calling "feminism"—work for everyone. Those men who fear them fear their own Moons. They are victims of the ancient lie. Those women who seek to possess the Moon exclusively for their gender fall, paradoxically, into the ancient *solar* disease of dominance, control, and obsession with territory. In recovering their Suns, they have succumbed to them. Either way, the real goal—the restoration of our lost wholeness—is missed.

Male or female, if you've read this book, you can call yourself a student of astrology. As such, you hold something precious: a blueprint for sanity, a link to the primordial feminine and the primordial masculine. Above all, you hold a language, a basis for communication. But it's not a language like English or Russian or French, with all their built-in assumptions about gender. In astrology there are no loaded words such as "mankind," "effeminate," or "ladylike"—or the non-anatomical uses of "prick" or "pussy." There's nothing but the raw language of life, newborn and primitive. Try to keep it like that! Astrology's greatest asset is its capacity to address what is natural in us, both as unique individuals and as members of human species. If we allow the arbitrary values of our society to influence our view of the symbols too deeply, we've compromised astrology's objectivity and clarity.

Such compromise would be a loss under any circumstances, but that's especially so today. At this point in our history we need all the clarity we can muster. "Feminine" and "masculine," long separate, are converging. Other, parallel convergences are taking place. In discovering quantum physics and Einsteinian relativity, humanity has set the stage for the convergence of science and mysticism. In creating the global village, we are creating a convergence of Industrial and Third World cultures—another marriage of the archetypal masculine and feminine. With computers, cinema, and electronic musical instruments, we are developing art forms in which lunar imagination must converge with solar logic. Environmentalism reflects the same pattern: the lunar urge to nurture the earth is inextricably tied to solar ideals of scientific analysis and planning. The list is long. We live in an age of revolutions, all of which reflect perhaps the greatest single revolution humanity has ever known: the healing of the schism between Sun and Moon.

We astrologers are in a unique position to promote that healing. With our precise language, we can promote communication and reconciliation between the estranged parts of each individual. Recognizing the diseases of our times, we astrologers can speak supportively to women regarding the "masculine" parts of their birthcharts. We can help them make peace with Mars and Uranus and the Sun, while inspiring them with new respect for their socially devalued lunar instincts. We can speak gently, coaxingly to men about the Moon, Venus, and Neptune, encouraging them to nourish and strengthen those "feminine" dimensions of their own beings, without sacrificing their solar sense of initiative and honor.

If we remain true to the symbolism, reading it with integrity, wary of biases, we astrologers can use our craft to help ease people back into balance, into the pleasure and freedom of wholeness.

Committed relationships are perhaps the most perfect incubator for the reconciliation of Sun and Moon. But that reconciliation is a fiery, explosive process. The epoch in which marriage was essentially required of us is now over. Marriage, at long last, has become voluntary. Those who make such commitments today, those who "volunteer for marriage," are on the front lines. Nowhere else is there such a lack of escape routes from these questions—and these ancient angers. With time-honored mythologies collapsing all around their ears, such individuals are left with little but their own creativity to rescue them. Old answers are exploding like so many skyrockets. New answers are not yet invented.

Synastry can help them. A man and a woman who dare to form a bond in the contemporary world are on humanity's cutting edge. If their experiment is to be successful, communication is essential, both within their own individualities and between them. To suggest that they couldn't succeed without astrology would be misleading; but to suggest that they can't succeed without dialog is certain. Dialog—communication—is the heart of reconciliation.

If you choose to practice synastry, trust the symbols. Begin by letting them guide you deeper into yourself. Whatever your gender, find your maleness, find your femaleness. Let the inner dialog commence.

Then look up from the astrology books. Lift your eyes and face the source of it all: the mysterious sky. What do you see? Two great Lights: Sun and Moon. Ancient. Palpably archetypal. Enigmatic. But identical in their apparent size! Let those Lights be the same size in you too. Then you've tuned your instrument of perception, brought it into harmony with the message of the heavens.

With your instrument tuned, with heart and mind open, you are ready to speak the healing language of synastry in this wondrous, uncertain age.

APPENDIX ONE

IF YOU NEED AN EPHEMERIS IN BOOK FORM: Try ACS, 5521 Ruffin Rd., San Diego, CA 92123, 800-888-9983

GET FREE CHARTS ONLINE: For charts only, **with no interpretation**, if you have Internet access, our website has links to other sites, not ours, that can calculate charts for free. The Internet changes fast, but we'll try to keep those links current.

1. Go to our FAQs page: http://www.sevenpawspress.com/faq.html
2. Scroll down until you see, "What if all I want is a chart?"
3. Follow the links you will find there.

PLEASE VISIT OUR WEBSITE if you want to buy:

* computerized birthcharts, progressions, solar returns, relocation charts, or composite charts and synastry grids
* our lecture tapes, books (astrology, and fantasy fiction), and books by other authors
* our personalized, computerized, written reports on birthcharts, transits and progressions, and synastry
* astrological software by Alphee Lavoie's AIR Software

Also, please go to our website to:

* learn about our other astrological work, including a directory of evolutionary astrologers trained by Steven Forrest
* read some of astrological articles, our website newsletter, and our definitions of the Norse Runes.
* see our workshop, conference and lecture schedule
* learn where to order a copy of your birth certificate in all fifty states, and some foreign countries.
* get links to other astrology sites, and some interesting non-astrological ones, too.
* find out what famous people share your birthday, month by month!

For more information and secure ordering:

http://www.stevenforrest.com, http://www.jodieforrest.com, and http://www.sevenpawspress.com. All three of those URLs go to the exact same website. Not online? Write to us for a price list:

Alpha Lyra Consulting and Seven Paws Press
POB 2345, Chapel Hill, NC 27515-2345

APPENDIX TWO

The Principles of Evolutionary Astrology
as developed by Steven Forrest and Jeffrey Wolf Green

Evolutionary Astrology embraces paradigms and methodologies which specifically measure the growth of the soul from life to life. These methods invariably focus on the planet Pluto and its relationship to the Nodal Axis. While it is composed of a set of specific formal methodologies, evolutionary astrology is ultimately characterized less by a technical approach than by a set of philosophical principles defined by natural law. Different evolutionary astrologers may use somewhat different interpretive methods, but they can always be recognized by a devotion to the following core perceptions:

1. An acceptance of the fact that human beings incarnate in a succession of lifetimes.

2. An acceptance of the fact that the birthchart reflects the evolutionary condition of the soul at the moment of incarnation.

3. An acceptance of the fact that the birthchart reflects the evolutionary intentions of the soul for the present life.

4. An acceptance of the fact that the circumstances of the present life, both materially and psychologically, do not arise randomly, but rather reflect the evolutionary intentions and necessities of the soul.

5. An acceptance of the fact that human beings interact creatively and unpredictably with their birthcharts; that all astrological symbols are multi-dimensional and are modulated into material and psychic expression by the consciousness of the individual.

6. An acceptance of the fact that human beings are responsible for the realities they experience, both internally and externally.

7. A respectful intention to accept and support a person seeking astrological help, regardless of the evolutionary state in which such an individual finds himself or herself.

Steven Forrest's Twelve Elemental Principles of Evolutionary Astrology

1. Every astrological configuration, no matter how malefic it may be from the traditional perspective, represents a potentially positive, enlivening, consciousness-generating path for the individual who possesses it.

2. Every astrological configuration, no matter how benefic it may be from the traditional perspective, is capable of manifesting in negative, self-limiting ways.

3. Thus, positive and negative may be excellent words for describing human responses to astrological configurations, but they are useless words for describing the configurations themselves.

4. Consciousness is the prime variable; it is the consciousness of the individual which governs the human expression of the inherently multidimensional astrological principle.

5. The spectrum of expression available to any astrological configuration can be viewed in a six-fold pattern. Each configuration contains both conscious (evolutionary) and unconscious (non-evolutionary) expressions on three different planes: concrete biographical events, psychological attitudes and states, and spiritual meaning.

6. There is only one expression that no astrological configuration can possibly achieve: inaction. Every configuration MUST manifest, spreading its energy out through some combination of the six planes of expression, as determined by the will, consciousness and concrete choices of the individual.

7. Because consciousness itself directs the manifestation of astrological forces, its action transcends those forces and cannot be predicted through reference to them: thus, rigid prediction – especially negative prediction – tends to fail in direct proportion to the intensity of the consciousness in the person for whom the predictions are being made.

8. The more conscious the person, the less precisely rigid astrological determinism describes his or her attitude, experience, and biography.

9. The less conscious the person, the more effectively his or her attitude, experience and biography can be foreseen by conventional astrological theory.

10. The role of the astrologer lies centrally in the task of encouraging and supporting conscious, evolutionary choices on the part of his or her client.

11. While evolutionary astrological counsel must involve frank consideration of lower possibilities, those considerations must be framed as cautions rather than as "predictions."

12. Rather than an embarrassing source of predictive errors, the infinite unpredictable creativity potentially inherent in each human being is the glory of astrology and the soul of the system.

To place an order for books or astrological reports by

STEVEN and JODIE FORREST
at Alpha Lyra Consulting & Seven Paws Press:

Our website has a *secure* order form. Go *directly* to it at:
https://www.stevenforrest.com/secure/orderformAL.htm

Internet: www.stevenforrest.com, email info@sevenpawspress.com
Mail*:* POB 2345, Chapel Hill NC 27515.
Phone: 919.929.4287. Please leave a message; the answering machine is always on.
Fax: 919.929.7092. Busy? Try later; we use that number to get online.

We accept checks, money orders in US funds, VISA and MC
(sorry, Visa & MC are the only credit cards we accept).
If ordering by credit card: please include card number, expiration date, phone number & address.
If ordering reports: please include birth date, place, and exact time (remember a.m. or p.m.) for all charts every time you order.

Book and report prices are indicated on the following pages.

Add postage for books & reports sent in the US by priority mail:
for orders totaling under $50.00, add $6.00.
for orders from $50.01 - $75.00, add $9.00.
for orders from $75.01 - $100.00, add $10.00.
for orders from $100.01 - $150.00, add $11.00.
for orders totaling $150.01 - $200.00, add $13.00.
for orders totaling $200.01 - $300.00, add $15.00.
for orders totaling $300.01 - $500.00, add $17.00.
Please inquire regarding US priority mail on orders over $500.00.
Orders sent in the US by Fed Ex 3 day if available, add $8.00 to rates above.
Orders sent in the US by Fed Ex standard overnight if available, add $20.00 to rates above.
Orders sent outside the US:
by surface mail, add $7.00 to rates above.
by US air mail, add $20.00 to rates above.
by Fed Ex 3 day if available, add $35.00 to rates above.
by Fed Ex standard overnight, add $60.00 to rates above.
North Carolina residents: Please add 6.5% NC sales tax.
Thank you for your business!

BOOKS AND REPORTS BY THE FORRESTS.
NC residents, please include 6.5% sales tax.

Priority shipping: for orders totaling under $50.00, add $6.00; totaling $50.01-$75.00, add $9.00; totaling $75.01-$100.00, add $10.00; totaling $100.01-$150.00, add $11.00; totaling $150.01-$200.00, add $13.00; totaling $200.01-$300.00, add $15.00; totaling $300.01-$500.00, add $17.00. See previous page for rates outside of the US, or Fed Ex. Rates subject to change without notice.

THE "RHYMER" TRILOGY:
NORDIC-CELTIC HISTORICAL FANTASY by Jodie Forrest.

"Tomas would sometimes consider, in later years, whether there was any chance that his Fate might have been different. Yet only upon occasions of the greatest rarity would he so wonder, when gripped by a black and somber mood, perhaps, or perhaps when drifting through the gates that link wakefulness to sleep—or Elfland to other realms. For Tomas had grown to understand, far better than most mortals, that to questions about Fate there are no true answers. There are only, sometimes, reasons."

THE RHYMER AND THE RAVENS: THE BOOK OF FATE, by Jodie Forrest. Explore the tangled genesis of the modern world. Set in the collision zone of Norse beliefs, the Celtic mythos and Christianity. Read the tale of Tomas the Rhymer, kidnapped by the Queen of Elfland and returned to our world with psychic powers, a total inability to lie, and a Mission... Seven Paws Press, **$13.95.**

THE ELVES' PROPHECY: THE BOOK OF BEING, by Jodie Forrest. (Sequel to *The Rhymer and the Ravens*.) In which Tomas the Rhymer learns to become a Mage. Meanwhile, there's something vitally important that the Elf Queen hasn't told him, about a certain prophecy affecting them both. Seven Paws Press, **$16.95.**

THE BRIDGE: THE BOOK OF NECESSITY, by Jodie Forrest. (Final volume of the trilogy.) The story of Tomas's twin children, whose Fate is to build a bridge between our world and Elfland. Seven Paws Press, **$16.95.**

"Forrest's writing is rich, lyrical, intricate: her books are a treasure."—R.A. MacAvoy, author of *The Book of Kells* and *The Lens of the World.*

"The best historical fantasy I've ever read. Forrest writes lyrically, descriptively and with a sword's deft touch."—Poppy Z. Brite, author of *Lost Souls* and *Drawing Blood*

"Should certainly be read by anyone interested in High Fantasy or mythologically-based fantasy. Should be on the shelf with Kushner's and Jones's treatments of the Rhymer's story, as well as such Celtic-Christian conflicts as Bradley's *The Mists of Avalon*."—C.W. Sullivan III, *Science Fiction Research Association Review*

COLLECTED ARTICLES ON ASTROLOGY, by Jodie Forrest and Steven Forrest. Over the years, we've written a number of technical articles for various astrological journals. We offer 36 of them in this photocopied, spiral-bound seventy-page compendium. **$10.00.**

THE INNER SKY, by Steven Forrest. Published to almost immediate critical acclaim. Assuming intelligence, motivation and complete ignorance of astrology on the reader's part, the book introduces all the astrological basics—signs, planets, houses, aspects—and pulls them together in a strategy for synthesis. ACS, **$14.95.**

"As intelligent and cogent as it is poetic."—Sting

THE CHANGING SKY, by Steven Forrest. Enters the realm of astrological prediction while remaining true to the principles of personal freedom, creativity and responsibility. Working primarily with the techniques of transits & progressions, Steven depicts a universe where we have a series of choices. ACS, **$14.95.**

SKYMATES: LOVE, SEX AND EVOLUTIONARY ASTROLOGY, Volume One, by Jodie Forrest & Steven Forrest. Revised and expanded version of the synastry classic. Learn the relationship dynamics in any chart, and how two birthcharts—two people—interact. Philosophical emphases remain on the power of individual imagination, determination and choice. Seven Paws Press, **$19.95.**

SKYMATES: THE COMPOSITE CHART, Volume Two, by Jodie Forrest & Steven Forrest. Revised and expanded version of the synastry classic. Learn the relationship dynamics revealed by the couple's composite chart. Philosophical emphases remain on the power of individual imagination, determination and choice. Coming from Seven Paws Press in 2003.

THE NIGHT SPEAKS, by Steven Forrest. Addresses astrology's dreadful public relations problem. Written in an accessible style, this is the book to buy your skeptical friends, or yourself, to offer perspective and encouragement in your own use of astrology. Containing science, philosophy and personal experience, it's the book Steven feels he was born to write. ACS, **$12.95.**

THE BOOK OF PLUTO, by Steven Forrest. Learn how your Plutonian wounds, once acknowledged, might become your most energizing strengths. Covers natal Pluto by sign, house, aspect, transits and progressions. Gutsy writing that unflinchingly looks the Dark in the face, but we think you'll come away from it inspired. ACS, **$15.95.**

AWAKENING TO THE SKY: Imagining the Astrology of Deep Space. Steven Forrest. Transcript of a talk presented to the Boston chapter of the National Council for Geocosmic Research in 1994. What might quasars mean, astrologically? Globular clusters? What if you have one on your ascendent? Poetically delivered, groundbreaking lecture with both hard and speculative science. Spiral-bound, signed edition. Seven Paws Press, **$19.95**

MEASURING THE NIGHT: EVOLUTIONARY ASTROLOGY AND THE KEYS TO THE SOUL, Volume One, by Steven Forrest & Jeffrey Wolf Green. Astrology, psychology and reincarnation come together in the hands of two of the bestselling authors in turn of the millenium astrological publishing. Based on a series of workshops the authors gave together. A warm and informal lecture format with audience comments. Steven and Jeffrey team up to analyze the chart of a volunteer from the audience. Seven Paws Press/Daemon Press, **$19.95.**

MEASURING THE NIGHT: EVOLUTIONARY ASTROLOGY AND THE KEYS TO THE SOUL, Volume Two, by Jeffrey Wolf Green and Steven Forrest. Volume Two of this groundbreaking new work by Green and Forrest, with all new material from their workshops together. Seven Paws Press/Daemon Press, **$19.95.**

"Some of astrology's most lively and provocative work is being modeled by Steven Forrest and Jeffrey Wolf Green."—Mary Plumb, *The Mountain Astrologer.*

"A collection of useful insights and interpretive techniques designed for the evolutionary astrologer . . . fascinating reading."—Chris Lorenz, *Dell HOROSCOPE*

"Reading these volumes is like having a private workshop with two powerful and commanding transformational coaches in your own home."
—Stephanie Forest (no relation to Steven Forrest), *Considerations*

COMPUTERIZED ASTROLOGICAL REPORTS . . .

. . . provide a safe, inexpensive stepping stone between Sun signs and heart-to-heart astrological counsel. All reports are laser-printed, spiral-bound with cardstock covers, and based on your individual birth data. **Please include complete birth data for each report every time you order.**

THE SKY WITHIN: Steven contracted with Matrix Software to write a birthchart interpretation text based on his book, *The Inner Sky*. "The Sky Within" is a personalized, 15-20 page booklet analyzing a birthchart's major features in positive, choice-centered language. **$20.00.**

SKYLOG: Steven and Matrix Software wrote a more sophisticated report on astrological "current events"—transits and progressions. "SkyLog" is based on Steven's book, *The Changing Sky*. Booklets vary in length, depending on how many astrological configurations affect someone at a given time, and focus on freedom, choice and personal responsibility. **Can be ordered in different lengths: three months, $25.00; six months, $35.00; nine months, $40.00; one year, $45.00.**

THE SKY WE SHARE: The Astrological Dimensions of Your Relationship. A joint project with Alphee Lavoie's AIR Software, with text by Jodie Forrest and Steven Forrest. Written in the spirit of the Forrests' synastry book *Skymates*, "The Sky We Share" offers an imaginative, choice-centered, positive and humanistic approach to the astrological analysis of a couple. About 35 pages. **$49.95.**

THE SINGLE SKY: Don't have a partner yet? Then order "The Single Sky," a report geared just to your own intimacy profile. A joint project with Alphee Lavoie's AIR Software. Text by Jodie Forrest and Steven Forrest. About 20 pages. **$24.95.**

Steven Forrest's Astrological Apprenticeship Program

The work is oriented toward the realities of actual astrological counseling—no rigidity, no power-tripping, no fortune-telling. The language is psychological and metaphysical, and always comes back to the client's own power to make choices. If you have a basic knowledge of astrological symbolism and a choice-centered attitude, please feel welcome to attend. If you've digested the Forrests' books, for example, you have the knowledge you'll need to understand the material. The Programs are limited in size (under thirty people in southern CA, and under forty-five in the Bay Area), and the first openings go to continuing students. We work primarily from real-world situations with class members' charts. Always, the aim lies in encouraging students to find their own voices. If you are interested in Steven's evolutionary, psycho-spiritual approach to astrology, we'd love to have you join us.

As of December, 2001, there are two Programs. Each meets twice each year, lasts four days and runs from approximately 9:00 a.m. to 5:30 p.m. Both programs are supplemented with a strong private Internet community and access to tapes and written materials available nowhere else. For detailed information about specific meetings, including dates, times, locations, topics, lodging, meals and fees, please contact the Program coordinators and visit their websites:

Marin County/Bay Area AP Group:
Vinessa Nevala, Aquarius Moon, POB 22045, San Francisco CA 94122, vinessa@aquariusmoon.com, www.aquariusmoon.com.

Southern California AP Group (near San Diego):
Ingrid Coffin, 13743 Blue Sky Ranch Rd., Lakeside, CA 92040, tel. 619.561.5436, indy333@earthlink.net, www.blueskyranch.org.

Also, please visit the Forrests' own website, www.stevenforrest.com, particularly the pages with AP Group information:
www.stevenforrest.com/apprentice.html
www.stevenforrest.com/workshop.html